Cities, Citizens, and Technologies

Routledge Research in Cultural and Media Studies

Cities, Citizens, and Technologies

Urban Life and Postmodernity

Paula Geyh

Routledge
Taylor & Francis Group
New York   London

First published 2009
by Routledge
270 Madison Ave, New York, NY 10016

Simultaneously published in the UK
by Routledge
2 Park Square, Milton Park, Abingdon, Oxon OX14 4RN

© 2009 Taylor & Francis

Library of Congress Cataloging in Publication Data
Geyh, Paula.
　　Cities, citizens, and technologies : urban life and postmodernity / by Paula Geyh.
　　　p. cm. — (Routledge research in cultural and media studies ; 22)
　　Includes bibliographical references and index.
　　1. Sociology, Urban.　2. City and town life.　3. Postmodernism—Social aspects.
　　4. Cities and towns.　I. Title.
　　HT151.G44 2009
　　307.76—dc22
　　　　　　　2008037545

ISBN10: 0-415-99172-2 (hbk)
ISBN10: 0-203-88047-1 (ebk)

ISBN13: 978-0-415-99172-8 (hbk)
ISBN13: 978-0-203-88047-0 (ebk)

for Arkady

Contents

Illustrations

Acknowledgments

I am deeply grateful to my colleagues, students, friends, and family for their support throughout the many years in which this book was in the making. I would like to thank in particular:

my Yeshiva University colleagues, most especially Joanne Jacobson, Richard Nochimson, Joan Haahr, Adam Zachary Newton, Lauren Fitzgerald, Barbara Blatner, and Ellen Schrecker;

Dean Fred Sugarman, Dean David Srolovitz, Provost Mort Lowengrub, and Yeshiva University for their generous support for this project, including a Summer Research Grant and junior leave, and funds for travel and expenses;

my students in the Metropolis class, from whom I have learned so much;

and Neil Goldman, my exceptionally talented and resourceful research assistant.

I was fortunate to receive a Summer Stipend Award from the National Endowment for the Humanities in 2005, which was instrumental for my work on this book. I would also like to acknowledge its support of the NEH Summer Institute on "The Built Environment of the American Metropolis" at the University of Illinois at Chicago in 1999, in which I was a participant. I thank Robert Bruegmann and my fellow participants in the Institute for lively and productive discussions.

I am grateful to Routledge Press, and to Erica Wetter and Ryan Kenney, my editors, and Liz Levine, editorial assistant at the Press, for their work in bringing this project to its published form.

I would like to thank Stephen Kern, Brian McHale, Sally R. Munt, Jean-Michel Rabaté, Thomas H. Schaub, Carl Smith, and John Unsworth for their help and important exchanges at different stages of the project. My special thanks to Marsha Plotnitsky, Inge-Vera Lipsius, Rens Lipsius, Crystal Bartolovich, Astrid von Baillou, Hilene Flanzbaum and Geoff Sharpless, Jeanne Ewert and Terry Harpold, Christina de Lancie, Laura de Toledo, Marcelo Toledo, James F. English, Vicki Mahaffey, Jane Cogie and Ed Brunner, Paula Bennett, and Leslie Brown and Tony Steinbock for their friendship and invaluable intellectual companionship. I am grateful to my family, Alison and Edward Geyh, Drew Gibson, Sarah Horn and Michael Selmon, Joyce and Arthur Geyh, Emmy and Bob King, and Leola and Graham King for all their years of encouragement and support.

And finally, my thanks to Arkady Plotnitsky, for everything.

Credits

IMAGE CREDITS

1.1. Museum of the City of New York. The Byron Collection; 93.1.1.18137.
1.2. Museum of the City of New York. The Byron Collection; 93.1.1.18404.
1.3. Courtesy of George Eastman House.
1.4. © Culver Pictures.
1.5. © Andy Warhol Foundation for the Visual Arts/ARS, New York. Photo by Billy Name/OvoWorks, Inc.
1.6. We Don't Need Another Hero, Barbara Kruger, 1987. Commissioned and produced by Artangel.
1.7. © 2008 Jenny Holzer, member Artists Rights Society (ARS), New York. Photo Lisa Kahane, NYC.
2.1. Courtesy of Bob Thorne.
2.3. © *Atlas of Cyberspace*. Martin Dodge and Rob Kitchin. Harlow, UK: Pearson Education Limited, 2001.
2.4. City of News, 1997. A dynamically growing 3D Web browser created by Flavia Sparacino at MIT.
3.1. *Creating Defensible Space* was originally published by the U.S. Department of Housing and Urban Development, Office of Policy Development and Research. Reproduced here with the Department's permission.
4.1. Harry Ransom Humanities Research Center, The University of Texas at Austin. Courtesy the Estate of Edith Lutyens Bel Geddes. Photo courtesy of the Estate of Margaret Bourke-White.
4.2. Le Corbusier. Paris: Plan Voisin 1925. © FLC/ARS, 2008.
4.3. © 2008 Alex S. MacLean/Landslides.
4.4. Photo by Irfan Khan. © 2002, *Los Angeles Times*. Reprinted with Permission; 4.5 RKD, The Hague.
5.1. Image by Corbis.
5.2. © Steve Raymer/Corbis.
All reasonable efforts have been made to contact copyright holders.

Introduction
From Postmodern Culture
to Postmodern City

This book is about the contemporary city and those who live in it. It is thus also about the urban world of the era (extending roughly from the 1960s to the present) that we see as *postmodern*. Most especially, the book explores how the urban spaces of postmodernity and postmodern urban subjectivities (and communities) respond to and create each other. "Urban spaces" are conceived broadly here, so as to include buildings, plazas, parks, streets, and sidewalks. These structures, moreover, are seen as *creating* space and making it variable and multiple, rather than as merely *being placed in it*. Thus understood, urban spaces embody in their concrete, material forms the ideas and ideologies of the social formations they house and represent. They are designed or acquire the capacity to act upon those who inhabit and move through them, and thus to elicit or, conversely, inhibit particular forms of existence, thought, and action. In the process, they become strategic, disciplinary mechanisms or "machines," although they may have other functions as well. Their effects, both intentional and unintentional (things do not always turn out as planned), can be positive or negative for individuals or groups or society as a whole, but they are rarely neutral. City dwellers may respond to such spaces in the ways they are expected to respond, or they may resist the disciplinary demands of these spaces by deploying one strategy or tactic or another (including deliberate forms of "misuse"), or they may re-imagine and reshape the urban spaces they inhabit for their own purposes. Indeed, while there is much in this book about what makes a city "postmodern" (culturally, technologically, politically, and economically), my primary focus is on how the postmodern city is experienced and understood by its inhabitants. The book thus deals not only with empirical descriptions of how the physical economies and spaces of the city are changing, but also with epistemological descriptions of how the postmodern city changes our ways of knowing and perceiving the world and ourselves as postmodern urban subjects.

1. POSTMODERNITY AND POSTMODERNISM

This investigation inevitably takes place within the larger contexts of *postmodernity* itself, as a historical era, and of *postmodernism*, the era's

Zeitgeist, constituted by the ideas and practices (scientific, philosophical, aesthetic, political, or still other) that define postmodern culture. The term "postmodern" has been and remains controversial. There are several reasons for this controversy, beginning with the negative reaction to anything labeled as "postmodern" by the majority of mainstream culture, public and academic, even though the contemporary academy is often seen by public culture as being dominated by threatening postmodernist ideas and teaching practices. Also, by now, after nearly half a century of postmodernity and postmodernism, there are so many ways of understanding both terms, and they are used by so many people in so many disparate ways, that they seem almost to mean or describe everything, and therefore some of the critics of postmodernism would say they mean nothing. While it is true that as these terms proliferate they acquire new meanings (hardly an uncommon situation), it is not true that they describe everything, and it is especially not true that they mean nothing. For, insofar as postmodernism affects so much of the world we inhabit, and the ways in which we (some of us) see the world, it designates a particular, and hence specifiable, set of ways of living in, perceiving, and understanding the world. Thus, while this specification is not immediate or easy and may not ever be exhaustive, and while the term does mean many things, it does not mean everything. Indeed, such "criticisms" often mask attempts to avoid confronting the real meaning and impact of postmodernist ideas and cultural practices—philosophical, aesthetic, ethical, and political. Admittedly, some uses of the term are superficial and discountable, and some may even be seen as abuses of it. Others, however, are effective and productive, and by now difficult to dispense with. For, however negatively one may feel or think about postmodern phenomena and the language of the "postmodern," they have long been parts of our life and culture, and it may, by now, be too late to avoid them. One might, however, do well to specify how one uses this language and how one understands postmodernity and postmodernism, and I shall do so in this section of my introduction. I shall discuss postmodern spaces, subjects, and cities themselves in the next section.

I begin by commenting on *modernity* and *modernism,* terms that are often as fluctuating and contentiously debated as *postmodernity* and *postmodernism.* These debates, however, are rarely accompanied by the same degree of acrimony, in part because modern and modernist phenomena have been around for much longer and some of them are by now in our past, and hence are less troublesome and disturbing for mainstream thinking. In this study, I shall use modernity as a broad cultural category, referring to a longer (over several centuries) period in the history of Western culture. Modernism will be used to designate a more narrow, mostly aesthetic and intellectual, category, referring to certain key developments in late nineteenth- and twentieth-century art, and some philosophical and scientific thinking. Thus understood, modernity is similar to but encompasses a longer temporal span than postmodernity, and, as a manifestation of a certain *Zeitgeist* of its historical period, modernism is similar to but somewhat more narrow than postmodernism. The actual temporal span of modernity is a complex and much debated matter. One may roughly (but sufficiently for my purposes) associate modernity with four interrelated developments, often still referred to as "revolutions" (although each was protracted, sometimes taking more than a century): (a) the rise of industrial capitalism; (b) the transformation of our cosmological and mathematical-scientific view of the world, in the wake of Nicolaus Copernicus, Johannes Kepler, and Galileo Galilei; (c) the emergence, beginning with René Descartes, of a new philosophical view of subjectivity and of our relations, as subjects, to the world; and (d) the gradual emergence of new political ideologies and practices (most especially Western democracy), as manifest in the ideals of the Enlightenment and the American and French Revolutions.

Other, although in many ways related, aspects of modernity as a cultural category are important as well, both in general and for this study, for example and in particular, Bruno Latour's understanding of modernity in his *We Have Never Been Modern*. According to Latour:

> Modernity is often defined in terms of humanism, either as a way of saluting the birth of "man" or as a way of announcing his death. But this habit itself is modern, because it remains asymmetrical. It overlooks the simultaneous birth of "nonhumanity"—things, or objects, or beasts— and the equally strange beginning of a crossed-out God, relegated to the sidelines. Modernity arises first from the conjoined creation of those three entities, and then from the masking of the conjoined birth and the separate treatment of the three communities while, underneath, hybrids continue to multiply as an effect of this separate treatment. The double separation is what we have to reconstruct: the separation between humans and nonhumans on the one hand, and between what happens "above" and what happens "below" on the other. (13)

This understanding leads Latour to his idea of "hybrid objects," such as the ozone hole or HIV virus, which are irreducibly both scientific (natural) and cultural, and which have come to play a central role in postmodernity. Postmodernity and its many hybrids have made us more sharply aware of the *impossibility* of the separation of "humanity" and "nonhumanity," which was the defining separation of modernity or what Latour calls "the constitution of modernity," although this impossibility was arguably in place all along: hence Latour's title thesis, "we have never been modern." Perhaps, on the other hand, we have been postmodern throughout modernity. Latour himself does not quite think so, since he sees postmodernism as continuing to subscribe to the constitution of modernity even in the face of hybrid objects. By contrast, as will be seen below, Jean-François Lyotard argues that postmodernism precedes (in the logical rather than ontological

or historical sense) modernism, if not modernity, both of which he understands closer to the more general lines sketched earlier.

With this discussion of modernity and modernism in hand, I am ready
to consider postmodernity and postmodernism, concentrating on postmodernism as the animating *Geist*, spirit, of postmodernity. For the reasons
already explained, the meaning I shall give to these terms is not exhaustive, but it is, I believe, sufficiently comprehensive. The key set of features
defining postmodernity and postmodernism may termed "techno-epistemological," by virtue of the (postmodern) relationships between new technologies, particularly information and communication technologies, and
epistemology—a transformation in the character of thinking and knowledge under the new technological *conditions* that define the postmodern
world. These are the postmodern technologies of this study's title. The
postmodern techno-epistemological situation thus defined was established
by Lyotard in *The Postmodern Condition: A Report on Knowledge* (1979)
and related works.

Lyotard understands modernity as Enlightenment or as the culmination
of Enlightenment thought. While this narrows somewhat the historical
scope of modernity as just defined here, conceptually this difference is not
that crucial, since Enlightenment thought and culture absorb most of this
history of modern thought and culture. "Postmodern," for Lyotard, "designates the state of our culture following the transformations which, since
the end of the nineteenth century, have altered the game rules for science,
literature, and the arts" (*The Postmodern Condition* xxiii). "Game rules"
are understood by Lyotard (via Ludwig Wittgenstein's concept of language
games) as referring to the fact "that each of the various categories of utter-
ance can be defined in terms of rules specifying their properties and the
uses to which they can be put" (10). This view of knowledge in terms of
language games is itself a postmodern move, insofar as it problematizes,
first, the alleged independence of nature or thought from language and,
second, the possibility, even in principle, of the unity of knowledge and, by
implication, culture. His study, Lyotard says, "will place these transformations in the context of the crisis of narratives" (xxiii). Lyotard then, in his
most well-known characterization, defines the *"postmodern* as incredulity
toward metanarratives," most especially the grand narratives of modernity,
which sought to explain the world through particular legitimating historical or political teleologies, such as those, dominant from the Enlightenment
on, grounded in the progress of science (xxiv).

Lyotard opens the main text of his "report on knowledge" by defining his "field" as that of "knowledge in computerized societies," which
expands both the epistemological reach of the postmodern and its economic, cultural, and political base (although some of this expansion is
apparent already in his "Introduction"). He then offers "a working hypothesis," which analogously expands his formulation just cited (the hypothesis
itself has, I would argue, been amply confirmed since then): "Our working

hypothesis is that the status of knowledge is altered as societies enter what is known as the postindustrial age and cultures enter what is known as the postmodern age" (*The Postmodern Condition* 3). The computerization of certain Western societies (keeping in mind that Lyotard is writing in 1979) and, more generally, the revolutions in information and communication technologies establish "the [postindustrial] postmodern condition" of Lyotard's title. This revolution is analogous to the industrial revolution that established the condition or, in any event, one of the main conditions of modernity (which qualification may apply to Lyotard's postmodern condition as well). In the postindustrial age, First World national economies have shifted from a manufacturing to an information and services base, concurrent with the rise of transnational corporations and the intricately interconnected global economy. The techno-industrial revolution of postmodernity radically transformed the practice and the very nature of our knowledge, a transformation that is most immediately manifest in the new (postmodern) mathematics, sciences, and technologies, but that extends across contemporary culture in all of its aspects, including its economic, political, ethical, and aesthetic aspects (*The Postmodern Condition* 3–6). In part following but also significantly departing from Lyotard, Fredric Jameson, in his *Postmodernism, or, the Cultural Logic of Late Capitalism*, aims to give postmodernism a (Marxist) economic base by seeing it as "the cultural logic of late capitalism," which he views negatively as an extension of the global cultural domination of capitalism. In his theorization of postmodernity, the culture of postmodernity emerges as a result of certain transformations of material structures of technologies and global economies, which subsequently drive and *govern* other transformations and new features in our cultural productions: in literature, film, art, television, music, dance, and architecture. Other influential analyses of both modernity and postmodernity, and of the transition between them (also grounded in a Marxist understanding of the relationships between capitalism and culture), were offered by David Harvey in *The Condition of Postmodernity* and by Edward Soja in *Postmodern Geographies*. By contrast, while, as just explained, Lyotard does argue for a correlation and perhaps even *a certain causality* between the rise of new forms of information and communication technologies and the transformation of the nature and practices of knowledge and culture, his argument is not wedded to the Marxist causality, proceeding from the economic base to cultural superstructure. Indeed, the logic and language of causality are generally shunned by Lyotard. This is unsurprising since a radical questioning of causality is a major feature of new scientific knowledge, especially in quantum theory, or postmodernist philosophy, on both of which his analysis relies. In view of this epistemology, Lyotard's ethical and political views are different from those of Marxists. Nevertheless, ethics and politics are his ultimate aims in the book, albeit coupled to this postmodern epistemology (*The Postmodern Condition* 65–67).

Lyotard extends the *Geist* of postmodernism to the twentieth century as a whole. Indeed, according to him this *Geist* in part arises from the *Geist* of modernism in *modernist* science, philosophy, and especially literature and art, such as that of James Joyce, the Cubists, or Marcel Duchamp, considered along these lines in Lyotard's more aesthetically oriented essay, "Answering the Question: What is Postmodernism?" Lyotard famously goes so far as to say that "a work [of art, or, by extension, of philosophy or science] can become modern [in present terms, modernist] only if it is first postmodern [in present terms, postmodernist]. Postmodernism thus understood is not modernism at its end but in the nascent state, and this state is constant" ("Answering" 79). Lyotard de facto extends this view to the philosophical thought of figures such as Friedrich Nietzsche and Ludwig Wittgenstein, and to the mathematics and science of (roughly) the twentieth century, or even to earlier artistic, philosophical, and scientific thinking of modernity, rather than only to modernism. Immanuel Kant, in particular, is viewed by Lyotard as "postmodern," or at least as an inspiration for postmodern thinking, in part in juxtaposition to the more "modern" Georg Wilhelm Friedrich Hegel ("Answering" 72–73). Lyotard's argumentation concerning the *logical* precedence of postmodernism over modernism and possibly modernity, developed throughout his work on postmodernism, is complex, and it is not possible to explain his reasoning in detail here. Arguably his most crucial point is the postmodernist character of the transformation of thought and knowledge enacted by certain *modernist* works (e.g., Joyce's *Ulysses*), a transformation that also brings with it a new set of attitudes. As he states, "the postmodern would be that which, in the modern, puts forward the un[re]presentable in [re]presentation itself; that which denies itself the solace of good forms, the consensus of a taste which would make it possible to share collectively the nostalgia for the unattainable; that which searches for new [re]presentations, not in order to enjoy them but in order to impart a stronger sense of the un[re]presentable" ("Answering" 81). It may be noted that this epistemology is automatically correlative to the postmodern incredulity toward metanarratives or grand narratives, since such narratives guarantee, at least in principle, an eventual elimination of the un(re)presentable. Now, the epistemology and the discursive enactment (narrative or other) of the un(re)presentable in (re)presentation may well be shared by (some) modernism and postmodernism. On the other hand, the postmodernist attitude toward the un(re) presentable expressed here is a more complex and subtler matter, and depends on the given figure and the given interpretation of the thought and work of this figure, which would establish such a figure as respectively modernist or postmodernist. Thus, Lyotard himself plausibly reads Marcel Proust as modern(ist) and Joyce as postmodern(ist) ("Answering" 80–81). But reading Proust along more postmodernist lines is not impossible, and has been done, and of course both Proust and Joyce can be read, with varying degrees of effectiveness, as modernist. While, however, certain figures or works can in principle be read either as modernist or as postmodernist, and while, as will be seen later in this study, the relationships between modernism and postmodernism are complex and multifaceted in general, Lyotard's point concerning the postmodernist epistemology of at least a significant portion of modernism is well taken. It will be especially important for my discussion in Chapter 2. It remains crucial, however, that the development, by whatever means, of postmodern ways of knowledge and new cultural attitudes goes hand in hand with the technological transformation of contemporary postindustrial society, defined by the rise of new information and communication technologies. Indeed, most of the modernist literary and art works and, even more so, the mathematical and scientific theories that are seen by Lyotard as epistemologically postmodern essentially relate to and, in the case of mathematics and science, facilitate this transformation. These relationships also further reflect complex causalities and a-causalities of the history of the transition between modernity and postmodernity, as against the Marxist single or, at least, uniquely dominant base-superstructure causality. The latter, however, plays its role, more limited but still important, in this history.

It would not be possible to consider here all of the features of the postmodern transformation of knowledge; Lyotard's 65-page report on postmodern knowledge required 231 notes, referring to nearly every conceivable field. I shall discuss some of these features and their role in postmodern urban life throughout this study. Arguably the greatest defining feature of postmodern knowledge remains the irreducible incompleteness of knowledge or the irreducible emergence of the un(re)presentable in (re) presentation, as just discussed, which also led to the irreducibly heterogeneous, if interactive, multiplicity of means—logical, conceptual, narrative, disciplinary, and so forth—by which we must pursue this knowledge. As will be seen in more detail in Chapter 2, this heterogeneity is correlative to and arises from the spaces of postmodernity, and thus, from a new, more material form of spatiality.

The power and prescience of Lyotard's *techno-epistemologico-political* analysis of postmodernity and postmodernism lie in bringing together the multiple threads just delineated and, again, the complex causalities and a-causalities relating or un-relating them as part of a network or set of networks. This network, shaped by the ideas, the *Geist* of postmodernism, *is* postmodernity; and it is, especially in its urban form, the main subject of this study. I add "political" to my characterization of Lyotard's analysis of postmodernity itself as techno-epistemologico-political because he also rightly links the techno-epistemological problematic of modernity to its ethico-political problematics, specifically to the question of justice. This link is in turn crucial for our understanding of urban postmodernity and hence for this study. Lyotard ends *The Postmodern Condition* by "sketch[ing]," in part against Jürgen Habermas's essentially modern argument, "the outline of a politics that would respect both the desire for justice and the desire for the unknown" (67). "The *desire* for the unknown," a quintessentially postmodern desire, also vis-à-vis even the quintessentially modern desire for knowledge, may be more conducive to justice than the epistemology of the Enlightenment. The cities and citizens of postmodernity must respect both desires as well and link them as part of urban life.

2. POSTMODERN SPACES, SUBJECTS, AND CITIES

The techno-epistemological or, again, techno-epistemologico-political transition from modernity to postmodernity was inevitably accompanied by a transformation of both spatiality and subjectivity—the first primarily for technological reasons of the development of information and communication technologies, and the second primarily for epistemological reasons of the radical change in the character of and attitudes toward knowledge. As discussed in Section 1, however, these reasons and, hence, their effects upon spatiality and subjectivity (and the relationships between both) are interactive. New ways of communicating enabled by new technologies, as Lyotard argues, have shaped the postmodern transformation and legitimation, or delegitimation, of knowledge as much as did these technologies themselves. Conversely, or reciprocally, postmodern forms of and attitudes toward knowledge are, in part via telecommunication, responsible for the rise of new forms of spatiality. The argument of this book, however, is that, while the technological and epistemological aspects of postmodernity may be more uniformly perceived in the postmodern world, the postmodern transformation of spatiality and subjectivity, and their mutually reciprocal constitution, can be seen most clearly in urban postmodernity—in urban spaces and urban subjectivities. This book also argues that, in view of the impact of postmodern cities as global cities, urban postmodernity is primarily responsible for making postmodernity global, geopolitical. Before I explain why such is the case, I would like to briefly discuss the question of postmodern subjectivity and spatiality, and their reciprocal, mutually constitutive, relationships.

Postmodern subjectivity radically departs from more "fixed" modern constructions, most especially Enlightenment subjectivity, developed philosophically from Descartes to Hegel, and defined by its alleged unity and by the dominant role of consciousness and self-consciousness in its constitution. Even the subjectivity of transcendental phenomenology, such as that of Edmund Husserl or (early) Martin Heidegger, while a major philosophical advance, tended more to reinforce than to dislocate the unity of the Enlightenment subject, or in any event did not sufficiently dislocate this unity. It should be noted that the thought of Husserl or Heidegger, or earlier figures crucial here, such as Descartes, Kant, and Hegel, is complex. In particular, this thought is suspended, proto-deconstructively and, as in Heidegger, deconstructively, between thinking the unity of subjectivity, or the primacy of consciousness or self-consciousness, and the impossibility of rigorously sustaining them. It is primarily in the hands of "followers" of these thinkers that the modern conceptions tend to acquire an unproblematized, uncritical form and are culturally transmitted in this form. Nevertheless, from their simplest and most uncritical to their most complex and subtle forms, the modern conceptions of the self are subjected to radical critiques by postmodernism. These critiques have been, first, undertaken analytically in the work of such earlier thinkers as Friedrich Nietzsche, Sigmund Freud (through the idea of the unconscious), and Martin Heidegger, and then in the work of Emmanuel Levinas, Jacques Lacan, Michel Foucault, Gilles Deleuze, Jacques Derrida, and Jean-François Lyotard. Secondly, they were enacted through postmodern practices of thinking and knowledge.

As a result, in the postmodernist view, as expressed by Lyotard, "a *self* does not amount to much, but no self is an island; each exists in a fabric of relations that is now more complex and mobile than ever before. Young or old, man or woman, rich or poor, a person is always located at 'nodal points' of specific communication circuits, however tiny these may be. Or better: One is always located at a post through which various kinds of messages pass" (*The Postmodern Condition* 15). Subjectivity or at least subjectivities do not disappear, but become radically and yet rigorously rethought, redelimited, and resituated, as such "nodal points," in decentered—heterogeneous but interactive—networks and postmodern spaces that are coextensive with these networks. Accordingly, as indicated earlier, postmodern spatiality, as the spatiality of postindustrial capitalism and its technologies (in particular, again, its information and communication technologies), and postmodern subjectivity become interactively correlated. This correlation gives spatiality a particularly important role in the emergence and the character of postmodern subjectivity. From Kant and, especially, Hegel to Heidegger and beyond, modern subjectivity and, with it, modernity itself, and most of modernism, were defined primarily in terms of temporality and history. By contrast, theorizations of postmodern subjectivity conceptualize it principally in spatial terms. These terms help, along the lines just explained, to articulate the postmodern subject as decentered, fragmented, and shifting among varied "positions," in parallel to and in interaction with the decentered material spaces and culture in which postmodern subjects live. The temporal contraction, the "disappearance" of time, due to instantaneous postmodern telecommunication, may be the most often invoked aspect of the dominance of spatial determination in shaping postmodern life and, hence, subjectivity. To cite Foucault's early response to this situation: "Our own era . . . seems to be that of space. We are in the age of simultaneity, of juxtaposition, the near and the far, the side by side and the scattered" ("Of Other Spaces" 22). This simultaneity of the postmodern remains important and has significantly contributed to the decentering of the cultural (and even phenomenal) spaces that we inhabit and, concomitantly, of postmodern subjectivity. There are, however, many other postmodern forces responsible for this decentering heterogeneity, for example, much larger and exponentially expanding *networks* of knowledge and communication, rather than only their speed. It is, accordingly, this decentering itself that defines most crucially the significance of spatiality, material and phenomenal, in the constitution of postmodern subjectivity.

It goes without saying (almost, because we like extreme pronouncements, such as that of the postmodern disappearance of time) that it is not a question of abandoning temporality in understanding postmodern subjectivity or, for that matter, postmodern spatiality. We still live in time, albeit a seemingly condensed time, and we are subjects of history, though no longer that history conceived as a forward march of human progress and development. We are still modern in this sense as well. But we are also postmodern, first, because of the greater role of spatiality in the constitution of postmodern subjectivity, but also because our temporality, or historicity, has changed as well. One might say that we live in a new type of "spacetime," which multiplies the actual spacetimes we inhabit, to adopt the language of Henri Lefebvre, borrowed by him from Albert Einstein's relativity theory, which is also in part defined by a general geometrization and thus spatialization of physics.

Relativity theory introduced not only the concept of spacetime, as a conjunction of space and time, but also, correlatively, a radical decentering of actual physical spacetimes. In Gilles Deleuze and Félix Guattari's words, such spacetimes are "pure patchwork[s], . . . heterogeneous, in continuous variation" (*A Thousand Plateaus* 485). Deleuze and Guattari technically refer to the so-called Riemannian spaces in mathematics (introduced by Bernhard Riemann in the nineteenth century); these spaces, however, are used by Einstein as well, especially in his general relativity theory, which combines his relativistic view of space and time as spacetime with gravity. Einsteinian physical spacetimes are, mathematically, Riemannian spaces. At the same time, as against Sir Isaac Newton's view of space as an ambient background space, and moreover as an absolute space, which things come to occupy, Einsteinian spaces are defined by the materiality of the physical bodies found in them, an idea that in part follows Gottfried Wilhelm Leibniz, who famously criticized Newton's concept of empty space. In short, the architectures of these physical spaces or spacetimes are, as it were, *formally* postmodern. The actual material spaces of postmodernity obviously involve a much greater complexity of materiality that defines their architecture (in either sense) and a much greater and more reciprocal role of decentered subjectivity in shaping this architecture.

I would argue, however, that most currently available theorizations of postmodernity, expressly those specifically concerned with the relationships between postmodern spatiality and subjectivity, have not so far sufficiently explained the reciprocity of these relationships. For, even as they have moved toward more spatial and more decentered conceptions of subjectivity, most theorists of postmodern subjectivity have usually considered it independently of the material spaces in which it exists. Conversely, even the best theorists of postmodern spatiality, such as David Harvey, Edward Soja, Manuel Castells, and Saskia Sassen, have generally (though not always) considered the spaces of the postmodern era as entities unto themselves, apart from the subjects who create and inhabit them. When such theorists do take up the effects of spaces on subjectivity, they either consider these spaces as exceeding the ability of subjects to adapt to them, as Jameson does, or else, in part, but only in part, following Foucault, they regard spaces as one-directional disciplinary mechanisms through which power acts upon pliant or unresisting subjects. I qualify these connections to Foucault because Foucault's own thinking concerning "power" and its effects is conceptually closer to my view, even though he does not quite develop the reciprocal dynamics in question, especially in the urban or postmodern, or most crucially for the present study, postmodern urban context.

By contrast, as must be apparent from the preceding discussion, one of the aims of this study is to explore space and subjectivity as fundamentally interrelated and mutually constructing, and in the first place to properly define them as such. It is in order to achieve this goal and specifically to examine how these interrelationships work "on the ground" in postmodernity that I shall focus on urban spaces and subjects. There are several reasons why urban spaces and subjects help one to pursue these tasks. The twentieth century was the greatest period of urbanization in human history: In 1900, only 14% of the world's population lived in cities; by the year 2000, the total was 47%, and it passed the 50% mark in 2007—the first time in human history that the majority of the world's inhabitants were urban dwellers. The United Nations anticipates that "almost all the population growth expected for the world in the next 30 years will be concentrated in the urban areas"; by 2030, the proportion of the world's population that is urban is expected to exceed 60% ("World Urbanization" 11). The postmodern world is, increasingly, an urban world. It is in our global cities where the peculiarities of postmodern spatiality and subjectivity are most clearly manifest, where the local and global are most conjoined, space-transforming information and communication technologies most concentrated, and the forces of transnational capitalism and consumer society most powerful.

I shall now briefly sketch out those features that characterize the postmodern city and differentiate it from earlier forms of the city. It is important to note that this description applies primarily to the global cities of the First World—New York, London, Tokyo—which are the focus of this study. Readers will also notice a particular emphasis on New York City in this book, in part because it is in many ways an exemplar of the global postmodern city, but also, admittedly, because it is the city I know best—the source of my personal "urban knowledge base." As would be expected given the postmodern condition that prevails in our world, as considered earlier, the postmodern global city is largely defined by its postindustrial, information- and services-based economy. This economy draws labor and capital from around the world, so that these cities become nodes in the vast networks of transnational flows of people, resources, technologies, and cultures. Communication and information technologies play a particularly vital role in these cities, where a massive renegotiation of the boundaries between material space and cyberspace is well underway. These cities constitute, thus, particular assemblages of the global and the local, the continuous and the discontinuous, the real and the virtual. Characterized by a widening gap between polarities of extreme wealth and poverty, these cities are also the primary sites for several troubling social trends, among them the privatization of ever-larger numbers of previously public spaces; the political, economic, and social secession of much of the upper and middle classes, manifest, for example, in falling support for public services and a withdrawal into secured, homogeneous enclaves; and the proliferation of surveillance and other control mechanisms. The challenges these conditions present us with are considerable. The first is one of, to use a term borrowed from Jameson, the basic "cognitive mapping" of our urban spaces: how to discern where we are situated both locally within the configurations or circuits of our own daily networks and, more broadly, within the circuits of a global network whose organization is never fully available to us at any given moment. The second but related challenge is how we might reconceive our subjectivities in a more global, cosmopolitan way, and, finally, how we might, as postmodern cosmopolitans, reimagine and recreate both our ideas and realities of community and civil society in the spaces of our global cities and world.

As might be expected given the preceding discussion of postmodernity and postmodernism, the relationships between urban modernity and urban postmodernity are complex. The use of the terms "modern" and "postmodern" in this urban context requires qualification, vis-à-vis their use earlier in this introduction. Terms such as "modern city," "urban modernity," and the like usually refer, as they will here as well, to urban phenomena of roughly the first half of the twentieth century. These phenomena are thus coextensive historically and linked conceptually with the "modernism" (or "modernist") rather than the "modernity" (or "modern") of my earlier discussion. I shall, accordingly, qualify this usage whenever necessary in order to avoid any confusion, although my context usually makes the difference clear. I shall, however, also speak at certain junctures of "urban modernism," such as that of Le Corbusier and other architects and urban planners of the earlier part of the twentieth century (one of my subjects in Chapter 2), in juxtaposing it to the urban postmodernism of architects, urban planners, writers, artists, and cyberspace designers and visionaries (who often think in urban terms of cybercities).

For the moment, like other cities across time, the postmodern city is an entity of its own time while simultaneously retaining vestiges of earlier city forms and, though they are considerably more difficult to perceive, anticipations of its future forms. In particular, while postmodern architecture, cities, and spaces constitute a radical departure from modern architectural forms, they also contain continuations or outgrowths of these forms. The fabric of postmodern cities is a complex interweaving of modern and postmodern elements, as are most postmodern phenomena in relation to modernity or modernism preceding them (keeping in mind the different use of modern in the urban context, as already explained). The imposition of postmodern urban forms upon a given modern city does not, however, leave the preexisting modern urban forms untouched, because they are recontextualized and transformed by the presence of the postmodern in their midst. One of my aims in this study is to explore the intersections, collisions, and concatenations of the modern and postmodern in contemporary cities, and their ramifications for our experience of the postmodern city and the postmodern world. We cannot understand either otherwise, even (and perhaps especially) when our primary concerns are the present and the future of the city and the world.

My analysis proceeds by building upon the work of the urban theorists mentioned above, and, when necessary, by extending and revising their ideas concerning postmodern urban subjectivity and spatiality, and, again, most especially the relationships between both. My conceptualization of subjectivity is founded in part upon the insights of Freudian and then Lacanian psychoanalysis (including the critiques and alternative models provided by Luce Irigaray and other feminist theorists), with its emphasis on the "positioning" of the subject in the family and society. This conceptualization also involves the extension of Louis Althusser's concept of "interpellation"—the "summoning" or "hailing" of the subject by social institutions or their agents—to include the effects of the material structures of those institutions in the construction of certain forms of subjectivity. I draw upon Foucault's work on how institutions such as clinics, prisons, and schools create particular types of subjectivity through their spatial organization (i.e., the panopticon) and functioning. My aim, however, is to give a greater emphasis to how resistances to strategies and technologies of power, as Foucault called them, are played out spatially and to how new, more open structures emerge in particular urban sites. In this respect in particular (but also in other respects), my analysis takes its direction from the pioneering work of Henri Lefebvre, Guy Debord and the Situationists, Michel de Certeau, and Gilles Deleuze and Félix Guattari on the strategies and tactics of resistance subjects deploy in everyday life. These strategies and tactics may now proliferate and mutate amid the material spaces of the postmodern city, which serve as both material frames for everyday life and as sites for the production of social differences of various kinds.

This book is, accordingly, a study of real-world urban spaces (again, in the broad sense in which this concept is understood) in the complex interweaving of their many components, from the architecture of buildings and their interiors to urban art to cyberspace and virtual reality. The book gives particular attention to cyberspace and virtual reality as two of the most distinctively postmodern features of contemporary urban life. It is also a study of representations of these spaces in contemporary literature, film, television, art, and advertising. My use of these representations is not based on an assumption that their depictions of the city and its inhabitants are literally true, but instead on the view that they convey, in complex and sometimes indirect forms, fundamental features of the city and its subjects and their interactions at particular historical moments. Statistics and other quantitative data (and this study contains a fair sample of such data) can tell us much about cities, but literature, film, and art can tell us what it is like to live in them, to experience them as living, moving, thinking, and dreaming subjects. They can often capture, far more tangibly than tables, charts, and graphs, the lived realities of cities past, present, and, quite likely, future.

At the same time, these representations themselves have powerful, real-world effects: they doubtlessly influence our experiences of the city and shape our perceptions and ideas of what it is and should or might be. Nor are these representations unimportant for those with the power to make decisions that can transform the concrete reality of urban spaces, including politicians, urban planners, developers, banks, investors, corporations, activists, and business and neighborhood associations. It would be naïve to think that the ideas that shape those decisions come only from narrow self-interest (though this might well often be the preeminent consideration) or from academic studies and theories of the city. When the popular representations of cities present them as corrupt sinks of iniquity, for example, these attitudes will inevitably influence the political and economic decisions that affect them, from support for mass transit and urban schools to capital investment and real estate development.

Literature and the other arts can also serve a proleptic function, anticipating and proposing new forms, as was the case, for example, with H.G. Wells's 1933 novel *The Shape of Things to Come* (and the 1936 William Menzies/H.G. Wells film *Things to Come*), which prefigured the architecture of the quintessentially postmodern Portman hotels. Similarly, William Gibson's 1984 novel *Neuromancer* predicted the transference of the spatial logics of the postmodern city to cyberspace and then demonstrably influenced the subsequent design of actual cyberspace environments. Indeed, literature and art tend to fare better in portraying and theorizing postmodernity than do our theories, which are more often than not contradicted or too quickly superseded by the fast-moving reality of postmodernity. Literature and art succeed in this not only by reflecting postmodernity but also by actively participating in and even creating it by continuously shaping and reshaping our experience and understanding of it. Art can, for example, function as a form of intervention in the space of the city, as it does in the work of the postmodern artists Jenny Holzer and Barbara Kruger, to be discussed in Chapter 1. Accordingly, the book's focus on real-world spaces and their literary and artistic representations helps to develop its theoretical arguments, rather than only to provide illustrations of them, and in the process to extend and revise prevailing theorizations of the postmodern city and citizens, and of postmodern urban life.

In sum, my argument in the book concerns the multifaceted relationships among the lived experiences of postmodernity, postmodernist literature, film, and art, and postmodern theory. It would not be possible to pursue the project of this book otherwise, since it is through these relationships, in all their multifaceted aspects, and only through them that one can understand the urban life of postmodernity—or live this life.

1 Legible Cities
Urban Signs and Subjects

> Your gaze scans the streets as if they were written pages: the city says everything you must think, makes you repeat her discourse.
>
> However the city may really be, beneath this thick coating of signs, whatever it may contain or conceal, you leave . . . without having discovered it.
>
> —Italo Calvino, *Invisible Cities*

While architecture has always been in part a semiotic art, the twentieth century saw an unprecedented convergence of signs and architecture. Since the early 1920s, the architectural spaces of American and European cities have been awash in texts and images—advertising, street signs, newspaper headlines, political posters, and graffiti. These signs have arguably become the dominant constituents of urban space, filling our perceptual fields, obscuring the streets and buildings that once defined the city. The emergence of this textualized *city of signs* marks a historical shift from the previous formation, which might be called the *city of things*. Although this opposition is to some degree qualified, the transformation itself is crucial for the emergence of the postmodern city and postmodern subjectivity, and their reciprocal relationships. It is, accordingly, fitting to devote the first chapter of this study to tracing this history in three novels: from the city of things in Theodore Dreiser's *Sister Carrie* (1901), through the early emergence of the city of signs in John Dos Passos's *Manhattan Transfer* (1925), to the early twenty-first-century culmination of the city of signs in William Gibson's *Pattern Recognition* (2003).[1] My analysis of these works is supplemented by brief discussions of several other modernist novels, such as F. Scott Fitzgerald's *Tender is the Night* and Virginia Woolf's *The Waves*, which allow me to support and amplify my argument, especially as it concerns the gendering of desire, a significant aspect of my argument throughout this chapter. Section 4 shifts to a broader cultural exploration of the themes developed in the preceding sections by considering various works of postmodern architecture, art, film, and television, which reflect, and in some cases have actually played a part in, the constitution of the postmodern city as the city of signs.

The transition from the city of things and its subjectivities to the modern and then postmodern cities of signs and their subjectivities, I argue, also involves concomitant changes in corresponding "economies" of signification and desire (using the term "economy" both in its direct sense and in a broader sense of the interplay and management of forces shaping a given phenomenon or process). Since a proper analysis of these economies (now, especially, in the direct sense of the term) inevitably involves the question of consumption of both things and signs, this chapter also examines how consumption impacts the urban environment, defines the relationships between the city and its inhabitants, and shapes the construction of urban subjects and their relations with one another.

My analysis is in part grounded in the argument that these formations of the city and of their corresponding subjectivities correlate with different stages of American capitalism: the industrial capitalism of mass-produced consumer goods, a capitalism of *things*, which dominated the late nineteenth and early twentieth centuries; and the postindustrial capitalism that began to emerge as early as the 1920s and came to dominate the late twentieth and early twenty-first centuries, a capitalism of *signs*. The capitalism of signs developed largely as a consequence of the unparalleled success of industrial capitalism's mass production, which spurred the increasingly sophisticated development of marketing devices as producers sought to generate demand for an unprecedented volume of consumer goods. Advertising (including signs identifying shops) and marketing in a broad sense have of course been around as long as marketplaces. It was in the twentieth century, however, that advertising and marketing became major urban industries. As these industries and the new media (radio, film, television, the Internet) that depended on them for financial support developed one after the other throughout the twentieth century, the character of the city was transformed. The *city of things* gave way to the *city of signs*, and the emphasis of the actual economies of major cities largely shifted from the production of goods to the production of signs, including advertising. Accordingly, the consumption of commodities also shifted to the consumption of signs. As Jean Baudrillard argues, most commodities are now consumed primarily as signs and only secondarily as things. Consumption in advanced capitalist societies, he contends, is best understood as "an active manipulation of signs, a sort of bricolage in which the individual desperately attempts to organize his privatized existence and invest it with meaning" (5). By the beginning of the twenty-first century, this transformation might be seen to be nearly complete in the hypertextualized postmodern city represented in Gibson's *Pattern Recognition*. The novel depicts the postindustrial economy based largely upon the production, manipulation, and exchange of signs (in print and broadcast media, finance, marketing, and so forth).[2]

These changes, like the transformations in the economic base that help to bring them about, are inevitably complex and uneven. The modern city becomes the postmodern city only gradually, over decades. The relationships between the city of things and the city of signs are, in part as a result, equally complicated, requiring some qualifications. One rarely encounters unconditionally defined entities or separations—one moment the city of things, the next the city of signs—but instead an intricate balance (different in each case) of both things and signs in the modern and then postmodern city. Being an inherent part of any capitalism, things and the consumption of things remain essential to modern and postmodern capitalism, urban capitalism included, even though today things are generally not made in American cities but in foreign cities that structurally resemble the industrial cities of late nineteenth- and early twentieth-century America. The American city itself, however, still constitutes a vast market and marketplace of signs and things alike. These complexities are also reflected in the literature and art discussed in this chapter. As in the actual world of the cities depicted by each novel, there are signs in Dreiser's depictions of Chicago and New York (notably the lights of Broadway and the billboards featuring Carrie), and there are vast quantities of things in both Dos Passos's Manhattan (the novel opens with a detailed description of the detritus floating around the bow of a ferry) and in Gibson's global cities (though the things there are almost always attached to a consumer brand). One might nevertheless argue, as I shall do here, that these three novels reflect the change in the balance in the relationships between things and signs—from the dominance of things in the modern city to the dominance of signs in the postmodern one, again, with a further shift toward the consumer-brand form of signification—which marks the history of urban postmodernity.

Published one year after Thorstein Veblen's *Theory of the Leisure Class*, which gave us the terms "conspicuous consumption" and "pecuniary emulation," *Sister Carrie* depicts clothing and accessories as the principle objects of desire and mediums of seduction. These commodities speak (quite literally) for capitalism, and their discourses are narratives of desire—desire for the *production* of an idealized subjectivity through the acquisition of things that will signal one's status in the social hierarchy. Dreiser's turn-of-the-century Chicago and New York are carefully mapped assemblages of department stores (the novel mentions five by name) and assorted showplaces (streets, theaters, restaurants, hotels) where the subjectivities of his protagonists are established through their purchases and public displays of consumer goods.[3] All of the novel's urban locales—from the factory floors where the goods are made to the department stores where they are purchased to the streets where they are on parade—are thronged with things.

The Roaring Twenties New York of John Dos Passos's *Manhattan Transfer* is, in contrast, a city of signs, and its inhabitants are the subjects of a relentless semiotic address issuing from the agencies of capital. These discourses also offer narratives of potential subjectivity that are sometimes adopted and sometimes resisted by the characters in the novel. Although both characters enact the consumerist narratives offered to them by capitalism, Dos Passos's Ellen Thatcher shifts among conceptions of herself that are filtered through and produced by her consumption of the signs of capital and the discourses of advertising, as against the consumption of actual things that defines Carrie's subjectivity. By contrast, the failed newspaperman Jimmy Herf struggles to create a sense of self in opposition to the commercial narratives that surround him in "the city of gilt letter signs" (Dos Passos 351). But both Ellen and Jimmy represent consumerist subjectivities that are shaped less by a desire for things than by a desire for and consumption of signs—"textualized" subjectivities.

The inhabitants of the First World global cities of William Gibson's *Pattern Recognition* are also shaped by a desire for and consumption of signs. In the postmodern world of Gibson's novel, however, nearly a century after Dos Passos's *Manhattan Transfer*, the nature of these signs has acquired a new defining dimension: advertising signs have become brands, and they produce a form of subjectivity that might be best described as "branded." As marketing has infiltrated nearly every public and private space, major corporations have come to see themselves less as purveyors of products than as purveyors of brands, expansive corporate images that seek to encompass ways of being and thinking—entire "lifestyles," sets of experiences, and systems of values. As brands have spread across the globe, our cityscapes have increasingly come to resemble one another: a relentless reiteration of Coca-Cola, McDonald's, Starbucks, Nokia, Sony, Samsung, and Nike illuminating the urban night. Gibson's protagonist Cayce Pollard, a "cool-hunter" with a phobic aversion to brands, seeks to construct her own, independent subjectivity in opposition to the "branded" subjectivities that surround her, in the process revealing both the difficulties and the potential of such an enterprise in the early twenty-first-century postmodern city.[4]

The emergence of this new (even for postmodernity) *pattern* of urban spaces and subjects, and the relationships between them, is my subject in Section 4, where this pattern is considered more in its own terms, through visual art and media, which are, however, themselves also part of this pattern. I shall in particular discuss the HBO television series *Sex and the City*, Sofia Coppola's *Lost in Translation*, and the conceptual art of Barbara Kruger and Jenny Holzer.

1. "WOMEN ON THE MARKET": CAPITALISM AND DESIRE IN *SISTER CARRIE*

> In the modern community there is also a more frequent attendance at large gatherings of people to whom one's everyday life is unknown, in such places as churches, theatres, ballrooms, hotels, parks, shops, and the like. In order to impress these transient observers, and to

retain one's self-complacency under their observation, the signature of one's pecuniary strength should be written in characters which he who runs may read.

. . . expenditure on dress has this advantage over most other methods, that our apparel is always in evidence and affords an indication of our pecuniary standing to all observers at the first glance.

—Thorstein Veblen, *The Theory of the Leisure Class*

Two years after his arrival in New York, Theodore Dreiser, writing about the city's 1896 sweatshop strikes in his column "Reflections," compared the city to "a sinful Magdalen," who "decks herself gayly, fascinating all by her garments of scarlet and silk, awing by her jewels and perfumes, when in truth there lies hid beneath these a torn and miserable heart, and a soiled and unhappy conscience" (411). Warning admirers of the city "that what delights you is only the outer semblance" (410), Dreiser reminded his readers of "the sorrow and want the ceaseless toil upon which all this is built," and the "countless miseries which these great walls hide" (411). Three years later, in writing *Sister Carrie*, one of the great novels of the American city, Dreiser began to work out these themes—the surface allure of the city, its harsh economic and social calculus of rise and fall, and, not incidentally, the role played in both by clothing and other items of conspicuous consumption.

Although the novel is set in the same decade in which outdoor electric signs, first used in New York in 1891, became commonplace, Chicago and New York in this period are, above all, cities of things. Period photographs of New York show streets that, from a contemporary perspective, are curiously bereft of signage (with a few dramatic exceptions, especially Broadway, which at night was transformed into "the Great White Way" by electric advertising).[5] Things and people, however, are everywhere. In the iconic 1898 photograph of the Hester Street market (Figure 1.1), one can see the plethora of pushcart goods set out for sale amid the crush of Lower East Side tenement dwellers. The 1897 photograph of the interior of the Siegel-Cooper department store (Figure 1.2), a lavish 1896 addition to the "Ladies' Mile" (Broadway and Fifth Avenue from 14th Street to 23rd Street) that advertised itself as "the largest store in the world," suggests that even in the more refined spaces of the new department stores, goods were not so differently displayed: the aesthetic is one of plenitude or even excess rather than rarity or exclusivity.[6] Department stores of this (and perhaps any) era functioned as purveyors and de facto celebrants of the wonders of mass production.[7]

Dreiser's protagonists navigate highly detailed urban milieus (the narration frequently provides addresses and even directions and itineraries), in which the emphasis is always on the consumption and display of consumer goods, particularly clothing and accessories. Veblen himself noted that

Figure 1.1   "Hester Street," 1898. (Museum of the City of New York. The Byron Collection; 93.1.1.18137.)

"conspicuous consumption claims a relatively larger portion of the income of the urban than of the rural population, and the claim is also more imperative" because "the provocation to this line of evidence [of wealth and status], as well as its transient effectiveness, are more decided in the city" (54). It is, therefore, no surprise that, as Stuart and Elizabeth Ewen observe, "the city provided a fertile soil within which mass fashion took root. As a mobile and personalized form of display, fashion was particularly suited to a society characterized, more and more, by mobile individuals" (142). The walk up Broadway, as Carrie discovers soon after her arrival in New York, "was a very imposing procession of pretty faces and fine clothes. Women appeared in their very best hats, shoes, and gloves, and walked arm in arm on their way to the fine shops or theatres strung along from Fourteenth to Thirty-fourth streets. Equally the men paraded with the very latest they could afford. . . . It was literally true that if a lover of fine clothes secured a new suit, it was sure to have its first airing on Broadway" (226). The mobility here is both literal (the walk up Broadway) and metaphorical (the climb up through the social hierarchy).

Carrie's first close encounter with mass fashion comes with her initial visit to the Fair, a Chicago department store. In this scene, she is only window-shopping because she has no money, yet she is "much affected by the remarkable displays of trinkets, dress goods, stationery, and jewelry. Each separate counter was a show place of dazzling interest and attraction.

Figure 1.2   "The Bargain Counter at Siegel-Cooper Department Store," 1897. (Museum of the City of New York. The Byron Collection; 93.1.1.18404.)

She could not help feeling the claim of each trinket and valuable upon her personally. . . . There was nothing there which she could not have used—nothing which she did not long to own" (17). Her own "shortcomings of dress," she painfully realizes, "make clear to all who and what she was" (17). As she intuitively understands, in this (capitalist) economy of desire, to lack desired things is to lack the desired self.

The items of clothing Carrie sees on display in the department stores, restaurants, hotels, and streets are for her objects of both conscious and unconscious desire, but this desire is unrelated to any biological need. The clothes are useful primarily as indicators (or in Veblen's terms, as objects of pecuniary emulation) of what Carrie might have and be, but they are also, at that moment, indicators of what she is not, of her class-bound status as a daughter of working-class parents, and thus of all that exceeds her grasp.[8] In this way, the clothing Carrie desires functions both as a thing (or in Saussurean linguistic terms, the referent) and, inevitably, as a sign, but her consumption of this sign always involves the referent, the material thing. In contrast, the signs in *Manhattan Transfer* are, as will be seen, consumed as signs, apart from their material referents (things). Accordingly, at work in these two novels are two different economies of consumption and of the relationships between consumption and signification.

This difference can be understood most clearly in light of Ferdinand de Saussure's theory of the sign. He articulated the concept of the sign as composed of the signifier (the word or sound-image) and the signified (the concept or meaning), bound together and linked to the referent (the thing referred to by the sign). Although Saussure acknowledged the arbitrary nature of the bond between the signifier and the signified, it was left to subsequent theorists (most importantly Jacques Derrida, and, in the case of the role of signification in the functioning of desire, Jacques Lacan) to explore additional complexities of their relationships to one another and of both to the referent.[9] These complexities involve possible shifts in the hierarchical relations between the signifier and signified (as against privileging the latter over the former, as in Saussure and elsewhere), the ways in which signifiers can become detached from their signifieds and "float," and, finally, how signs themselves can become detached from their referents and take on, in effect, a life of their own. In these respects, Derrida and Lacan depart from or at least (deconstructively) radicalize Saussure.

I would argue that in Dreiser the functioning of the sign is closer to Saussure's view of signification, insofar as signifiers, signifieds, and things (as referents) are more firmly linked together, and insofar as signifieds and things dominate this economy (in either sense).[10] On the other hand, the functioning of signs in Dos Passos and Gibson can be seen as manifesting or artistically staging the kind of departure from Saussure that Lacan and Derrida articulate analytically. In Dos Passos and Gibson, signs leave things, signifiers leave signifieds and float, and are thus ready to reattach themselves differently or continue to remain detached and exist independently. Even when the consumption of things in Dreiser's *Sister Carrie* also involves a consumption of signs (for example, clothing as a sign of wealth and status), it is nonetheless the signified that dominates the economy of this consumption; and, as noted earlier, in this novel, the consumption of signs almost always involves the consumption of things.[11] By contrast, in Dos Passos's *Manhattan Transfer*, not only does the consumption of things (or the consumption of signs via commodities) become essentially secondary to the consumption of signs via discourses on commodities (especially advertising), but also and most importantly the signifiers (the words) now come to dominate the economy of the sign in a proto-postmodern fashion. In short, to the degree that Dreiser's city of things is also a city of signs, it is primarily a city of *signifieds*; while Dos Passos's city of signs is also a city of things, it is primarily a city of *signifiers*.

In the city of things, the channeling of Carrie's desire—its direction into particular systems and structures of meaning which can be said to produce the specifics of what she wants and when—is determined by various economies: capitalist, political, social, and familial. From this perspective, the two economies of desire at work in the city of things and the city of signs— the Freudian and the Lacanian, respectively—may be seen as largely arising from industrial capitalism and postindustrial capitalism. Desire, constituted as lack—that is, defined and driven by the unattainability of the desired object—in both of these models, is "a function of market economy," as Deleuze and Guattari argue in *Anti-Oedipus: Capitalism and Schizophrenia* (28). This function "involves deliberately organizing wants and needs (*manque*) amid an abundance of production; making all of desire teeter and fall victim to the great fear of not having one's needs satisfied" (28). In the Freudian model, which Deleuze and Guattari argue is intimately bound up with the structures of capitalist society and the nuclear family as constituted within it, the multiplicity of desire of the pre-Oedipal, polymorphously perverse child is channeled by the Oedipal complex into an Oedipal economy of desire that is characterized by lack. This lack is precipitated by an anticipated (on the part of the boy) or perceived (on the part of the girl) loss of the penis, a material thing. Desire in the market economy of Dreiser's city, I argue, retains this characteristic focus on things and signs (their signifieds and their signifiers) that are connected and defined by them.

"Quick to understand the keener pleasures in life, [and] ambitious to gain in material things" (2), Carrie is drawn to men who can offer her both. This attraction is, crucially, always mediated by dress—his and hers. At Carrie's first encounter with Drouet on the train from Columbia City to Chicago, his clothing (the details of which are elaborately described in the text) and manner "built up for her a dim world of fortune, of which he was the centre" (6). Drouet is a "drummer," a traveling salesman, and his flashy dress speaks to Carrie far more eloquently than Drouet himself.[12] It is effectively part of his sales pitch: it advertises his success and, by extension, the success of the companies and products he represents.[13] But potential customers are not the only ones he is pitching. His dress is also, and not tangentially, "calculated to elicit the admiration of susceptible young women" (3).

Drouet's seduction of Carrie, like all the other seductions in the novel, then, turns upon the issue of dress—initially his and subsequently hers. Urging her to take the money he offers, he promises, "I'll see you through all right. Get yourself some clothes" (47). In turn, Carrie perceives the money in terms that seem to conflate it with Drouet himself: "The money she had accepted was two *soft*, green, *handsome* ten-dollar bills" (47; my emphasis). Money, desire, and seduction merge as, having accepted the money, Carrie "felt bound to him by a strange tie of affection now" (47).

The next day, "*possessed* of the means, *lured by desire*" (51; my emphasis), Carrie takes the twenty dollars and returns to the Fair department store (Dreiser's "possessed" is carefully chosen and significant here). As an impecunious job-seeker, she had previously wandered dreamily among the store's "remarkable displays of trinkets, dress goods, stationery, and jewelry. . . . She could not help feeling the claim of each trinket and valuable upon her personally, and yet she did not stop" (17). One can see here a shift from a desire that begins in a sense of attraction and plenitude (one that "does not stop") to a desire underscored by lack: all of the things she saw "touched her with individual desire, and she felt keenly the fact that not any of these things were in the range of her purchase. She was . . . an outcast" (17). As Deleuze and Guattari argue, "from the moment we place desire on the side of acquisition, we make desire an idealistic (dialectical, nihilistic) conception, which causes us to look upon it as primarily a lack: a lack of an object, a lack of the real object" (*Anti-Oedipus* 25)—and, one might add, a lack of a real subject, the subject produced (however ephemerally) by possession of the object.

This shift is also evident in the later scene in which Carrie returns to the store with money in her purse. Yet, interestingly, she is again not initially focused on acquisition—or on lack. She is in "that middle state in which we mentally balance at times, possessed of the means, lured by desire, and yet deterred by conscience or want of decision. . . . Now she paused at each individual bit of finery, where before she had hurried on. Her woman's heart was warm with desire for them. How would she look in this, how charming that would make her!" (51). Here her desire begins in plenitude and only subsequently turns to lack: "What would she not have given if she could have had them all! She would look fine too, if only she had some of these things" (51).

One might read the shifts within each of these two primal shopping scenes as a movement between two different models of desire. Each of the scenes begins amid a form of desire defined by connectivity or what Deleuze and Guattari term a "connective synthesis" (*Anti-Oedipus* 5–6) that then gives way to the Oedipalized disjunction or lack that follows. The original desire is based on what they describe as a "schizophrenic" proliferation and multiplicity of desire that is situated outside the Oedipal economies of Freudian and Lacanian desire, and hence is not restricted to the lack that defines those economies. Such desire is arguably what Hurstwood has in mind when he imagines that Carrie "was too full of wonder and desire to be greedy. She still looked upon the great maze of the city without understanding" (91–92). Her desire appears to him inchoate, unfocused, or unchanneled—characteristics it shares with her perception of "the great maze of the city," whose economies of desire are still largely unknown to her. This desire of hers, however, is supplanted by an Oedipally shaped field to which she is returned by Drouet and Hurstwood, and by money—Oedipus cum capitalism.[14] One might also compare this "primal scene" of shopping with the one that occurs in F. Scott Fitzgerald's *Tender is the Night*, in which Nicole Diver and Rosemary Hoyt go shopping together:

With Nicole's help Rosemary bought two dresses and two hats and four pairs of shoes with her money. Nicole bought from a great list that ran two pages, and bought the things in the windows besides. Everything she liked that she couldn't possibly use herself, she bought as a present for a friend. She bought colored beads, folding beach cushions, artificial flowers, honey, a guest bed, bags, scarfs, love birds, miniatures for a doll's house and three yards of some cloth the color of prawns. She bought a dozen bathing suits, a rubber alligator, a traveling chess set of gold and ivory, big linen handkerchiefs for Abe, two chamois leather jackets of kingfisher blue and burning bush from Hermes—bought all these things not a bit like a high-class courtesan buying underwear and jewels, which were after all professional equipment and insurance— but with an entirely different point of view. (54–55)

Nicole's shopping might be read as the ultimate display of conspicuous consumption, enabled by her immense wealth. And yet, the nature or the structure of Nicole's desire, enabled by wealth as it is, becomes subtly, even if only partly, de-Oedipalized.[15] To use this model to approach Dreiser's, Fitzgerald's, or Dos Passos's novels may be somewhat against the grain of their authors' own thought, but it may not be against what the novels and the world they depict so well tell us. All three characters (Dreiser's Carrie, Fitzgerald's Nicole, and Dos Passos's Ellen) exhibit at least some elements of this model of desire at certain points, signaling a potential, albeit never truly enacted or sustained, resistance to the Freudian and Lacanian econo- mies of desire the male world imposes on them. It is one of the strengths of these novelists' portrayals of the relationships between capitalism and desire that one finds in them the interplay and confrontation of different types of desiring-machines, in particular, the Oedipal (Freudian or Laca- nian) and schizophrenic (Deleuzean).

A Deleuzean economy of desire, especially (but not exclusively) by vir- tue of its radical juxtaposition to Freudian and Lacanian economies of desire based on lack, finds significant parallels in the work of a number of recent gender theorists, in particular Luce Irigaray and her conception of the female imaginary, based on a lack of (Lacanian) lack.[16] A key ques- tion posed by Irigaray and modern feminist and gender studies is how this history of the economy of desire, from ancient Greece, where the figure of Oedipus was born, to modern (and postmodern) Oedipalized capital- ism, is gendered, and how this economy might be both reimagined and re-gendered.[17] One can of course also see along these lines much of the pre- ceding history of feminism, beginning with Mary Wollstonecraft's medita- tions on political justice. Especially pertinent here, too, is Virginia Woolf's work, from her profound theoretical reflections to her many portrayals of London, where people "look at nothing but shop-windows" (*The Waves* 217). Like Dreiser's Chicago and New York, Woolf's London, especially in *The Waves*, is still a city of things (there are almost no signs in evidence), although more mysterious, more in the mist (literally and figuratively); it is also a city of images of things that are ultimately elusive.

At one level, the novel may even be read as a narrative of London itself, as asking the question: What is London? At the same time, Woolf's depic- tion of London and of the experience of London, and the way the economy of desire functions in this experience—her way of asking this question— could be seen along the lines of Deleuze and Guattari's understanding of desire, and they refer to *Mrs. Dalloway* in their critique of Freud's economy of desire in *A Thousand Plateaus*: "A very good schizo dream. To be fully a part of the crowd and at the same time completely outside it, removed from it: to be on the edge, to take a walk like Virginia Woolf (never again will I say, '*I am this, I am that*')" (29; *Mrs. Dalloway* 11).[18] Woolf appears several times and at important junctures of *A Thousand Plateaus*. She is described there, in the context of *The Waves*, as someone "who made all of her life and work a passage, a becoming, all kinds of becomings between ages, sexes, elements, and kingdoms," which economy of becoming and desire, Deleuze and Guattari rightly argue, is allegorized by the septet of characters in the novel (*A Thousand Plateaus* 252). London, too, becomes a city of many becomings. I shall further comment on Woolf's fiction in its, more proper, modernist context later in this chapter. For the moment, however, I would like to return to Irigaray, specifically to her analysis of the political economy of Oedipal desire and the role of women as commodities in it, which is especially significant in the context of Dreiser's novel.

According to Irigaray, "the economy—in both the narrow and the broad sense—that is in place in our societies thus requires that women [as commodities] lend themselves to alienation in consumption, and to exchanges in which they do not participate, and that men be exempt from being used and circulated like commodities. . . . Marx's analysis of commodities as the elementary form of capitalist wealth can thus be understood as an interpretation of the status of woman in so-called patriarchal societies" (*This Sex* 172). The question, accordingly, becomes "what modifications would it [the social order] undergo if women left behind their condition as commodities—subject to being produced, consumed, valorized, circulated, and so on, by men alone—and took part in elaborating and carrying out exchanges? Not by reproducing, by copying, the 'phallocratic' [Oedipal] models that have the force of law today, but by socializing in a different way the relation to nature, matter, the body, language, and desire" (*This Sex* 191). In other words, at stake here may be a program, closer to that of Deleuze and Guattari, of radically restructuring the economy of desire of male and female alike (each and their interactions now described as multiplicities of becomings), which, by the same token, also amounts in practice to an equally radical critique of capitalism.

The mechanisms by which consumer capitalism mobilizes Oedipalized desire to produce subjectivities are given a peculiar kind of agency throughout *Sister Carrie*. Clothing literally speaks a discourse of desire that evokes a corresponding desire and recognition in the subject, creating a relation through which the subject is interpellated and thus defined in particular (and highly commodified) ways.[19] "Fine clothes," the narrator observes, "were to her a vast persuasion; they spoke tenderly and Jesu-itically for themselves. When she came within earshot of their pleading, desire in her bent a willing ear" (75).[20] In *Sister Carrie*, "the voice[s] of the so-called inanimate" commodities are essentially the cajoling voices of lov-ers: "'My dear,' said the lace collar she secured from Partridge's, 'I fit you beautifully; don't give me up.' 'Ah, such little feet,' said the leather of the soft new shoes; 'how effectively I cover them. What a pity they should ever want my aid'" (75). More specifically, the discourses of the new shoes and lace collar are reminiscent of the thoughts and words of Drouet at important moments—the beginning and end—of his amorous relationship with Car-rie. Drouet believes the money he offers Carrie at their first dinner in the city is the solution to her dire financial straits, and it would indeed be (as the shoes say) "a pity" if she were to refuse his help. This help turns out to be quite substantial, as he reproachfully reminds her months later, when he confronts her with his knowledge of her clandestine relationship with Hurstwood. "I think I've done a great deal," he says. "I've given you all the clothes you wanted, haven't I? I've taken you everywhere you wanted to go" (165). His argument is as blunt as that of the lace collar: "I [out]fit you beautifully; don't give me up."

The fetishistic seductiveness—"Ah, such little feet . . . how effectively I cover them"—of the shoes' discourse is also remarkable for what it suggests about the transformation that the city has wrought in Carrie. Her desire for the shoes reveals no trace of her own, earlier relation to such things or of the grim realities of the conditions of their production. The "soft new leather" of the shoes evokes no memory of her days in the shoe factory where she had her first job, of her aching muscles, and the increasingly dis-tasteful repetitive action she was required to perform on the factory assem-bly line until it became for her "absolutely nauseating" (29). In a stunning demonstration of commodity fetishism, the shoes in the department store exist for Carrie solely as objects of seduction and allure, and all memory of the circumstances and human relations involved in their production are lost to her.

What attracts Carrie most is the transformative power of clothing, its ability to make her "look quite another maiden" (58). Mirrors—both lit-eral mirrors and the figurative mirrors of others' reactions to her—play a central role in this construction of identity, as Carrie sees reflected in them the Ideal-*I* she has always imagined lay within her.[21] "The mir-ror," the narrator observes, "convinced her of a few things which she had long believed. She was pretty, yes, indeed!" (58). The process of mirroring through which Carrie creates her identity is, however, not merely a matter of dress: It is also bound up with her natural acting ability. Able "to per-ceive the nature and value of those little modish ways which women adopt when they would presume to be something," Carrie mimics, mirrors, the gestures of those she admires: "She looked in the mirror and pursed up her lips, accompanying it with a little toss of the head, as she had seen the railroad treasurer's daughter do. . . . She became a girl of considerable taste" (78–79).

The urban environment itself offers numerous sites of such identificatory mirroring or interpellation, from the half-lit display windows of department stores in which one might see one's own ghostly reflection superimposed on that of the mannequins to posh restaurants like Sherry's, where "in every direction were mirrors—tall, brilliant, bevel-edged mirrors—reflecting and re-reflecting forms, faces, and candelabra a score and a hundred times" (235). Among the earliest documentations of the spectacular and subjectivity-producing effects of elaborate window displays in small shops and department stores are to be found in "Vitrines," a series of evocative photographs of Paris taken between 1912 and 1927 by Eugène Atget, one of the first great urban photographers. In "Bon Marché Department Store" (Figure 1.3), one can see how the city and passersby might be reflected by the window glass, simultaneously situating both the mannequins and the passersby in the same visual space, set against the background of the reflected city.

Properly positioned, the "window-shopper" can superimpose her own face upon that of the idealized mannequin, simultaneously assuming possession of its clothing and taking up the fantasy subject position it proffers

Figure 1.3 "Bon Marché Department Store," 1926–1927. (Photo by Eugène Atget. Courtesy of George Eastman House.)

amid the encircling panorama of the city street. The glass is, of course, also a barrier of sorts. As Carrie is well aware, how substantial a barrier is really a function of the consumer's means. The situation effectively reproduces the Lacanian mirror-stage moment in which the jubilant child "recognizes" herself in the "idealized" image in the mirror, at the center of the world around her. At the same time, other commodities on display in the window appear to float within the reflection of the surrounding city, creating a fantasy image of the city as a realm of magical things.

Drouet's purchase of clothing for Carrie (which was the occasion for Carrie's mirror epiphany) also triggers a subsequent conflict between mirror images: "She looked into her glass and saw a prettier Carrie than she had seen before; she looked into her mind, a mirror prepared of her own and the world's opinions, and saw a worse. Between these two images she wavered, hesitating which to believe" (70). The answer to Carrie's beleaguered conscience is ultimately quite simple and compelling: "She was alone; she was *desireful*; she was fearful of the whistling wind. The voice of want made answer for her" (70; emphasis added). It is lack, "want," finally, that silences the conflicted consciences of both Carrie and society itself.

There is, toward the very end of *Sister Carrie*, a scene that suggests a related form of mistaken identification or recognition, one that foreshadows the coming confusions of the city of signs. Cold, hungry, and homeless, Hurstwood decides to seek solace in the lights of what is now Times Square. There he encounters "blazing, in incandescent fire, Carrie's name," and overhead, "a large, gilt-framed posterboard, on which was a fine lithograph of Carrie, life-size" (362). He seems at that moment to confuse this sign of Carrie with Carrie herself: "'That's you,' he said at last, addressing *her*. 'Wasn't good enough for you, was I?'" (362; my emphasis). Through a triangulated desire, this misidentification heightens his own sense of lack, evokes in him a desire for what she's "got"—wealth, fame, social acceptance—all symbolized by that idealized "sign." "'She's got it' . . . 'Let her give me some'" (362). Pushed away from the stage door, "a fierce feeling against Carrie welled up," but in this moment it is reduced to a simple need: "'She owes me something to eat,' he said. 'She owes it to me'" (363). Having lost the "real" Carrie, Hurstwood is reduced to negotiating with her sign. While his confusion signals the depth of his disorientation and despair, it also points to how, in many ways, Carrie's own identity is now not much more than this sign, and that the theater has become the privileged site and the fitting symbol of her construction of her own identity.

The theater is also an essentially *urban* site and symbol of identity construction. Indeed, in many ways, the city and the theater prove to be interchangeable throughout the novel. As Deborah Garfield observes, "Dreiser labors to depict the city as a mega-stage, an extension of the theater . . . gradually defin[ing] the two as twin spheres—each a reflection of the other" (224). Den Tandt, Bowlby, and Fisher all link the theater to the urban economy, arguing that the theater mirrors (and naturalizes) capitalism's commodification of people and things. In "What Is a City?" Lewis Mumford took a more benign view of these connections: "the city creates the theater and *is* the theater. It is in the city, the city as theater, that man's more purposive activities are focused, and work out, through conflicting and cooperating personalities, events, groups, into more significant culminations" (185). Mumford's *idealism* (in either sense) is not entirely wrong or out of place. Dreiser's portrayal of the *reality* of the city as performative may ultimately be more convincing, however. As will be seen in the remainder of this chapter and throughout this study, much of this reality persists into the postmodern city and its theater of signs.

2. INTERPELLATIONS: SIGNIFICATION AND DESIRE IN *MANHATTAN TRANSFER*

> This is the principle of commodity fetishism, the domination of society by "intangible as well as tangible things," which reaches its absolute fulfillment in the spectacle, where the tangible world is replaced by a selection of images which exist above it and which simultaneously impose themselves as the tangible *par excellence*.

> The spectacle is not a collection of images, but a social relation among people, mediated by images.

> —Guy Debord, *Society of the Spectacle*

Manhattan Transfer is one of the first works of American fiction to capture the ethos of the modern and modernist American city, with its ceaseless circulation of capital, commodities, signs, and urban subjects. The streets of Dos Passos's Manhattan are constructed less of asphalt and paving stones than of advertising slogans, blaring newspaper headlines, snatches of popular songs, and fragments of conversation. We are seeing the emergence of the "textualized" city—the city of signs.[22] This new urban space is itself reflected in George Salter's illustration and cover design for the 1943 (and current) Houghton Mifflin edition of *Manhattan Transfer*, in which the book's title appears as a giant sign, perched on top of a tenement, against a background of looming skyscrapers. It may also be noted here that Dos Passos took the title of the book from a Pennsylvania Railroad interchange station where passengers could transfer between trains bound for Jersey City and those headed through the tunnels under the Hudson River to New York City's Pennsylvania Station. The Manhattan Transfer station, which could only be reached by train (it had no outside access), was located in the New Jersey Meadowlands. It was closed in 1937. The peculiar situation of the station may have been used by Dos Passos as part of his modernist allegory of the novel's "Manhattan," which is only a Manhattan *Transfer*, as opposed to the great cities of realist novels, such as those of Dreiser's *Sister*

Carrie, which are "real places" of arrival. Dos Passos's Manhattan is only an intermediate station, a place to which you arrive from somewhere (one lesser place or another) and from which you can depart to some envisioned and purportedly "real" Manhattan, as if trying to reach the thing or at least a signified (a real idea) starting from a signifier. You cannot, however, ever reach this destination. Such a place of transfer may become a place of final *destiny*, a better or worse one fulfilled at this transfer, but never a reachable *destination*.

The novel powerfully depicts how the massive proliferation of advertising in the 1920s (and the shift in its strategic appeals) transformed both the urban landscape and Americans' sense of themselves. In the 1920s and 1930s, Roland Marchand argues, "not only did the number of advertisements . . . and the media available to advertising expand dramatically; in addition, advertisements increasingly gave predominate attention *to the consumer rather than the product*. In their efforts to win over consumers by inducing them to live through experiences in which the product (or its absence) played a part, advertisers offered detailed vignettes of social life. This evolution toward an emphasis on consumer anxieties and satisfactions, which culminated by the 1930s, was what made American advertising 'modern'" (xxi–xxii; my emphasis). These new advertising vignettes presented a considerably more advanced technique for interpellating consumers by offering explicit subject positions in which they were expected to recognize and identify themselves. In the 1929 photograph of Times Square (Figure 1.4), one can see an example of this phenomenon in the billboard located in the center of the cacophony of signs crowding the square. It features an urbane "swell" looking genially out toward passersby, his cigarette pointing to the suggestion that they, too, "Graduate to Camels," that is, move up in the world, as he has already done.

A similar process of interpellation is encapsulated in a brief scene closing the first chapter of *Manhattan Transfer*, when an unnamed man pauses to study an advertisement for a Gillette razor in a drugstore window: "It was a highbrowed cleanshaven distinguished face with arched eyebrows and a bushy neatly trimmed mustache, the face of a man who had money in the bank, poised prosperously above a crisp wing collar and an ample dark cravat. Under it in copybook writing was the signature King C. Gillette. Above his head hovered the motto NO STROPPING NO HONING. The little bearded man pushed his derby back off his sweating brow and looked for a long time into the dollarproud eyes of King C. Gillette. Then he clenched his fists, threw back his shoulders and walked into the drugstore" (11). After purchasing the razorblades, he returns home and shaves off his beard. Then, the identification and transformation complete, he presents himself to his wife and children: "He turned towards them a face smooth as the face of King C. Gillette, a face with a dollarbland smile" (11). Throughout the novel, the thoughts of the inhabitants of Dos Passos's textualized Manhattan, "the city of scrambled alphabets . . . the city of gilt

Figure 1.4   "Times Square," 1929. © Culver Pictures.

letter signs" (351), are caught up in such vignettes and are intertwined with this welter of discourses and signs. Their identities, I shall argue, are largely produced in relation to these discourses and signs, though the process is frequently more complex than the response to the Gillette ad. I will focus on three of the best exemplars of this textualized, modernist subjectivity: the upwardly mobile Ellen Thatcher and her lover Stan Emery, and the downwardly mobile Jimmy Herf.

Ellen Thatcher may be seen as the consummate manipulator of the city's signs and of sign systems in general. Throughout the novel, Ellen's identity is in flux, as her frequent change of name indicates. She is first Ellie, then Ellen, then Elaine the lily maid of Astalot, then Elaine of Lammermoor, then Helena—each new name signaling a shift in her private or public persona and in the systems of signification she enters and responds to. Though Ellen is in some ways the most strong-willed of the characters in the novel and the one most in control of her own fluid identity, her conceptions of herself are incessantly filtered through and produced by her consumption of the signs of the city. When she overhears a fragment of conversation—"But she's made the biggest hit ever been made on Broadway"—she connects it to another sign, the familiar advertising slogan that has, by now, graced thousands of theater billboards, "Greatest Hit on Broadway" (154). The link sets in motion a remarkable fantasy of self: "Greatest hit on Broadway. The words were an elevator carrying her up dizzily, up into some stately height where electric light signs crackled scarlet and gold and green, where were bright roofgardens that smelled of orchids, and the slow throb of a tango danced in a goldgreen dress with Stan while handclapping of millions beat in gusts like a hailstorm about them. Greatest hit on Broadway" (154). Ellen, the up-and-coming actress, recognizes herself in and is interpellated by this sign. The process is propelled by desire—desire for ascendancy, for success, for sensual pleasure, for love, for adulation and recognition by others. The process involves both a fantasy identification (of the actress self with the "Greatest hit on Broadway") and a projection of her innermost desires.

Ellen's desire, like that of Dreiser's Carrie, is constituted within an Oedipalized (and capitalist) economy organized by lack, but it functions according to the Lacanian model of Oedipalized desire more than the Freudian model. For Lacan, desire is organized within the Symbolic Order that, while still Oedipal, is the order of language or signification (especially signifiers), and of relations, including social and economic relations; it is less grounded than it is for Freud in the material prototypes (for example, bodily organs) of signs or fetishes. In Lacan's conception of the Oedipal complex, what is lacked is not material (the penis) but rather symbolic (the phallus, a *sign* of sexual difference and of the powers and privileges of maleness), as is the nature of the anticipated or perceived castration.[23] Desire in the market economy of the city of signs, I argue, accordingly retains this characteristic focus on signs. In this, *postmodernist*, respect, in part helped by the realities of New York in the 1920s (but only in part, since there is an unquestionable aesthetic dimension to Dos Passos's vision of the city and the emergence of the cities of signs elsewhere), Dos Passos's novel may be seen as quite revolutionary, as against many works of his fellow *modernists*. Thus, Woolf's London in *The Waves*, for example, is as much a city of interpellation and desire (as the city where she inscribes the multiplicity of becoming), and of more radical, more Deleuzean, resistances to the Oedipal economy of desire as those found in Dos Passos. And yet, as noted earlier, it is still primarily a city of things and of the corresponding, (in this respect) more Freudian than Lacanian, economy of desire and resistances to Oedipalization. This is perhaps not surprising, given the prominence and even dominance of Freud's ideas in the Bloomsbury intellectual circle. While Woolf resists (Freudian) Oedipalization rather effectively, she nonetheless remains interpellated philosophically as concerns the (metaphysical) primacy of things over signs and, in particular, signifiers.

The primary sign defining Ellen's subjectivity and its economy of desire is the Danderine Lady, a roving advertisement for Danderine, a popular dandruff shampoo. Ellen first spots her in Lincoln Square: "a girl rode slowly through the traffic on a white horse; chestnut hair hung down in even faky waves over the horse's chalky rump and over the giltedged saddlecloth where in green letters pointed with crimson, read DANDERINE" (136). When Ellen is ogled soon thereafter by a pair of sailors, she summons the image of the Danderine Lady in a defensive mental maneuver: "All in green on a white stallion rode the Lady of the Lost Battalion. . . . Green, green, danderine . . . Godiva in the haughty mantle of her hair" (137; Dos Passos's ellipses). For Ellen, the Danderine Lady functions as a floating signifier, completely detached from its referent (dandruff shampoo) and acquiring a new set of meanings (signifieds) as it shifts along a signifying chain of associations. Ellen's identity and, to a great extent, her relations to the people and the city around her are, in turn, constructed within and along this same chain.

There is, thus, not just a different economy of desire in play here but also a different economy of signification than that operating in Dreiser's city of things. In *Manhattan Transfer*, the signs are largely detached from things, and, within the signs themselves, signifiers are largely detached from their signifieds. The social and psychological processes related to consumption and desire are governed primarily by signifiers, to which both signifieds and things (when they are involved) are subordinated.

In the preceding assemblage, the Danderine Lady is first transformed in Ellen's imagination into the "Lady of the Lost Battalion," and Ellen's identification with the image lifts her above the sailors' lascivious regard and renders her the romantic heroine of a martial legend. After returning briefly to "danderine," she slides further along the signifying chain of noble ladies on horses, summoning up another figure: Lady "Godiva in the haughty mantle of her hair"—noble, untouchable, and, of course, unregardable.

Ellen's images of these untouchable women on horseback (an image not without symbolic sexual connotations) might well be related to her failure to respond to any of the men who love her and to her own ambivalence regarding her sex, marked by her childhood insistence that "Ellie's goin to be a boy Ellie's goin to be a boy" (23). Yet she also harbors a romantic vision of love. A few more minutes after her glimpse of the Danderine Lady, Ellen launches into a poetic discourse inspired by the legendary figure: "When thou and I my love shall come to part, Then shall I press an ineffable last kiss Upon your lips and go . . . heart, start, who art . . . Bliss, this, miss . . . When Thou . . . When you and I my love. . ." (138; Dos Passos's ellipses). The fumbling rhyme and fractured syntax reflect both an ironic awareness of the falsity of the dream and her conflicting desires in regard to her love. The scene of loss and parting might also foreshadow the end of her relationship with her lover Stan Emery.

In her first conversation with Stan, Ellen remarks: "I saw the danderine lady this afternoon . . . She impressed me enormously. Just my idea of a great lady on a white horse" (140). Stan is quick to pick up on her identification with the figure. Misquoting the Danderine jingle, he renders it: "With rings on her finger and bells on her toes, And she shall make mischief wherever she goes" (140). The substitution of *mischief* for *music* is significant, for despite all her charm, Ellen produces few grace notes and indeed much havoc in the lives of the men who admire and love her. For her first husband John Oglethorpe, the theater producer Harry Goldweiser, her lawyer George Baldwin, and her second husband Jimmy Herf, she remains a tantalizing, unreachable figure.

The Danderine Lady functions not only to mediate Ellen's relationship to herself and the men in her life, as her conversation with Stan suggests, but also to mediate Stan's relationship to her. While Stan is the only man Ellen ever loves, he doesn't love her back. Caught up in his own despair and seeing Ellen more clearly than her other men, he mocks her attempts to help him: "'Rings on her fingers,' chanted Stan, pressing his buzzer, 'And bells on her toes, And she shall cure dandruff wherever it grows'" (143). Later, sitting on a bench on the Battery, Stan looks out over the water, away from the city, but its signs are inescapable: "His mind went on jingling like a mechanical piano. 'With bells on her fingers and rings on her toes / Shall ride a white lady upon a great horse / And she shall make mischief wherever she goes. . .'" (252; Dos Passos's ellipsis).

Just as Ellen adopts the Danderine Lady, Stan conceives of his own subjectivity partly through the image of Longlegged Jack of the Isthmus, the hero of a popular song. As he contemplates suicide, the song runs through his mind: "And it rained forty days and it rained forty nights / And it didn't stop till Christmas / And the only man who survived the flood / Was longlegged Jack of the Isthmus. . ." (252; Dos Passos's ellipsis). The last line in that section is his remark: "Kerist I wish I was a skyscraper" (252)—a wish not for the citadel of desire a skyscraper symbolizes for Jimmy or the triumphant pinnacle it represents for Ellen, but rather an inanimate tower of strength capable of withstanding the apocalyptic floods of the city's relentless demands. His failed identification with the phallic skyscraper is signaled by the image of "Skyscrapers go[ing] up like flames, in flames, flames" that precedes his self-immolation (253). His last thought, "The only man who survived the flood rode a great lady on a white horse," conflates the image of the Danderine Lady—Ellen, the great lady he cannot "ride," with that of the survivor, Longlegged Jack of the Isthmus, a role he is finally unable to assume (253). Ultimately, neither Stan nor, as we will see, Jimmy is able to forge a viable sense of self out of the materials offered by the deluge of signs and images that surrounds them.

Although Ellen easily adopts the signifiers of consumerism, this does not produce a satisfying sense of self or enable her to love the men who love her. As her marriage with Jimmy begins to falter, there is a moment when he imagines that he is conversing with "the Elliedoll" (301), an image that recurs in one of the novel's final scenes, when Ellen dines with George Baldwin and refuses his marriage proposal. Exhausted from the day, she takes refuge in the ladies' room. There, she "stayed a long time looking in the mirror, dabbing a little superfluous powder off her face, trying to make up her mind. She kept winding up a hypothetical dollself and setting it in various positions. . . . Suddenly she turned away from the mirror with a shrug of her toowhite shoulders" (374). Ellen's interlude before the mirror suggests the extent to which her identity is, like the "hypothetical dollself," a matter of "gestures . . . acted out on various model stages" (374). Yet her abrupt turn from the mirror seems to signal her dissatisfaction with any of these mirror images, and the shrug might be read as surrender. The "dollself" is ominously inhuman, inanimate, dead.

It is the newspaperman Jimmy Herf who is most resistant to interpellation by the forces of capital and the "textualized" subjectivity it produces. For him, the subjectivity-producing "city of shiny windows" that mirror some commercial version of an ideal self, "the city of gilt letter signs" that seem to promise so much, is also "the city of scrambled alphabets" (351). Like that of Ellen and many others, Jimmy's mind fills with the signs that surround him on his walks through the city. There appears to be no outside to this all-pervasive discourse of consumer capitalism: when Jimmy attempts to escape it on one of his long, despairing walks out of the city, he finds even the sides of barns covered with "peeling letters that spelled out LYDIA PINKHAM'S VEGETABLE COMPOUND, BUDWEISER, RED HEN, BARKING DOG" (113)—the product's very names, with their references to vegetables, hens, dogs—serving as an ironic gloss on the changing countryside and on the precession of the sign over the real wrought by capitalism and its desiring-machines.

Within this all-pervasive commercial discursive sphere, the urban subject's manipulations of semiotic codes—including those of image or of clothing—might, as Jonathan Raban proposes in *Soft City*, "register the city's immense and arbitrary range of choice. They announce simply that you have chosen, made your personal bid for a fantasy" (49). Jimmy appears to understand, however, that while this "range of choice" to which Raban refers might well be "immense," it is not quite "arbitrary": it is massively determined and often overdetermined by the exigencies of consumer capital. The possibilities are thus inevitably limited to those choices, also offered by means of and as signs, which the corporations of the era deem acceptable, that is, most profitable, and which they accordingly make available.

Jimmy responds to this welter of consumer discourse with revulsion: "With every breath [he] breathed in rumble and grind and painted phrases until he began to swell, felt himself stumbling big and vague, staggering like a pillar of smoke above the April streets" (352–53). He resists the city's hailing of him as yet another up-and-coming young professional. It may be that for him, as Deleuze and Guattari suggest is true of most subjects within a capitalist, Oedipalized economy, "what is missing is not things a subject feels the lack of somewhere deep down inside himself, but rather the objectivity of man, the objective being of man, for whom desire is to produce, to produce within the realm of the real" (*Anti-Oedipus* 27). Yet within the circuits and structures of capitalism, un-Oedipalized desire is repressed and diverted elsewhere, channeled through capitalist Oedipalization into lack-fueled fantasies of consumerist fulfillment. This channeling is at least partly prophylactic—a check on desire's revolutionary potential. "If desire is repressed," they observe, "it is because every position of desire . . . is capable of calling into question the established order of society" (*Anti-Oedipus* 116).

As a newspaperman, Jimmy himself is nonetheless complicit in the corruption of the public sphere by capitalism, as Oglethorpe scornfully points out to him, since "every sentence, every word, every picayune punctuation that appears in the public press is perused and revised and deleted in the interests of advertisers and bondholders. The fountain of national life is poisoned at the source" (195). Not long before he quits his job, Jimmy has a dream in which he is "writing a letter on a linotype": "The arm of the linotype was a woman's hand in a long white glove. Through the clanking from behind amber foots Ellie's voice Dont, dont, dont, you're hurting me so. . . . Mr. Herf, says a man in overalls, you're hurting the machine and we wont be able to get out the bullgod edition thank dog" (329; Dos Passos's ellipsis). The dream signals both the collapse of his relationship with Ellen, who is conflated with the machine, and his nascent desire to "monkeywrench" the production process. The anticipated outcome of these conflicts with Ellen and the machine itself is ominously depicted in the most Freudian terms: "a gulping mouth with nickelbright rows of teeth, gulped, crunched" (329).

After Jimmy quits his job, he wanders through the city, imagining himself disrupting the ceaseless flow of consumerist discourse, writing "cusswords on typewriters between the stenographer's fingers, mix[ing] up the pricetags in departmentstores" (353). Yet he has no alternative method of self-creation. His sense of self seems to disintegrate amid the oversweet flavors of the language all around him: "Inside he fizzed like sodawater into sweet April syrups, strawberry, sarsaparilla, chocolate, cherry, vanilla dripping foam through the mild gasolineblue air," until finally, "he dropped sickeningly fortyfour stories, crashed" (353).

The reference to the forty-four-story skyscraper here is part of a complex of meanings concerning the skyscrapers of Manhattan in the novel. Jimmy appropriately reads these edifices—the Pulitzer Building, the Woolworth Tower, and the Flatiron Building—as concrete advertisements for the power of business. As the architectural historian Piera Scuri argues, "if we begin with the assumptions that churches are the expression of religious power and castles of aristocratic power, and that architecture is the expression of the society that creates it, then it follows that skyscrapers must be considered to express the power of multinational corporations" (ix). They also carry (symbolically and literally) these corporations' signifying power; they are signs no less than things, although they are certainly things as well, and also signify by this thingness, by their materiality. Citing the skyscraper's "great potential as an advertising image" (ix), Scuri believes "the transformations undergone by [the skyscraper's] powerful image correspond to a courting of public opinion, achieved by means of the seductive power of the image itself, and above all by one of the most powerful images that can be set before human eyes: the architectural image" (2).[24] (It should be noted that this image is also, inevitably, phallic, a signifier of more than just economic power.) This intersection of architecture and capitalism, along with and alongside the architectural developments made possible by the creation of new materials and technologies, are explored at several points in *Manhattan Transfer*, particularly in the discourse of the architect Phil Sandbourne, who envisions "the skyscraper of the future'll be built of steel and glass. . . . He's got a great sayin about some Roman emperor who found Rome of brick and left it of marble. Well he says he's found New York of brick an that he's goin to leave it of steel . . . steel an glass" (75).

Amid the litany of advertising discourse surrounding Jimmy appears a series of material components, the stuff of skyscrapers: "Wrought steel, monel, copper, nickel, wrought iron," and then, ironically, "*All the world loves natural beauty.* LOVE'S BARGAIN that suit at Gumpel's best value in town. Keep that schoolgirl complexion" (351), a slippage between the skyscraper and the figure of Ellen that links the skyscraper to a somewhat different form of phallic desire than that suggested previously. Throughout his long days and nights of wandering the city, Jimmy is obsessed with a particular skyscraper, "a grooved building jutting up with uncountable bright windows falling onto him out of a scudding sky," from which "typewriters rain continual nickelplated confetti in his ears" (365). This edifice is simultaneously an embodiment of the city's alluring consumer discourse and a signifier of (commodified) sexual desire: "Faces of Follies girls, glorified by Ziegfeld, smile and beckon to him from the windows" (365). The desire involves more than the appeal of the Ziegfeld girls, however, for Ellen, who has married and then left him, is up there too, contained within the phallic skyscraper of Jimmy's desire, "in a gold dress, Ellie made of thin gold foil absolutely lifelike beckoning from every window," but, now, forever inaccessible (365). The skyscraper now appears as the image, the signifier, that finds its signified in the nightmare reality of the doors that are impossible to find or the dead end of the lost faith in words, and perhaps more than only words. In his imagination, Jimmy "walks round blocks and blocks looking for the door of the humming tinselwindowed skyscraper, round blocks and blocks and still no door. Every time he closes his eyes the dream has hold of him, every time he stops arguing audibly with himself in pompous reasonable phrases the dream has hold of him. . . . 'If only,' he thinks, 'I still had faith in words'" (365–66). Finally unable to reach Ellen, and unwilling or unable to forge a sense of himself in the face of the over-load of semiotic overtures offered by the city, he leaves it behind, headed nowhere in particular, but "Pretty far"—the last words of the novel (404).

In contrast to Jimmy, Ellen is very much the product of the city signs that circulate around her, though she finds that these only allow for simulacra of identity. It would be tempting and easy, perhaps too easy, to juxtapose these simulacra to some authentic human identity, for which, say, Jimmy or Stan search, equally in vain, though for different reasons. In the city and beyond, if there is such a beyond anymore (how far can Jimmy go?), an identity is inescapably a mixture of the thing and the simulacra, of the human and the material, including the textual, and finally of identity and difference, in short, of us, each and together, and of our cities. Jimmy and, to a much lesser extent, even Stan might represent emerging forms of what Deleuze and Guattari refer to as anti-Oedipal desiring-machines, presented to us as models of resistance, however unsuccessful, to the despotic Oedipal desiring-machines of the state and of capitalism that so thoroughly ensnare Ellen and, earlier, Dreiser's Carrie, Drouet, and Hurstwood. They would need, however, to deploy alternative economies of desire to succeed, since theirs are still too complicit with capitalism and its Oedipalization.

As Deleuze and Guattari point out, it is in the nature of desiring-machines to break down, even as they run (*Anti-Oedipus* 31–32). Modernist litera-ture provides plenty of examples of this phenomenon, from the radical disjunctions and disruptions of Joyce's *Ulysses* to Dos Passos's *Manhattan Transfer* and *U.S.A.* trilogy. Surveying the wreckage of the lives of Dos Passos's protagonists, and not a few of Dreiser's, we discover that "the artist is the master of objects; he puts before us shattered, burned, broken-down objects, converting them to the régime of desiring-machines. . . . Even more important, the work of art is itself a desiring-machine" (Deleuze and Guattari, *Anti-Oedipus* 32). *Sister Carrie* and *Manhattan Transfer* are not only remarkable portrayals of American cities on their way from cities of things to cities of signs, or in their complex existence between things and signs. They are also powerful interventions that make us rethink and resist the processes by which capitalism summons and forms us as subjects.

3. TRADEMARKS AND FRAGMENTS: MARKETING AND DESIRE IN *PATTERN RECOGNITION*

> Where every prospect pleases, man is at his vilest when he erects a billboard.
>
> —David Ogilvy, founder of the Ogilvy & Mather advertising agency, *Confessions of an Advertising Man*

> The graphic sign in space has become the architecture of this landscape.
>
> —Robert Venturi, Denise Scott Brown, and Steven Izenour, *Learning from Las Vegas*

William Gibson's postmodern novel *Pattern Recognition* explores the early twenty-first century apotheosis of the city of signs and of the sign-constructed urban subjectivities that began to emerge early in the twentieth century. Unlike either Dreiser's *Sister Carrie* or Dos Passos's *Manhattan Transfer*, which taught us to navigate the cities of things and signs, of department stores and text-saturated streets, *Pattern Recognition* takes our utter immersion in the city of signs for granted. Here, the department store is itself a "logo-maze," and the hypertextualized postmodern city outside, "more of the same" (18).

Our global cities can be seen as present-day incarnations of the "architecture of communication over space" described by Robert Venturi, Denise Scott Brown, and Steven Izenour in their influential 1972 study, *Learning from Las Vegas*. "This architecture of styles and signs is antispatial," they observe of the sign-based architecture that came to dominate the city of Las Vegas, since "communication dominates space as an element in the architecture and in the landscape" (8). This new urban milieu, they argue, constitutes "not chaos, but a new spatial order relating the automobile and highway communication in an architecture which abandons pure form in favor of mixed media" (75). This architecture is the offspring of the acceleration of both automobiles and of consumer culture, for it is primarily commercial messages that compose this new architecture of signs, this "new symbolic order . . . determined by movement, isolation, and consumerism" (Schwarzer 91). In contemporary global cities, this dominance of signs over space now occurs at all levels—those of cars, buses, trains and subways, and also of pedestrians.

On the verge of postmodernity, in the early 1960s, pop artists such as Andy Warhol and Ed Ruscha signaled the extent to which the cityscape had already been transformed into a virtual signscape. Andy Warhol's 1964 installation, "Campbell's Soup Cans, Del Monte, and Heinz 57 Boxes," at the Stable Gallery in New York evokes an urban geography of towers of brand-name boxes and cans (Figure 1.5).

Ed Ruscha's iconic 1968 painting of the Hollywood sign looming against the vast Pacific sky and his photographic series of "For Sale" signs capture the essence of the Los Angeles cityscapes as signscape, in which the buildings no longer define the urban space. "Whenever I come upon a Ruscha, I am suddenly there, palpably there, as if I were about to turn on the radio, ease into the traffic on Santa Monica, and let the world float across my brain pan," Mark Stevens wrote of a Ruscha exhibition in 2004. Even "his more abstract images or words and phrases," he continued, "create the same, mysterious sensation of the city" (58).

This "branding" of the urban landscape through the proliferation of advertising signs and logos has profound implications for its inhabitants. As architecture critic Herbert Muschamp argues, "architecture is also a medium of mental conditioning as well as a form of art or social practice" ("Service" 36). This mental conditioning, the internalization of the exterior world, also helps to generate subjectivities that are increasingly contingent

Figure 1.5 Andy Warhol, "Campbell's Soup Cans, Del Monte, and Heinz 57 Boxes," Installation at Stable Gallery, New York, 1964. (©2008 Andy Warhol Foundation for the Visual Arts/ARS, New York. Photo by Billy Name/Ovo Works, Inc.)

not just upon the consumption of signs, but specifically upon the consumption of "brands." The contemporary, postmodern city and the "branded" subjectivities of its inhabitants are in many ways the creation of the most recent stage of postindustrial, sign-based capitalism and the global economy shaped by it.

In this economy, the financial, marketing, media, and culture industries— industries that all involve the production, manipulation, and exchange of signs of various kinds—are centralized in a few First World postindustrial cities, while the actual manufacturing of material goods takes place elsewhere, wherever raw materials and labor are most accessible and least expensive, generally in the Third World. These cities—New York, London, Tokyo, and Paris—constitute the leading, first-tier "global cities," the primary nodes in the global economic network, and it is in these four cities, along with the transitional city of Moscow, that Gibson has set the plot of *Pattern Recognition*.[25] (The Third World production sites, where industrial and consumer goods are manufactured, are nearly invisible in the novel, as they are in reality for most inhabitants of the First World global cities.)

With the emergence of transnational capitalism has come a global (though by no means universal) consumer culture of music, movies, fashion, celebrities, advertising, and brand names—an evolving, Westernized culture produced in global cities whose landscapes increasingly resemble one another. As Gibson's narrative follows the movement of its New York-based protagonist Cayce Pollard between New York, London, Tokyo, Moscow, and Paris, it becomes apparent that, despite minor local differences in the styles of things (milk, coffee, cars, appliances), these cities are all saturated with the same consumer signs and brands. Capital, as Marx observed, "creates a world after its own [monotonous] image" (213). In London, Cayce emerges from the Underground and spots a Starbucks; in Tokyo, she can find her way by keeping a Gap billboard in sight; in Moscow, she encounters a giant Prada logo; in Paris, Tommy Hilfiger is on prominent display in the Galleries Lafayette. Inscribed across cityscapes around the world, brands are the postmodern lingua franca, and corporate logos its *logos*.[26]

In *No Logo*, Naomi Klein links the spectacular rise in resources devoted to marketing, particularly the marketing of brands (as opposed to individual products), in recent decades with the expansion and concomitant deindustrialization of First World economies. She asserts that "the astronomical growth in the wealth and cultural influence of multinational corporations over the last fifteen years can arguably be traced back to a single, seemingly innocuous idea developed by management theorists in the mid-1980s: that successful corporations must primarily produce brands, as opposed to products" (3). In this postmodern realization of Marx's observation that "all that is solid melts into air," marketing displaces manufacturing (which is contracted out, often to Third World entities), and corporations now "compet[e] in a race toward weightlessness: whoever owns the least, has the fewest employees on the payroll and produces the most powerful images, as opposed to products, wins the race" (Klein 4).

This shift in emphasis from production to marketing seems the inevitable result of the mass production of consumer goods that first set the development of modern marketing in motion. As legions of identical goods streamed off production lines, persuading consumers to purchase a particular product required marketers to differentiate it from competing products, even when, as is the case with soaps, the differences among them were negligible. Marketers use several (sometimes concurrent or overlapping) pitch strategies to accomplish this. One emphasizes the material attributes of the product and seeks to distinguish it on that basis—"Dove is one-quarter moisturizing cream" or "Ivory is 99 44/100 percent pure"— however specious the attributes might be. "It floats!", for example. (It floats almost like a signifier, ready to enter the economy of consumer desire, for which it offers a promise of fulfillment.) This type of marketing generally emphasizes use value over exchange value. A second strategy, explained in Section 2, focuses more on consumers' needs or "lacks," and offers fantasy vignettes involving the product. Here a symbolic and imaginary exchange value takes precedence over any actual use value the product might have for the consumer. The third strategy, known as "branding," has two primary goals: first, to "develop the brand," to create a compelling corporate (as opposed to product) image that engages the consumer's imagination and desires, and second, to encourage "brand loyalty," not just to individual products but also to families of products identified with that brand (often extremely extended and diverse families—Starbucks, for example, now sells not just coffee but also music and movies). The degree of this "branded" engagement of the consumer's imagination and desires goes far beyond a vague romanticizing of the product's real-world utility (floors that "sparkle and gleam," for example) or even any fantasy vignette, though it is related to and sometimes involves this type of marketing. As Klein notes, corporations now conceive of their brands "not [as] a product but a way of life, an attitude, a set of values, a look, an idea" (23). What they seek to create, in effect, are "branded" subjectivities and "branded" lives.

As First World urban economies have made the transition from an industrial to a postindustrial base, with a concomitant shift in emphasis from production to consumption as the engine of economic growth, the conception of identity or subjectivity has also changed. No longer finding or even expecting to find self-definition and fulfillment primarily through work, many (perhaps most) people now, with the prompting of marketing, define themselves less and less through what they produce and more and more through what they consume. It is consumption that defines their "lifestyle" (a term that owes its genesis to marketing): what kinds of food they eat (and where), what kinds of houses they live in and how they are furnished, where they vacation, what styles of clothing they wear, what movies they watch and music they listen to, and so forth. The ways in which these things are defined, understood, and imagined are almost entirely the creation of advertising and other forms of marketing, which have set out to brand those lifestyles and all of the things, ideas, and experiences that they comprise. This conceptual expansiveness of branding is matched by the unprecedented extent of its promotion and dissemination. As global advertising spending has skyrocketed from a conservatively estimated $27 billion in 1970 to $604 billion in 2006 (of which the U.S. accounts for $292 billion), marketing in a multitude of forms has seemingly infiltrated nearly every space—physical, cultural, and mental—of contemporary life.[27] In Gibson's *Pattern Recognition* and in many current films and artworks, we can see how these forces are shaping both the cities and the subjectivities of the postmodern world.

Cayce Pollard makes her living as a "cool-hunter." A preternaturally acute reader of the market and the mechanisms of its manipulation, particularly advertising and branding, she advises manufacturers and marketers on emergent trends and on corporate and product logo design. The exquisitely tuned sensitivity that allows her to anticipate the currents of consumerist desire and response, is, however, actually "closer to allergy, a morbid and sometimes violent reactivity to the semiotics of the marketplace" (2). Product labels, trademarks, logos, and advertisements—the "signs" of marketing—all induce in her a profound, visceral nausea, of which her ability to function as "a very specialized piece of human litmus paper" is a side effect (13). It is this side effect of her resistance (which is essentially phobic in nature) that makes her useful to the forces of global capital, her very outsiderness that makes her, perversely, the ultimate insider. Cayce's revulsion is the dark mirror of others' consumerist desire; her attempted creation of her own "unbranded" subjectivity, the inverse of the postmodern branded identity.

A liminal figure, Cayce alternates between the urban nexus of global capital and the few remaining unbranded, oppositional interstices, some of which she herself helps to create. Early in *Pattern Recognition*, there is a scene in which Cayce, dressed in her own, resolutely no-fashion, unbranded (or, more accurately, de-branded) clothes, sees her reflection in the window of a Soho boutique, surrounded by an array of vintage mod apparel which her practiced eye instantly identifies. The contrast is striking, and it marks a refusal of the fantasy subject positions the clothing and accessories in the window offer, of their potential interpellation—but it also, inevitably, emphasizes the extent to which she is nonetheless simultaneously immersed in the branded consumer scene. Cayce has developed her own wardrobe, her "CPUs" (Cayce Pollard Units), as a kind of defense or reaction against the "reactor-cores of fashion" (8) to which she is constantly exposed. She affects a minimalist, monochromic, determinedly generic look that is reinforced by her erasure of every brand marker from her white t-shirts, gray pullovers, and black Levi's, on which "even the buttons . . . have been ground flat, featureless" (2). In this conversion of clothing to CPUs via scissors, seam-rippers, and other tools, it is as if she is attempting to detach the things from their signs, to reestablish a realm of concrete, perhaps authentic things that might somehow have been produced outside the realm of consumer fashion.

The contrast here is implicitly to the inauthentic fashion that inevitably induces Cayce's allergic reaction, like the Tommy Hilfiger that is a sort of fashion mise-en-abyme, a "simulacra of simulacra of simulacra. A diluted tincture of Ralph Lauren, who had himself diluted the glory days of Brooks Brothers, who themselves had stepped on the product of Jermyn Street and Savile Row" (17). Yet Cayce's own minimalist tastes are not without their contradictions. Her attachment to her black Buzz Rickson's jacket, itself "a fanatical museum-grade replica of a U.S. MA-1 flying jacket," suggests that even she is susceptible to the right kind of sartorial simulacrum, despite her assessment of it as "purely functional," and "having nothing at all to do with anything remotely like fashion" (11–12). And her own position as "a design-free zone" is itself fraught, since she's "a one-woman school of anti whose very austerity periodically threatens to spawn its own cult" (8).

In her role as "cool-hunter," Cayce is involved, implicated, in the "productization" of styles, things, and, ultimately, people. Recognizing the emerging "group behavior pattern around a particular class of object" that constitutes "cool," she "point[s] a commodifier [manufacturer] at it. . . . It gets productized. Turned into units. Marketed" (86). Often, such a cool object involves a "consumer repurposing" or détournement of some commodity that is identified by someone like Cayce, and then, in turn, re-commodified and recuperated by capital, and subsequently disseminated, via advertising and other forms of marketing, around the globe.[28] This process is one of the principal reasons that the streets of global cities increasingly resemble one another, creating a sort of generic uni-city. Cayce is uneasily aware that her profession makes her complicit in this erasure of the unique character of each city, or for that matter the unique character of everything, her own identity included, which her resistance to and handling of brands in her own clothes can only partially mitigate.

It is of some interest in this context and more generally that Cayce's encounters with mirrors are almost always uncomfortable, summoning up images of inauthentic selves. Gazing into a bathroom mirror, "she sees a black-legged, disjointed puppet," the image conjuring the memory of being compared by an old boyfriend "to Helmut Newton's nude portrait of Jane Birkin" (3). Unlike Dreiser's Carrie, whose mirror image "convinced her of a few things which she had long believed" about herself, Cayce finds only a strangely alien (though easily identifiable) image (58). Like the "hypothetical dollself" Ellen confronted in the mirror toward the end of *Manhattan Transfer*, Cayce's images—the puppet and the Helmut Newton portrait of Jane Birkin, the British 1960s film actress whose first role was as one of the models in Michelangelo Antonioni's *Blow-Up*—are objectified (and commodified) ideals, manipulable yet inert. Later, when Cayce again confronts her mirror image, backed by square white tiles, she observes that "she looks like something snipped from a magazine and placed on a sheet of graph paper. Not such good work with the scissors" (77). In other words, her identity at least partially dissolves into a brand image, if not product. In contrast to Dreiser's Carrie, who recognizes in the mirror her Idealized-*I*, Cayce's confrontations with mirror images (or their equivalents) suggest a flawed or failed identification with commercial ideals and, of course, brands. Such discordant confrontations have, in fact, become a common feature in contemporary literature, film, and television, where they continue to represent the economy of desire as part of the political economy of subjectivity and urban spaces. As we have seen earlier in this chapter, they also inevitably pose the problem of the inscription of gender within this economy, which, interestingly, persists even into later postmodernity, in spite of and sometimes because it has led to a much more diverse and heteromorphous landscape of desire.

Advertising is not, however, solely focused on the construction of individual subjectivities and on the production of the desire for an idealized self or lifestyle. In many instances, it seeks to channel a much less focused, characteristically urban desire that circulates freely among citydwellers—a longing or desire (not always or necessarily sexual) for the Other or for otherness. This desire and whatever sexual components it might involve can be mobilized and directed by marketers in a multitude of ways. In London department stores, the disembodied voices of "designer ghosts" haunt the elevators (described by Cayce, significantly, as "coffins"): "'I'm feeling rather excited,' a woman says, breathily, as the door closes, though Cayce knows she's alone in this upright coffin of mirror and brushed steel. . . . 'Mmmm,' purrs the male of the species" (18). The effect here is simultaneously voyeuristic (or perhaps more accurately, auralistic), since the discourse of the "designer ghosts" puts one in the peculiar position of an inadvertent eavesdropper, and interpellative, since one is intended to respond to excitement with excitement, to join the couple in eager anticipation of some sexual or consumerist consummation. As in *Sister Carrie* and *Manhattan Transfer*, the discourses of sexual and consumerist desire are nearly always entangled, though here they have taken on a peculiarly postmodern, indirect and spectral, and sometimes uncanny, quality.

This quality distinguishes the advertising "product" of Blue Ant, the "globally distributed, more post-geographic than multinational" agency for which Cayce works as a consultant (6). Their marketing strategies involve a high degree of subterfuge and, again, the entanglement of sexual and consumer desire: sexual desire used to generate consumer desire and a concomitant sexualization of consumer desire itself. Perhaps nowhere is this quite so evident as in the mechanisms of "viral marketing," as produced by a Blue Ant subsidiary called "Trans," which takes place in the sexually charged milieus of nightclubs and wine bars.

Essentially a kind of organized "word of mouth," viral marketing deploys attractive young men and women to chat people up in carefully selected, fashionable clubs and bars, and then, at some point in the course of the conversation, casually mention a product. The goal, at this point, is not to sell the product to this particular receiver of the message, but to turn him or her into transmitters themselves: "They recycle the information. They use it to try to impress the next person they meet" (85). Thus, virus-like, in the proper medium or milieu, the "information" (i.e., sales pitch) is transmitted from person to person, along a sexually charged chain (which presumably culminates in consumption of the product at some point in the future). In this way, the marketing comes to covertly mediate romantic relationships. The result (aside from product sales, of course) is yet another variation on the reduction of the self and others, and the interactions between them, to "product."

Processes of commodification and consumption affect not just our "local" relations to ourselves and to those close to us, however. Consumption, Manuel Castells argues in *The Urban Question*, "concretizes at the level of the relations of distribution the oppositions and struggles determined by the relations of production," relations that are increasingly global (455). Our consumption, thus, also shapes what might be seen as our globalized selves—our own places in and relations to the systems of global capitalism, and how they are, in turn, connected to those of others who are ensnared in the same systems. In the postmodern world, these relations are often, as Fredric Jameson and others have observed, difficult to map, cognitively or otherwise. While this difficulty is partly a function of their complexity, these relations have also tended to be deliberately obscured whenever possible. Revelations of sweatshops in Third World cities, like those that have been plaguing Nike in recent years, are generally met first with denials and then with reluctant promises of reform. In *Pattern Recognition*, the focus is much more on the final stage of production as marketing and on consumption than on the conditions of production of the things themselves. Yet these nonetheless do appear in Cayce's fantasy of the "bouncing sperm"-like symbol (the Nike swoosh?) she's been asked to assess, "work[ing] its way into [the] dreams" of "the countless Asian workers who might . . . spend years of their lives applying versions of this symbol to an endless and unyielding flood of footwear," their children "chalk[ing] it in doorways before they knew its meaning as a trademark" (12). The Third World is equally susceptible to the allure of brand names, though the actual (or authentic) products might be out of reach. In such cases, there are substitutes, as the journalist Rory Stewart discovered in his walking tour of Afghanistan in 2002: in the city of Herat, "on the street corner, [he] watched men unloading tablecloths from China and Iranian flip-flops marked 'Nike by Ralph Lauren'" (18).

Tactics of resistance to the all-pervasive consumerism of the postmodern city primarily involve variations on "consumer repurposing," the appropriation and détournement of already existing consumer artifacts, including media products like films and music. The practice of guerilla re-editing—a creative form of "recycling" in which films, advertisements, and songs are recut and reassembled into new configurations—is particularly significant because it intervenes in processes of production, marketing, *and* consumption. Cayce's boss Bigend advocates artists riding the wave, rather than attempting to hold it back. Clever musicians, he opines, "put new compositions out on the web. . . and wait for other people to anonymously rework them. . . .It's as though the creative process is no longer contained within an individual skull, if indeed it ever was. Everything, today, is to some extent the reflection of something else" (68).[29] These "reflections," can, however, pose uncomfortable challenges to their sources. Slogans from the international anti-Nike movement (frequently scrawled across Nike's own advertising billboards), for example, include "Just Don't Do It," "Nike, Do It Just," "Justice. Do It, Nike," and "Just Boycott It" (Klein 366–67).[30]

By a peculiar reciprocity that will reemerge throughout this study, however, the Web can also become the *site* of a very different form of "networking" and community. Given Gibson's earlier cyberpunk fiction, this vision of the Web is unsurprisingly central to *Pattern Recognition* as well and ultimately governs its plot and defines *Cayce's* character, her *case*. Cayce's primary sense of community, however, arises out of her attachment to "the footage," 134 fragments of what appears to be a film-in-progress, and to the community of devoted fans, the "footageheads," that has grown up around it. Created by an unknown "maker" and secreted in obscure corners of the Web, the footage fragments are discovered by the footageheads and endlessly discussed and debated in an on-line forum to which Cayce is a frequent contributor.

The footage constitutes the principal site of resistance to consumer culture in the novel. Anonymous, free, and uncommodified, the footage exists outside the circulation of capital; its circulation occurs within a different economy of desire (and also, as will be seen, offers a very different vision of urban space). The footage functions, in effect, as a new kind of desiring-machine. With Cayce as the point of convergence (or collision), the conflict between these forms and machines of desire turns out to be the primary engine of the novel's plot.

Fascinated by the phenomenon of the footage, Bigend decides to trace it to its source so that he can "productize" and then "monetize" it. As Bigend mobilizes his formidable worldwide network of resources (one of which is Cayce herself) to locate the source of the footage, Cayce tries to throw him off the track while racing to find the mysterious maker before he does. She hopes to warn the maker of the threat Bigend poses and thus to prevent him from co-opting the footage and destroying the virtual community to which she belongs (the only community to which she truly belongs).

Cayce's attachment to the footage itself arises, in part, out of its uncommodified quality: it is a "dream," but, unlike the dreams proffered by advertising and branding, the dream that is the footage somehow avoids any possible connection to the world of merchandise. Lacking any identifiable fashion or style through which they might be placed in a particular period, the clothing and hairstyles of its protagonists, for example, are timeless: "He might be a sailor, stepping onto a submarine in 1914, or a jazz musician entering a club in 1957. There is a lack of evidence, an absence of stylistic cues, that Cayce understands to be utterly masterful" (23). As one of Cayce's friends observes about the footage, "it's no-name . . . Like your trademark thing" (94–95).

The footage is not only uncommodified: it might also be uncommodifiable. Cayce notes that "whenever the media do try to pick it up, it slides like a lone noodle from their chopsticks. It comes in mothlike . . . a species of ghost" (52). Yet this aspect of the footage is also what Bigend finds, from his very different vantage point, so interesting. Having captured the attention of millions around the globe without any attempt at promotion by its unknown maker and distributor, the footage is, as Bigend sees it, "the single most effective piece of guerilla marketing ever . . . The most brilliant marketing ploy of this very young century" (64–65).

Once one knows what one's looking at, the footage pops up with startling frequency. Cayce spots stills from the footage on lampposts and walls across New York.[31] These fragments are signs, not just of the existence of the footage itself, but also of the community it has created. On the subway, she spots a still from the footage pinned to a woman's uniform and, recognizing one another as "fellow followers," Cayce is comforted by "this suggestion of just how many people might be following the footage" (52). The footage forum is "a second home" (65) for Cayce, "like a familiar café that exists somehow outside of geography and beyond time zones" (4).

Cayce's attempts to find the source of the footage, however, cause the universe of the footage forum to "evert," bringing Cayce's virtual relationships and the people she's forged them with into the physical world. She is aided in this endeavor (and finally rescued) by a man she knew only as "Parkaboy," her footagehead friend and virtual soulmate. Following a trail of clues Parkaboy has helped to turn up, Cayce finds the disseminator of the footage and, ultimately, through her, the maker.

The disseminator is Stella Volkova, a young Russian woman whose sister Nora makes the footage by appropriating and digitally editing scraps of found video (at least some of it from surveillance cameras), erasing from it all markers of identity, time, and place. Wounded in a bombing that killed her parents, Nora has a T-shaped fragment of shrapnel embedded in her brain, and the creation of the hauntingly beautiful footage is her only activity and her only engagement with the world. She does not speak. Her sister Stella, who is eager for Nora's work to be shared but also wants to keep her safe, thus has sought to disseminate the footage while still protecting her sister's identity. Stella cannot, however, solve the mysteries of the footage: She does not know what her sister thinks or intends.

While the footage fragments, "having been endlessly collated, broken down, reassembled, by whole armies of the most fanatical investigators, have yielded no period and no particular narrative direction," they are, nonetheless, products of an identifiable aesthetic sensibility (Nora's) and so at least parts of *something* (24). Or, once they are sent out onto the Web (and taken up by whomever can find them), *somethings*: "Zaprudered into surreal dimensions of purest speculation, ghost-narratives have emerged and taken on shadowy but determined lives of their own" (24). Viewers can make of them what they will—the fragments seem infinitely combinable. In this respect, the footage might be seen to resemble both postmodern narratives such as Julio Cortázar's *Hopscotch* and, perhaps more pertinently, a radical form of hypertext narrative in which the links between lexias (hypertext "pages") are *created* by the readers, rather than only navigated (in whatever order) by them.

By virtue of a type of anti-Oedipal overdetermination, Deleuze and Guattari also link, via the question of fragmented narrative, as posed by Maurice Blanchot, the anti-Oedipal landscape of desire to the question of fragmentation and new relationships between "the whole and its parts" (*Anti-Oedipus* 42–50.) Their argument there makes it possible, in closing, to bring together, even if without in turn completely unifying them (which is, it follows, impossible and even counterproductive), the threads of the economies of desire and of urban spaces and subjectivities that this chapter has followed from Dreiser to Dos Passos to Gibson. For, as Deleuze and Guattari say, "it is only the category of multiplicity, used as a substantive and going beyond both the One and the many, beyond the predicative relation of the One and the many, that can account for desiring-production: desiring-production is pure multiplicity, that is to say, an affirmation irreducible to any sort of [single] unity" (*Anti-Oedipus* 42). That does not of course mean that all coherence and wholeness, narrative or other, are lost, but only that they in turn are multiple and may not be manifest, or at least not immediately manifest.

Whether there might exist, in Nora's mind, an intended narrative thus remains unknown, and perhaps unknowable. Yet, as Cayce discovers, there is at least one identifiable form of structure underlying Nora's work. Encoded in each piece of footage is a number that maps its location in a T-shaped city, at once an echo (or perhaps, as Alex Wetmore suggests, a re-appropriation) of the fragment of shrapnel lodged in Nora's brain and a geography of some new cosmopolis known only to her. The number can also, it seems, be used to track the dissemination of the footage and thus to produce a different kind of map: a map of a virtual community. In the first e-mail Cayce writes to the anonymous maker, she tells her, "We don't know what you're doing, or why. Parkaboy thinks you're dreaming. Dreaming for us. Sometimes he sounds as though he thinks you're dreaming us" (255). Or dreaming as we must. And perhaps he is right. For in our postmodern moment, we must seek our own ways of reassembling our fragmented cities into diverse yet coherent wholes, inscribing new geographies of desire and maps of meaning across the plural urban landscapes of the globe.

4. TEMPTATIONS OF SIGNS AND SIGNS OF RESISTANCE: ADVERTISING, ARCHITECTURE, AND ART

Gibson's *Pattern Recognition* reflects and depicts remarkable transformations of the cityscape—of urban cities and subjects—during the decades of postmodernity, even compared to earlier stages of postmodernity itself. The shift from advertising signs to advertising brands is one of these transformations, but only one of them, and I would like now to further explore this shift and other phenomena defining the postmodern city at its current stage, both directly and via contemporary architecture, art, film, and television. I shall still be primarily concerned here with "the city of signs," and with how these signs, especially in their postmodern aspects, transform the city and how the postmodern city reciprocally transforms them and the very nature of signification. I shall explore other aspects of this self-transforming urban postmodernity in subsequent chapters.

It is true that, while the late twentieth-century paradigm of the advertising image as architecture now dominates most urban spaces, the previous paradigm in which architecturally distinctive skyscrapers were conceived as expressions of corporate power—architecture as advertising image—has not entirely disappeared. Indeed, given the number of high-profile, high-concept buildings by such architects as Renzo Piano, Santiago Calatrava, Rem Koolhaas, and Frank Gehry that have recently been constructed in London, New York, Tokyo, Madrid, and Barcelona, it appears to be undergoing a resurgence. Yet there has been a shift since the 1980s: in the new paradigm of architecture as advertising, it is not so much the corporations (or their brands) that are being promoted as the architects themselves, or rather, the architects *as* corporate brands. The recent proliferation of branded condominium developments by celebrity architects (among them, Richard Meier, Philippe Starck, Charles Gwathmey, and Robert Siegel) in New York City is effectively a continuation of a 1980s trend of, as architecture critic Paul Goldberger puts it, "treat[ing] internationally known architects as the equivalent of Hermes or Gucci or BMW. . . . Commission a Michael Graves. It's all the same" ("Architecture View"). The transmogrification of architects into fashions has been accompanied by a transmogrification of some fashion designers into interior designers. Giorgio Armani's expansion into interior design with Armani-Casa, for example, has been extended to the branding of "20 Pine Street-The Collection," a New York condominium whose public spaces and apartments were both designed and furnished by Armani/Casa. "It's very comforting for the buyer to know he is part of a long-lasting, long-sustaining brand," the condominium's promoter Michael Shvo explained to a *New York Times* reporter (La Ferla).

The new, high-profile branded architecture of Gehry et al. must still, however, contend against the relentless, all-pervasive onslaught of advertising signage and the continual shrinking of "unmarketed" or unbranded spaces as corporations seek to insinuate advertising into every public and private space imaginable.[32] Recent innovations in intrusive selling techniques include, for example, ads on restroom signs and positioned above urinals and hand dryers in public restrooms; ads on school buses and on protective wrappers for elementary and high-school textbooks; ads on college campus bicycle racks; ads blaring from overhead monitors in airports and train stations and on planes and trains; ads on airsickness bags, trays used in airport baggage screening, and baggage carousels; ads in hospital and doctors' office waiting rooms, including on examination table paper covers; ads on bus shelters and subway turnstiles; ads stenciled onto the white spaces between parking places; ads projected onto sidewalks, the exteriors of buildings, and the floors and elevator doors inside office buildings and malls; ads for cars, soft drinks, and deodorants interspersed among the "previews" (also, of course, ads) in movie theaters; Army recruiting ads on pizza boxes; ads that interrupt your phone conversations in exchange for "free" long-distance calls; and advertising stamped on eggs and on the plastic bars separating your groceries from the next guy's at the supermarket check-out counter. There is, apparently, no interior or exterior space that is safe from the advertiser's intrusion, and the extent of this intrusion tends to intensify in population-dense areas such as cities. "We never know where the consumer is going to be at any point in time, so we have to find a way to be everywhere," explained Linda Kaplan Thaler, chief executive of a New York ad agency; "Ubiquity is the new exclusivity" (Story). Present-day marketing is distinguished not only by its spatial invasiveness, however, but also by its psychological invasiveness.

This invasiveness lies not just in the rhetorical strategies deployed by marketers (the focus on the consumers and their needs or "lacks" and so forth), but also, and perhaps more fundamentally, in the mechanisms by which marketers track, construct, and target consumers to begin with. Chief among these is the marketing science of geodemographics, which uses sophisticated demographic research and models to construct consumer identities on the basis of geographic locations (usually by neighborhood or zip code) and consumption patterns (lifestyles).[33] The fictional portraits of "geographically typical" consumers produced by geodemography are not only descriptive, however; they are inevitably prescriptive as well. In his article "'We Know Who You Are and We Know Where You Live,'" Jon Goss argues that "the genius of geodemographics is that it systematically *produces such life-styles both from us and for us*: it presents descriptions of our consuming selves that are actually normative models, or mean characteristics of our consumption (stereo) type to which we are exhorted to conform. Geodemographics enables marketers to make, within known levels of statistical confidence, that most psychologically effective of marketing pitches, that beginning with 'People like you . . . '" (214; my emphasis). Big Brother not only wants to keep an eye on you: he also wants to sell you things.

Cities have, of course, always been centers of consumption. Yet historically that consumption has been balanced by production, and cities defined themselves in relation to both. Though the postindustrial economy obviously involves production of a kind, cities increasingly define themselves *primarily* as centers of consumption, indeed, they are frequently presented as commodities in their own right. This emphasis on consumption, in turn, has radically reshaped both the experience of the city and the ways in which people understand themselves as citydwellers: "Human beings are no longer citizens of the city in which they live," Steven and Malcolm Miles argue in *Consuming Cities*, "but rather they are consumers in and consumers of that city" (11).[34] The complex relations and disjunctions between capitalism and urban citizenship are taken up at length in Chapter 5, but here it is nonetheless worth emphasizing that consumption is deeply, inescapably ideological—it is one of the principal means by which we are shaped and interpellated by capitalism as individuals, and it mediates our relations to one another in complex ways.

To understand how some of these interactions work in real-life, material urban spaces, we might consider the experience of shopping in both Niketown and Diesel Jeans stores, spaces constructed by marketers of two of the biggest contemporary clothing brands. These shopping environments, which are distinguished by the information overload they impose on their customers through a barrage of sensory stimuli in the form of both (visual) signs and sounds, present us with intentionally overwhelming and illegible environments.[35] "To the uninitiated, walking into the Diesel jeans store on Union Square West feels a lot like stumbling into a rave," *New York Times* reporter Warren St. John writes: "Techno music pounds at a mind-rattling level. A television plays a videotape of a Japanese boxing match, inexplicably" (1). Once customers make their way back to "the denim bar" where the jeans are assembled, they find a daunting array of types and styles. The strategy here, he explains, "is based on the unconventional premise that the best customer is a disoriented one. . . . Indeed, it is just the moment when a potential Diesel customer reaches a kind of shopping vertigo that members of the company's intimidatingly with-it staff make their move. Acting as salesmen-in-shining-armor, they rescue—or prey upon, depending on one's point of view—wayward shoppers" (1). The disorientation elicited in this environment is quite similar to that created in Niketown (whose name indicates that it aspires to being rather more than a store), where the sensory overload is compounded by the store's mall-like, multilevel structure. Customers are intended to be "lost" here—and not just spatially. Both of these spaces aim to destabilize the customers' sense of self. (These spaces thus operate rather like the standard advertising pitch which, John Berger argues, "steals her [the consumer's] love of herself as she is, and offers it back to her for the price of the product" [135].)

This type of store design, media critic Douglas Ruskoff notes, "is a new take on an old trick. In the 1950s, the shopping mall designer Victor Gruen realized that when shoppers were distracted by confusing mall layouts and grandiose visual stimuli, they seemed more prone to impulse buying" (St. John 6).[36] I would argue that this impulse buying might be seen as an attempt to re-situate oneself, to create an anchored subject position through the identification with the purchased object (as Berger suggests), and to reestablish, through that purchase, one's lost sense of agency and control. In Niketown, the immense, heroic images of sports figures (in the early 1990s, the one devoted to Michael Jordan hung behind the basket in a half-size replica of a basketball court) provide compensatory "sites of identification" in which the subject can be reconstituted—a process consummated in the purchase. In Diesel Jeans, the process involves the intervention of the "hip" salesclerk who, as Ruskoff explains, is hip because he "know[s] how to navigate the space" (St. John 6).

"Adopted" by his new "shopping friend," the disoriented Diesel customer is assessed, "psychographically profiled" by the salesclerk on the basis of his "clothing, attitude and friends," and then the clerk "recommends a number of styles he hopes will suit the customer" (St. John 6). This is, in effect, yet another version of the geodemographic "loop" that "produces . . . life-styles both from us and for us" (Goss 214). Yet more is happening here than a salesclerk's attempt to match a pair of jeans with a customer's own, personal style. There is an important element of identification involved, as the disoriented shopper identifies with the hip, oriented salesman, what St. John describes as the "retailing equivalent to the Stockholm syndrome, whereby captives bond with their captors" (St. John 6). He emphasizes the potentially erotic nature of this bond, which "is not always limited to the sales floor," but one should remember that the Stockholm syndrome involved not only bonding and identification, but also the alliance of captives with their captors and the creation of loyalty to them (which puts an interesting spin on the concept of "brand loyalty" here) (St. John 6). In this context, it's also worth remembering the expansiveness of branding: "At Diesel Jeans," president and founder Renzo Rosso opines, "we don't sell a product, we sell a style of life. I think we have created a movement. . . . The Diesel concept is everything. It's the way to live, it's the way to wear, it's the way to do something'" (qtd. in Klein 23–24).

The subjectivities constructed in the contemporary milieu of the post-modern city seem remarkably formulaic. In *Manhattan Transfer*, the signs of the city infiltrate the minds of its inhabitants, becoming part of the signifying chains of their thoughts and being used by them to structure their narratives of self and of their lives, but in these processes, the signifiers are generally detached from both their original signifieds or meanings and from their referents, the products to which they refer. In our branded contemporary cities, by contrast, it seems to be increasingly difficult to effect this detachment, so all-encompassing have brands become. It is, precisely, the brand that we seek to consume now, not the product, or rather we seek to consume all of those things that the brand represents for us. "Consumers do not have an insatiable desire to consume," Colin Campbell argues in *The Romantic Ethic and the Spirit of Modern Consumerism*, "but rather they seek to experience in reality what they have already experienced in their imaginations. From this point of view, consumers are, above all else, imaginative creatures and the cultural products offered for sale in modern societies are in fact consumed because they serve as aids to the construction of day-dreams" (92). In Don DeLillo's *White Noise*, Steffie Gladney, one of the children depicted in the novel, repeats "Toyota Corolla, Toyota Celica, Toyota Cressida" like a mantra in her sleep (155, 167). Brand names and fragments of advertising float randomly through the narrative—disembodied discourses that are part of the all-pervasive white noise of the branded postmodern world: "The Airport Marriott, the Downtown Travelodge, the Sheraton Inn and Conference Center" (15), "Dacron, Orlon, Lycra Spandex" (52),

"Mastercard, Visa, American Express" (100), "Tegrin, Denorex, Selsun Blue" (289). Colonizing our dreams, these brands propose to become the lenses through which we see and experience our lives.

Like literature and art, advertising creates for us a vocabulary, a repertoire of imagery (perhaps the greatest popular repertoire of imagery today, even beyond that of film or television) through which we might know the world. As Berger observes, "advertising adds up to a kind of philosophical system. *It explains everything in its own terms.* It interprets the world" (149; my emphasis). As we have seen, however, advertising is also about the self-image jointly created by both the ad and the buyer in a "magic mirror" that both create first. Thus, advertising is also about confrontations with mirror images that suspend one's consciousness and unconscious, and hence one's space of desire, between the fantasy of success and the reality of failure, as Lacan argues. The postmodern difference is that the fantasy is not only that of the identification with a more glamorous self-image: Warhol's "fifteen minutes of fame" is also part of this fantasy, the desire for and illusion of the possible dissemination of this image of one-self. This dissemination is in turn captured in the multiplying images in Warhol's celebrity portraits, or at the other end of this spectrum, of such objects as the electric chair—a nightmare celebrity image. The confrontation with the mirror image remains, however, a constant of our relationships with advertising.

One of the more memorable confrontations of this kind in recent popular culture occurs in the opening credits of the long-running HBO sit-com *Sex and the City*, which was originally uninterrupted by TV advertising, which might, however, have been rather superfluous in any event. (In its syndicated run on TBS, the series was edited—episodes were both shortened and bowdlerized—and interrupted by advertisements.) The series, which critics often derided for its lack of realism, remarkably begins every episode with an ironic, cautionary depiction of the unbridgeable gap between the alluring images and fantasy lifestyles of commercial discourses (of both advertisements and brands), and our actual experiences of ourselves and our lives. The scene, which is the series' title sequence, opens with a montage of shots of a smiling Carrie Bradshaw (an allusion to the Carrie of Dreiser's novel is not inconceivable), played by Sarah Jessica Parker, walking through the streets of Manhattan, inter-cut with shots of street traffic and of the city's architectural landmarks—the Empire State Building, the World Trade Center, the Brooklyn Bridge, the Chrysler Building. As she glances up to catch a glimpse of the gleaming spire of the Chrysler Building, the camera cuts to a close-up of a car wheel zooming through a puddle at the curb and sending up a plume of muddy water. Then we see Carrie, reacting in horror as the water drenches her from head to toe. As she turns to watch the car speed away, she comes face to face with her own image on an advertisement spread across the full length of the side of a city bus. It is an ad for her column, the eponymous "Sex and the City," and it features Carrie reclining in a glamorous, Odalisque-like pose. The tagline reads, "Carrie Bradshaw knows good sex." As the bus and Carrie's ad recede into the distance in the final shot, she remains, dripping. Although the experience is not uncommon (as any urban pedestrian on a rainy day can attest), there is something particularly arresting about this scene. Much of its power lies in the utterly abject state to which Carrie is reduced at its end: her face spattered with mud, her long blonde curls dripping, her pale pink dress drenched in filth. (The dress, which strongly resembles a ballerina's tutu, is itself a sign of idealized femininity; in it, Carrie looks almost like a little girl playing dress up.) The scene is a stunning portrayal of the allure of the idealized image and—the inevitable flaw in the identification process—the unhappy insistence, here virtually an eruption, of the reality principle. The contrast is not just between Carrie's glamorous and sexy advertising image and her sodden, bedraggled appearance: it is also between her branded (and Carrie is, in her way, a brand) fantasy existence, implied by the ad, and her actual lived experience. Not only do our outward appearances fail to measure up to the idealized images of advertising (a plight arguably more painful for women than men, given the premium society puts on women's appearance), now we also suffer the considerably more all-embracing failure to inhabit the fantasy lives or lifestyles presented by brands.

Sofia Coppola's 2003 film *Lost in Translation* can, in many respects, be read as an extended commentary on both of these forms of failure. In the film, Bob Harris, played by Bill Murray, is a slightly over-the-hill actor who has come to Tokyo to make a Suntori whiskey commercial. Jet-lagged, sleepless, and culturally disoriented, he is perpetually caught in and wryly aware of the ironic contrasts between the debonair and assured man of the world (complete with black tie and a glass of Suntori on ice) he is expected to portray and his current state, both physical and existential. Receiving a constant barrage of bulletins about the chaos back home from his furious and estranged wife, he proves incapable of successfully playing the suavely self-satisfied role the commercial demands. Completely, comically unable to divine what the Japanese director of the commercial has in mind, Bob segues desperately from approach to approach (James Bond and Dean Martin are only two of the many masculine paradigms he seems to be successively channeling), take after take. Meanwhile, the director speaks passionately, furiously, and at great length. Then, the interpreter offers—a word or two. (Much, apparently, is "lost in translation.")

In between disastrous attempts to shoot the commercial, Bob aimlessly wanders the neon-saturated, congested streets of Tokyo. At one point, he encounters a huge electronic billboard bearing his own image amid a welter of other shifting, glaring images. It is him in black tie, relaxing in a club chair with his glass of Suntori on ice—the same scene that they are still, unsuccessfully, trying to enact for the television commercial.[37] As Bob regards the image, his expression is puzzled, as though he cannot quite "place" the person in the ad, out of context and lost in translation. His disorientation is, in this instance, both temporal and spatial. Like the audience, Bob must be struck by the uncanny nature of this perfect, completed image, which appears to have been taken directly (as a freeze-frame or simultaneously shot still) from the commercial that has not yet been shot: a literal precession of the simulacra (though the "real" of the commercial shoot will, finally, also produce a simulacrum of its own). Spatially, the distance between Bob and the towering image overhead is similarly immense, and he seems somehow like the earthbound "remainder" left behind by his own ascendant image. In the postmodern city of signs and brands, reality never quite measures up and experience appears always at odds with our dreams (particularly the commercial ones).

Urban signscapes have long been contested sites, particularly when they have been appropriated by noncommercial interests. The history of the subway and mural graffiti that flourished in cities like Philadelphia, New York, and Los Angeles from the late 1960s through the early 1980s (when art galleries and museums began exhibiting it) has been extensively documented and discussed, so I will not explore it in detail here. It is worth noting in this context, however, that this graffiti was primarily name- or "tag"-based, and thus can be seen as an application of the logic of the market to the individual, a form of advertising the self—the production of auto-celebrity. "Your name is your brand, and writing your name is like printing money," Jeff Chang, a historian of graffiti and hip hop observes. "Quality (aesthetic style) and quantity (the number of trains and walls you've hit) are the primary ways that the brand gains market share. If you're the biggest name on a line or in an area, then you're the king" (qtd. in Ehrlich and Ehrlich 51). Here I will focus on counters to the sign discourses of the market and government in the interventions in the urban signscape by artists like Barbara Kruger and Jenny Holzer, and, not least, by casual passersby.[38]

Kruger is a conceptual graphic artist who appropriates images, many of them taken from advertising and news and documentary photography, and overlays them with slashes of red-framed slogans (visually, the effect is reminiscent of both Dada photomontage and, perhaps more recognizably, Soviet avant-garde art of the 1920s). Relying on the semiotic dissonance between the image and the words (which are often plays on popular clichés and on advertising and political slogans), the works demystify the images, exposing the ideological messages and power relations embedded within them. Kruger's works almost always address or suggest particular subject positions—a "you" or an "I" or "we"—but the subject itself is never explicitly identified, and viewers must decide for themselves where they will stand, how they will position themselves in relation to it. The process makes one conscious of the ways in which such discourses (advertising and so forth) interpellate us and of how we might become "resistant readers" of them. "I'm interested in making an active spectator who can decline that You or accept it or say, It's not me but I know who it is," Kruger says (qtd. in Squiers 80).

Kruger's works are deliberately confrontational. Some focus on the power of the state. Her "flag installation," questions arranged in the form of an American flag, asks, "Who is beyond the law? Who is bought and sold? Who is free to choose? Who does time? Who follows orders? Who prays loudest? Who dies first? Who laughs last?" Kruger is fully aware of how dispersed ideologies are and how they function through a range of institutions (what Althusser would term "ideological state apparatuses") and discourses, and her work engages many of them beyond the government itself. Kruger's perception that there is "nothing outside the marketplace" and that she "live[s] and speak[s] through a body which is constructed by moments which are formed by the velocity of power and money" has made the discourses of the market and advertising frequent targets (Kruger, "An Interview" 131). Her work is often displayed in spaces usually reserved for ads—on billboards and bus shelters, on T-shirts and hats. The disruption, then, is twofold. First, there is the diegetic dissonance of the work itself: A picture of a particularly repulsive stuffed toy resembling a deformed Donald Duck overlaid with the slogan, "Buy me. I'll change your life." An image of a hand presenting a business card that reads, "I shop therefore I am." Emblazoned across a photograph of a ventriloquist's dummy, "When I hear the word culture, I take out my checkbook," and then, in miniscule type by the dummy's lips, "We mouth your words." Second, there is the extradiegetic dissonance of these messages appearing in "commercial" space, a placement that inevitably raises questions about the increasing domination of public space by private, commercial interests.[39]

Figure 1.6 Barbara Kruger, "We Don't Need Another Hero," 1987. (Commissioned and produced by Artangel.)

Also among the more interesting postmodern artistic interventions in urban space is the conceptual sign art of Jenny Holzer, whose first public project, "Truisms," appeared in early 1977. "Truisms" consisted of a series of small, offset posters bearing an alphabetized list of anonymous aphorisms that were pasted on walls, lampposts, parking meters, public phones, garbage cans, and manhole covers throughout Lower Manhattan. Strangely familiar and obviously related in form to advertising and political slogans, one-liners and clichés, the aphorisms and the intentions behind them were nonetheless mysterious. They seemed to issue from conflicting ideological viewpoints—what Holzer has termed "a universe of opinion":

ABUSE OF POWER COMES AS NO SURPRISE
AN ELITE IS INEVITABLE
ANY SURPLUS IS IMMORAL
MONEY CREATES TASTE
PRIVATE OWNERSHIP IS AN INVITATION TO DISASTER
SELFISHNESS IS THE MOST BASIC MOTIVATION

Like Kruger's slogans, these aphorisms seemed to require viewers to take up a position in relation to them. Some passersby paused and edited them, or crossed some out, or added their own aphorisms to the list, joining the cacophony of voices. In 1982, aphorisms from "Truisms" and two subsequent series entitled "Living" and "Survival" were displayed on the immense Spectacolor signboard in Times Square (Figure 1.7) and on the electronic billboards of the Las Vegas strip, disrupting the spaces of advertising and publicity with statements such as "PROTECT ME FROM WHAT I WANT" and "PROPERTY CREATED CRIME." As the news of the Reagan era slid past on the Times Square "zipper" and a nearby sign kept a running tally of the mounting national debt, Holzer's signs asked, "WHAT COUNTRY SHOULD YOU ADOPT IF YOU HATE POOR PEOPLE?", observed that "IT TAKES AWHILE BEFORE YOU CAN STEP OVER INERT BODIES AND GO AHEAD WITH WHAT YOU WERE WANTING TO DO," and advised us to "PUT FOOD OUT IN THE SAME PLACE EVERY DAY AND TALK TO THE PEOPLE WHO COME TO EAT AND ORGANIZE THEM."

More common than the project interventions of artists like Kruger and Holzer are spontaneous responses to events or images by anonymous passersby in the city. Some of these are variations on culture jamming—scrawling "feed me" across the images of models in Calvin Klein ads on subway walls, for example, or creating and disseminating one's own anti-ads.[40] Others react, sometimes whimsically, to changes in the urban environment, like the graffiti on the plywood-covered windows of a closed Manhattan supermarket that commemorated experiences that occurred there: "My parents forgot me here" and "Ian, in front of the oranges"; or editorialized on the causes of the supermarket's demise: "Lousy service is what put you

Figure 1.7 Jenny Holzer, "Truisms," Times Square sign, 1982. (© Jenny Holzer, member Artists Rights Society [ARS], New York. Photo: Lisa Kahane, NYC.)

out of business" and "The corporations are winning"; or simply lamented its absence: "I came here tonight to get my stuff for my famous six-hour tomato sauce and you are gone!" (Clines).

Commemoration on city streets is also found in the urban tradition of street memorials. In the U.S., pedestrians and bicyclists killed by automobiles are memorialized by body outlines on the pavement like those at crime scenes, annotated with the date and the victim's name. Memorials for young people killed in gang violence often include murals, flowers, and candles surrounded by notes and objects (stuffed toys, sports equipment, cans of beer). In New York City, in the days and weeks after 9/11, many of the thousands of posters of the missing attached to walls, lampposts, and bus shelters became improvised shrines, as people laid flowers, candles, flags, and messages beneath them.

It may, accordingly, be fitting to return in closing to *Pattern Recognition*, which, I have argued, captures the current, post-9/11 juncture of postmodernity. Cayce, making "the stations of some unthinkable cross," is one of those putting up posters of her father, who went missing in Lower Manhattan on 9/11 (186). These images punctured the anonymity of the city with both remembrance and recognition: "while producing her own posters," she "watch[es] the faces of other people's dead, emerging from adjacent copiers at Kinko's, to be mounted in the yearbook of the city's loss" (186). As she walks around Lower Manhattan, posting her signs, she finds that "more missing strangers had become familiar" (186). Yet, "she had never, while putting hers up, seen one face pasted over another"—an acknowledgment of both the personal and communal nature of the losses involved (186). Later that day, she joins the communal vigil at Union Square Park near the immense "organic accretion of candles, flowers, photographs, and messages" at the base of Washington's statue (186). As we have seen, however, Cayce and the novel ultimately move from memory to dream, from the past, however recent and close, to the future, perhaps quite distant as yet, in which we can glimpse a new image of the city and its citizens. This city might still be the city of both things and signs, and of the relationships between them, but hopefully in the service of a better urban community. It will not be easy to build, indeed it is not easy even to dream of it; but it is not impossible to do both.

2 Urban Grids and Urban Imaginary
City to Cyberspace, Cyberspace to City

The ordered swirl of houses and streets, from this high angle, sprang at her now with the same unexpected, astonishing clarity as the circuit card had . . . there were to both outward patterns a hieroglyphic sense of concealed meaning, of an intent to communicate. There'd seemed no limit to what the printed circuit could have told her (if she had tried to find out); so in her first minute of San Narciso, a revelation also trembled just past the threshold of her understanding.

—Thomas Pynchon, *The Crying of Lot 49*

—may each point of Heaven be mapp'd, or projected, upon each point of Hell, and vice versa. And what intercepts the Projection, about mid-way (reckon'd logarithmickally) between? why, this very Earth, and our lives here upon it. We only think we occupy a solid, Brick-and-Timber City,—in Reality, we live upon a Map.

—Thomas Pynchon, *Mason & Dixon*

This chapter offers a discussion of the grid in our urban imaginary and in our material urban spaces and practices, where it has played a crucial role, beginning literally with the very first cities ever built. I shall address some of this history, especially how the idea of the grid was shaped by and, reciprocally, shaped modernity and modern urban culture. The relationships between the grid and urban culture are crucial for my argument here, since some of these relationships extend into postmodernity. My main concerns in this chapter, however, are, first, the significance of the idea of the grid in the *postmodern* urban imaginary and, second, the practices defined by the continuing role, positive and negative, of the grid and by resistances to it in imagining and building our urban spaces. Most especially, I will consider the role of the grid in the interface between the city and cyberspace, which, as I argue here and in the next chapter, defines the postmodern urban imaginary and urban reality.

Section 1 discusses, by way of a general introduction to the chapter, the "city/cyberspace dissolve" as a postmodern icon and as a sign of the complex interrelations between these two spaces. Section 2 considers, first, the history of the idea of the grid and, more generally, coordination, as they took shape with Descartes and in their impact as part of the imaginary of the Enlightenment and modernity itself. Then, it examines some of the ramifications of the idea of the grid as it took material form in cities throughout history. Section 3 moves to the critique of this modern imaginary and its replacement by the postmodern imaginary, especially as it pertains to urban and cyber spatiality. This section also examines how this critique and replacement began to emerge within modernity and, especially, in the literary and artistic modernism of the twentieth century. Finally, Section 4 offers a discussion of the role of cyberspace in the urban imaginary and practices of postmodernity, present and future.

1. TRANSPOSING GRIDS: FROM PRE-HISTORY TO POST-HISTORY

One of the most striking and strikingly recurrent images in contemporary culture is that of the intricate grid of city streets dissolving into the luminous tracery of the computer-generated grid of cyberspace.[1] The image is prefigured in the passage that serves as my first epigraph to this chapter, taken from Thomas Pynchon's novel *The Crying of Lot 49*, which was written at the onset of the postmodern era in 1966, when the electronic hardware of transistors and circuit cards defined the frontier of technology and its cultural image. In the mind of the novel's protagonist Oedipa Maas, the city grid of San Narciso shifts into the printed circuit card (the hardware), rather than the virtual grid of cyberspace, as in the current incarnation of the image. Now, nearly half a century later, it is digital software and virtual reality that dominate our technology and world, and define their images. These images tend to make us forget the material hardware of our computers, our bodies, or our cities that makes possible the virtual world that we occupy and that occupies us (in both senses). Impressing upon us the transmutability or even interchangeability of real and virtual (cyber) space, the image of the city and cyberspace grids dissolving into each other also reflects the power of urban space as a conceptual model for cyberspace and, more obliquely, the immense influence the computer technologies of the virtual have come to exert over the spaces of postmodern cities. The reciprocal relationships that are developing and have already developed between these two spaces are my main subject in this chapter, along with the structure or, more fittingly, architecture of each space itself. Neither space, I shall argue, can any longer be considered apart from the other, even if they have not yet altogether dissolved into each other or merged into a single new form of reality, which may not be possible, although there are those who argue otherwise and even expect such a dissolution or merger to occur in the foreseeable future.

The 1982 Disney film *Tron* was arguably the first cinematic representation of the virtual world, conceived as a city, which used the image of the city/cyberspace dissolve. *Tron* opens with a shot of computer circuitry morphing into a shimmering night cityscape; a later shot dissolves from the printed circuit into the computer-generated cyberspace grid (here, the "game grid"), a vast Cartesian grid interspersed with towering monoliths and looming walls. The film thus marks the transition from the imaginary equation of city space and integrated circuit, invoked by Pynchon, to the equation of city space and the new, virtual space—cyberspace—made possible by the computer technology developed through the integrated circuitry of digital processors. Since the early 1980s, the image (depicting this dissolve in either direction from the city to cyberspace or from cyberspace to the city) has appeared in legions of films, television series, novels, newspaper and magazine articles, advertisements, and websites, especially those dealing with computer technology and cyberspace. Among the better-known examples are the television series *Max Headroom* (1987), which employed several versions of the city/cyberspace dissolve; the film *Hackers* (1995), which, like *Tron*, transitions among city space, lighted circuitry (inscribed on the *exterior* of an array of mainframes), and cyberspace; *Johnny Mnemonic* (1995); and the Wachowski brothers' *Matrix* trilogy (1999, 2003, 2003).[2] The image is equally common in the species of science-fiction literature known as "cyberpunk," of which William Gibson's early novel *Neuromancer* (1984) and Neal Stephenson's *Snow Crash* (1992), both to be discussed later in this chapter and the next, are perhaps the best-known exemplars.[3] It is also found with conspicuous regularity in print and television advertising, particularly for banks and computer software and services, such as the mySAP. com advertisement that bids you "Welcome to the City of e: A place where more than 10,000 companies from around the corner and across the globe are joined into one seamless, supercharged web of e-commerce." One could argue, then, that the image of the city/cyberspace dissolve, usually rendered more specifically as a "city-grid/cybercity-grid dissolve," has become an omnipresent icon, if not *the* icon, of our representations and even conceptions of cyberspace and the postmodern city, and their interfusion with each other.

This iconography carries a complex meaning and has a major significance. Much more than simply a compelling visual metaphor, the image reflects the fact that cyberspace is conceived both as being organized and functioning as a virtual city, while the material city increasingly acquires multiple elements of virtual reality. The works in which the image appears and our contemporary urban reality allow us to read this image in even stronger terms, as telling us that the boundaries between physical and virtual spaces are quite literally dissolving or, more accurately, are no longer decidable once and for all. Both spaces have become so interconnected that we can no longer simply or unequivocally dissociate them or their functioning in either domain. It makes sense, therefore, that the imagery of the city-grid/cyberspace-grid dissolve has come to represent the postmodern matrix of relationships between urban spatiality and information that is one of the defining features of the postmodern era and its cities.

While the intertwining of city and cyberspace is, like the creation of cyberspace, recent, the link between urban architecture and information, and even the architecture (organization) of information, is ancient, perhaps as ancient as the city itself. Cities and systems of writing appear to have emerged simultaneously. Indeed, scholars have argued that the creation of cities on any scale worthy of the name (and their concomitant political bureaucracies and large-scale commercial activities) necessitated the invention of writing. As Lewis Mumford writes in *The City in History*:

> It is no accident that the emergence of the city as a self-contained unit, with all its historic organs fully differentiated and active, coincided with the development of the permanent record: with glyphs, ideograms, and script, with the first abstractions of number and verbal signs. By the time this happened, the amount of culture to be transmitted orally was beyond the capacity of a small group to achieve even in a long lifetime. It was no longer sufficient that the funded experience of the community should repose in the minds of the most aged members. . . . In daily transactions, the same need for permanent notations and signs was even more obvious: to act at a distance through agents and factors, to give commands and make contracts, some extra-personal device was needed [i.e., a system of writing]. (97)

Writing made it possible to encode information in a way that could be transmitted both across space and through time. The medium on which this writing was inscribed was related, in turn, to the distance—spatial or temporal—through which it needed to travel. Clay tablets or (better) papyrus and parchment were portable and thus good for sending messages from place to place. In the inscriptions and images carved into the walls of the tombs and temples of ancient civilizations (including those of the Sumerians, Assyrians, Egyptians, Persians, Mayans, Olmecs, Toltecs, and Aztecs), however, we might discern the desire to transmit knowledge down through time, to the future inhabitants of the city.

Cities themselves might even function *as* writing: Many of these ancient peoples aligned the buildings and streets of their cities with celestial bodies, rendering cosmological knowledge and sacred symbolism concrete. Combining both writing on the city and the city as writing, the Renaissance philosopher Tommaso Campanella envisioned his utopian *City of the Sun* (1602), Trapobane, as an encyclopedia built of and inscribed upon stone. The city was constructed of seven rings or huge circles named for the planets, connected by four streets and gates laid out along the four points of the compass. Accessible to all the city's inhabitants, its walls were adorned with paintings and verses that conveyed all the accumulated knowledge of the human and natural sciences.

The city can serve as a memory template in a great variety of ways. As Kevin Lynch observes, the image of the urban landscape, "familiar to all, furnishes material for common memories and symbols which bind the group together and allow them to communicate with one another. [It] serves as a vast mnemonic system for the retention of group history and ideals" (126). Ancient Greek and Roman rhetoricians used the image of the city as the template for one of earliest technologies of memory—the creation of memory palaces (also known as the "method of loci"). Described in detail by Cicero and Quintilian, the technique involved the imprinting of a familiar locus—usually a large building or several buildings—on the individual's memory. One then formed mental images of the things one wished to remember and placed the images, like furnishings, one by one, into these imaginary buildings. The first might be left on the threshold, the second affixed to a pillar, the third set in a corner, and so on. When one wished to recall the memory, one would imagine walking through the memory palace, retrieving each image in turn. Extended feats of memory might require many buildings arrayed along a street, or even an entire city. Revived in the Renaissance, this art of memory reached its apotheosis in the architecture of a great memory theater envisioned in the mid-sixteenth century by the scholar Giulio Camillo, which was to have contained "all the things that the human mind can conceive" (Yates 132).

In the postmodern era, memory is often seen in computer terms, and the computer in effect functions as an electronic memory prosthesis, which is not surprising since the conception of computer memory and the "database" arose from a conception of human memory as a storage house of information (impressions, images, ideas, and other knowledge) to be retrieved, deliberately or spontaneously, later. Yet memory is still envisioned in architectural form as well, interactively with seeing it in terms of digital hardware (as, for instance, in descriptions of the neural networks of the brain) and software, the *architecture* of digital hardware and software, which, I argue here, is in turn often conceived and imaged as a city.

Cyberspace, a memory system as capacious as those envisioned by Campanella and Camillo, is described in Gibson's *Neuromancer*, for example, as "a graphic representation of data abstracted from the banks of every computer in the human system. Unthinkable complexity. Lines of light ranged in the nonspace of the mind, clusters and constellations of data. Like city lights, receding" (51). When *Neuromancer*'s protagonist Case enters cyberspace, he sees computer-generated data analogues of transnational corporate headquarters and governmental agencies in distant, fortress-like architectural forms: "the stepped scarlet pyramid of the Eastern Seaboard Fission Authority burning beyond the green cubes of Mitsubishi Bank of America, and high and very far away . . . the spiral arms of military systems, forever beyond his reach" (52). At the same time, for Case, the urban landscape is itself information, as the city often is for all of us: "it was possible to see Ninsei as a field of data . . . Then you could throw yourself into a highspeed drift and skid, totally engaged but set apart from it all, and all around you the dance of biz, information interacting, data made flesh in the mazes of the black market" (16).

Neal Stephenson's *Snow Crash*, less than a decade but nonetheless a cyberspace "generation" later than *Neuromancer*, depicts the virtual world of "the Metaverse" as a vast urban landscape dominated by the Street, "a grand boulevard going all the way around the equator of a black sphere . . . considerably bigger than Earth" (24). When the protagonist Hiro enters the Metaverse and surveys the Street, he "sees buildings and electric signs stretching off into the darkness, disappearing over the curve of the globe" (25). "Downtown is a dozen Manhattans, embroidered with neon and stacked on top of each other" (26). The essence of the Metaverse might be distilled into street, buildings, and electric signs. So, too, Hiro's description of Los Angeles: "The hazy sprawl is ringed and netted with glowing lines . . . Streams of red and white corpuscles throb down highways . . . Farther away, spreading across the basin, a million sprightly logos smear into solid arcs" (190). Three years after *Snow Crash*, the film *Hackers* (1995) depicted cyberspace as a virtual "City of Text," a cityscape/signscape of gleaming skyscrapers laid out along the regular pathways of a printed circuit. Packets of data, like pulses of light, shoot through the air between "buildings," moving from one "file" to another.

Figure 2.1 *Hackers*, "The City of Text." (Courtesy of Bob Thorne.)

The postmodern link between city and cyberspace might have initially arisen metonymically out of the striking resemblance between aerial views of urban spaces and the computer's integrated circuit "microchip," a resemblance that, as Scott Bukatman notes, "is no coincidence—the chip, like the city, is designed for ease of circulation, constant flow, and a dense maximization of available space" (110). Or, as Allesandro Aurigi and Stephen Graham suggest, it might be that "so woven is the notion of the city into the mindset of the modern condition that [one] can simply use some idealized urban metaphor as a legible interface for Internet services which are, in fact, scattered across host computers distributed right across the planet" (492). The history of the design of graphic interfaces for online communities, from Apple's eWorld and Alpha World in the mid-1990s to SimCity and Second Life today, suggests that they are correct about the appeal of the "urban metaphor." As I argue here, however, the connection, so evocatively captured by the images of city and cyberspace dissolving into one another, is more than merely metonymic or metaphoric. There exists, between these two spaces, a complex and multifaceted array of conceptual and material interrelationships, interrelationships that are increasingly important in shaping postmodern cities and our experiences of them.

2. COORDINATIONS, MODERN AND POSTMODERN

With the rise of modernity, grids and their transpositions from one domain to another, for example, from mathematics to city planning, became a common logic and technology of culture. The beginnings of this process can be traced to Descartes, whose thought philosophically inaugurated modernity, and his most famous invention, the coordinate "grid," known as the Cartesian coordinate system ever since. Although part of human civilization throughout its history, the grid in this deeper and broader conceptual and, ultimately, ideological sense of coordination of spaces, events, configurations, and so forth is one of the hallmarks of modernity. The logic and technology of the grid in this broader sense were especially crucial to the mechanisms of social discipline of the eighteenth and nineteenth centuries, powerfully examined by Foucault in his late works in terms of "technologies of power." Many of these mechanisms continue into the present, in part producing the complexity of the relationships—the continuities and discontinuities—between modernity and postmodernity. The continuities are defined by the persisting role of these mechanisms, and the discontinuities by the transformations of these mechanisms and the rise of new ones, in particular those that, according to Deleuze, lead to a gradual shift from "disciplinary societies" (and their institutions) to "societies of control." This shift, Deleuze argues, is in part brought about and enforced through the digitalization of our information. It may thus be seen as part of a broader transformation, as defined by Lyotard, from modernity, defined by the industrial revolution, to postmodernity, defined by the revolution in information technology (*The Postmodern Condition* 3–6). As Lyotard writes, "along with the hegemony of computers comes a certain logic, and therefore a certain set of prescriptions determining which statements are accepted as 'knowledge' statements." Accordingly, "knowledge in the form of an information commodity indispensable to productive power is already, and will continue to be, a major—perhaps *the* major—stake in the world-wide competition for power" (4–5).

The conjunctions and interactions of the material and cyber spaces in which mechanisms of power are embedded and through which they operate are, I argue, among the significant forces of this cognitive and cultural transformation. As the transformation of urban spaces, this transformation is thus also a shift from modern to postmodern city grids or, in the postmodern city, sometimes the near dissolution of these grids, yielding to what Deleuze and Guattari call "smooth"—de-coordinated and de-striated—spaces. These spaces enable more uninhibited movement of the kind we encountered in the case of the flow of Deleuzean desire, discussed in Chapter 1, or in parkour, to be discussed in Chapter 4. This dissolution is never absolute, and it both retains some of the older (modern) grids and striations, and creates new (postmodern) ones, leading to a great complexity of the interactions between the smooth and the striated in postmodern urban spaces.

These spaces, thus, comprise multiple local spaces, smooth and striated, which may be related (via transitions between them, for example) but are in general heterogeneous, and thus resist and ultimately defeat any complete, global coordination of individual subjects, groups, or events in a particular postmodern landscape. Given the role of striation in the local spaces involved, however, it is not surprising that, while now localized as well, the grid, as a common part of most actual striated spaces, retains its significance as one of the foundations of urban architecture, both material and conceptual. It is, inevitably, the character of urban architecture that enables the transfer or translation of the grid and particularly the urban grid into cyberspace, making it a cybercity. (The transfer is accomplished in part through the phenomenal and specifically visual imagery shaping urban architecture.) In general, this kind of transfer need not be that of the postmodern conceptual space defined by the multiple local interactions of the smooth and the striated, and thus by different local grids, and possible connections or disjunctures of local subspaces. The rise of cyberspace, however, coincides with the rise of postmodern urban spaces, conceptual and material. Hence the relationships between postmodern urban spaces and urban-like cyberspaces are equally defined by the postmodern spatiality of the smooth and the striated, as just explained. It is, moreover, not only a question of parallels or isomorphisms between both types of spaces. In the postmodern city, both types of spaces, and thus the grids that support them and are supported by them, are interconnected and indeed are no longer always unequivocally dissociable in their form or functioning.

In order to understand these relationships and the forms of social discipline and control or freedom they entail, it may be helpful, first, to look more closely at how these forms of spatial organization relate to knowledge and, in particular, at the changes that computer technologies have led to in the forms and uses of information in the postmodern world. To do this requires a brief excursion into the practices of mapping (broadly understood as the technology that links space and knowledge) and, specifically, the coordinate grid, the conceptual structure that undergirds so many of our modern and postmodern cities, and our "real" and imaginary cyberspaces. As just explained, even though the postmodern city and cyberspace finally move beyond the grid towards smooth urban spaces, they do not and perhaps cannot leave the grid behind altogether, in either its negative or positive aspects. It is important that the grid can also play a positive, shaping role in the postmodern city, as shown by Lynch in his analysis of the grid's "legibility," to which I shall return in the next section.

Descartes's idea of the coordinate system extended the Euclidean vision of mathematics and the world, and gave this vision a more powerful encoding and mapping technology. This technology enabled the progress of multiple material technologies that were often based on mathematics, along with physics, which Descartes and, following him, Galileo and Newton also brought together, in part by using coordinate systems to map and analyze the physical world. Descartes's system allows one to locate particular events relative to the orthogonal (and hence easily measurable) lines of coordinates. It also, and conceptually more crucially, allows one to coordinate different events with one another within the same spatial and temporal frame of reference. In physics, this "coordinate dream" was fully realized, or was believed to have been fully realized, in Newton's mechanics, grounded in Newton's vision of absolute space and absolute time, which coupled this coordination of physical events to a strict causality. It may be noted that, as was quickly realized by mathematicians, a coordinate system can be curvilinear, as is the one we use on the surface of the globe in geography. This fact eventually helped in the discovery of non-Euclidean geometry. This discovery was one of the key steps in the process that eventually (it took a while) brought about the end of Newton's dream of classical physics and of the universe governed by its laws or, as William Blake would have it, "Newton's sleep."[4] The coordinate dream, sometimes becoming the coordinate nightmare, has persisted for much longer in mathematics and science or, in its broader form, elsewhere in our culture. In philosophy, Descartes's and Newton's dreams were questioned from the outset, specifically by Leibniz, who astutely understood the philosophical problems involved in Newton's vision of space (as absolute space). As noted in the introduction, Leibniz did not believe that it is possible to rigorously define the concept of absolute space or, to begin with, empty space, coordinated or not, which would then serve as an ambient space for material bodies. According to Leibniz, space and whatever coordinate systems could be introduced there could only be defined by a given configuration of material bodies. This view, as Einstein was to eventually discover through his relativity, ultimately implies the impossibility of, correlatively, both Newton's absolute space and a unique coordination of all physical events.

Such philosophical problems notwithstanding, the role and impact of Cartesian coordination was momentous and extended far beyond mathematics and physics, or geography (where the idea was of course especially helpful) and other scientific and technological applications, to the modern understanding of human thought and culture, and to modernity's self-understanding and even self-definition. Inevitably, in this broader domain the concept also took on more complex, including metaphorical, dimensions, and was coupled to a series of broader philosophical conceptualities, beginning with that of Descartes himself, now as a philosopher (especially a philosopher of conscious thinking, the *cogito*), and his contemporaries, such as John Locke. Extending to the key figures of the Enlightenment, such as Jean-Jacques Rousseau, Kant, Hegel, and beyond, this philosophical grounding of Cartesianism gave it a greater conceptual power and amplified its impact. With the help of philosophical thinking, the concept of the coordinate system led to both actual models of organization, such as that of particular cities built or rebuilt according to a coordinated and often rectangular grid, and a general model of defining human subjects and their behavior, and hence society, in relation to a proper system of coordinates. The coordinates could be economic, cultural, political, religious, or other, and they could be variously adjusted or subdivided within each of these categories. New coordinates could be and have been continually added as well, and different coordinate systems and transitions between them could be possible, just as they were in Newtonian physics. What was crucial, however, was that, as in Newtonian physics, everything would be seen, at least in principle and (hopefully) potentially in practice, as subject to overall global coordination. These coordinate systems were connected to or built around actual grids, those of material structures, such as those in cities, or institutions, such as churches, schools, prisons, hospitals, and offices, which were located on the city grid and thus partly defined this grid itself, culturally or even physically. The grid was also reproduced within many of these institutions, as analyzed by Foucault. By the nineteenth century, the power and impact of this thinking permeated the fabric of modernity and provided some of its strongest and most pronounced threads. Then, and sometimes even now, it appeared unassailable, even though (as Foucault's analysis also demonstrates) it was only a dream or a "sleep," albeit one with powerful and sometimes devastating real effects.[5]

It is not surprising that, even while reconfigured and often redeployed differently in postmodern urban spaces, the coordinate grid persists in and is one of the primary modern conceptual structures found in the postmodern city. Euclidean geometry and Newtonian physics largely remain our conceptual and practical models for "human-scale" urban spaces or cyberspace (primarily because our phenomenal spatiality appears to be Euclidean and Newtonian), and they shape our phenomenal image of the world and, as a result, our visualization of cyberspace accordingly. The "spaces" of modern physics, especially those of quantum theory, are nonvisualizable phenomenally, and ultimately even the very denomination of space may no longer apply to them.

Besides, the ideology of and the desire (for example, Oedipal and/as capitalist desire) for global grids or striations continue to persist. As a result, powerful ideological apparatuses and desiring-machines that aim at such global grids and striations threaten our desire for and our attempts to create new spaces defined by the complex interplay of local smooth spaces and striations or grids. As indicated earlier, the idea of this type of space or of smooth space, to begin with, has been given a mathematical conception by Riemann and his followers, which provided a mathematical model both for Einstein's general relativity (his theory of gravitation) and for Deleuze and Guattari's philosophical vision (*A Thousand Plateaus* 485). The idea of smooth space has also grounded Deleuze and Guattari's anti-Oedipal conception of desire and their critique of the complicity between Oedipal desire and capitalism in *Anti-Oedipus*, as considered in Chapter 1. Whether in the field of desire or elsewhere in human practice, it does not appear to be possible, however, to ever fully realize a completely smooth space. Only mathematical spaces and certain mathematically idealized physical models can be seen as rigorously enacting smooth spaces; but for better or worse, we do not live in purely mathematical spaces. Our practices defined by the idea of the smooth-space movement of desire do make it possible for us, however, to create spatial architectures in which striations are always local and are subordinated to smooth spaces and smooth motions, to the degree, hopefully the maximal degree, to which these smooth spaces and motions are realizable. Our postmodern conceptions and realities of the city and of cyberspace inevitably reflect these complexities of the relationships between the smooth and the striated, from the persistence of the desiring-machines pursuing global striation to the shifts between the smooth and the striated within the alternative machines of (smooth) desire. These complexities are amplified by the fact that our postmodern urban spaces and, in subtler ways, our cyberspaces (given the digital codes on which they depend) emerge amidst modern or still earlier spaces, striations, grids, ideologies, and desiring-machines, and cannot avoid coexisting and interacting with them. Indeed, as noted earlier, as a base for urban design, the grid is ancient, and some of the premodern aspects of it still have their effects even in the postmodern city. To some degree, the "fortress" part of the postmodern control logic involves some of these effects, as the term "fortress" indicates. My main concern for the moment, however, is Cartesianism and its impact on modernity, and with modernity itself, on postmodernity and its urban spatialities, actual and phenomenal, or virtual, such as those of cyberspace.

In *The Radiant City: Elements of a Doctrine of Urbanism to Be Used as the Basis of Our Machine-Age Civilization* (1935), the great modernist architect and urban planner Le Corbusier lays out his philosophy, principles, and plans for the city of the future, a "Cartesian city" of cruciform "Cartesian skyscrapers" arranged in ranks and files amid vast green lawns overlaid with a grid of elevated highways.[6] His treatise is a model of high-modernist architectural thought and design, conceptually and materially founded upon the concept of the Cartesian grid. In the midst of his chapter entitled "Is Descartes American?" (the answer to this would be no, since Le Corbusier repeatedly contrasts the Cartesian order of his Radiant City to the chaotic disorder of Lower Manhattan), he interrupts his discourse on the history of architecture with a meditation on mathematical calculation, measurement, and the formula in order to ground his new vision. His meditation essentially reveals the Newtonian conception of the world considered earlier, arguably in its most triumphant form reached in the nineteenth century, perhaps especially in France. "A formula," he asserts, "can . . . be used in place of a reality that is itself too cumbersome to deal with . . . Such formulas . . . contain the laws of the cosmos, and they will not finally solidify into a unity until the mixture reaches a perfect conformity with all the universal laws involved" (*The Radiant City* 130–31). These formulas link "the mathematician, the inventor, and the artist (the true artist!). Everything comes to the same thing in their mediating hands: a reabsorbence of chaos into harmony. . . . This accomplished, man . . . is a demiurge. He has the power of decision over *future events*. Once his calculations are finished, he is in a position to say—and he does say: '*It shall be thus!*'" (*The Radiant City* 131; his emphasis).[7] In other words, as in Newtonian mechanics, the future is determined and is determined in the right way once one sets the initial conditions properly (in this case, doing so is the affair of humans, as against Newtonian physics, where these conditions are set by nature), has the right laws, and performs one's calculations correctly. It should be noted, however, that Le Corbusier is well aware of the fact that this seemingly divine power of calculation "is only the mirror of our own very *human* divinity" and should not be worshiped in a religious manner (*The Radiant City* 131; emphasis added). It can, he believed, and should be deployed not only to understand the world but also to change it, as Marx would have it in famously juxtaposing philosophy and revolutionary practice in his final thesis on Feuerbach.[8]

For Le Corbusier, as for the urban planners who preceded and followed him, the grid constitutes a Cartesian "rationalization" of the space of the city, the creation or, in cases of an already-existing urban fabric, imposition of order. The grid carries with it, above all, the advantages and disadvantages of particular forms and functions of *visibility* or *legibility*. Both simple and

Figure 2.2 Le Corbusier, model of the Plan Voisin. (From Pierre Chenal's film, *L'architecture d'aujourd'hui*.)

replicable to any scale, the grid facilitates the imaging, mapping (both literal and conceptual), and navigation of the city; the commodification of urban space by dividing land into abstract units that can be easily bought and sold; and certain municipal operations, including governance by precinct or borough, zoning, taxation, and security. Thus, the grid simultaneously serves the interests of individuals (sometimes), capital, and the state.

For individual inhabitants of the city, one of the primary advantages of the grid is its navigability. "Way-finding," Lynch writes in *The Image of the City*, "is the original function of the environmental image" (125), and the "legibility" of the cityscape can be measured by "the ease with which its parts can be recognized and can be organized into a coherent pattern" (2–3). The image of the city, however, "is valuable not only in this immediate sense in which it acts as a map for the direction of movement; in a broader sense it can serve as a general frame of reference within which the individual can act, or to which he can attach his knowledge. In this way it is like a body of belief, or a set of customs: it is an organizer of facts and possibilities" (125–6).

What the form of the grid itself can tell us about a particular city or society is, however, not necessarily clear or uniform. As discussed earlier, as an urban form, the grid predates Descartes by at least eight thousand years, and throughout history, it has appeared in cities ruled by every economic and governmental system known to man. Its role has been shifting and often ambiguous in the past, and it remains complex and ambiguous in postmodern cities as well. In particular, despite the claims of recent advocates of the grid "as traditional, nonhierarchical and, perhaps, even democratic," it may well be that, as Jill Grant argues, "the grid and other patterns of urban form that derive from geometric principles and surveying technology [are] more frequently associated with the concentration of military power and wealth rather than with egalitarian traditions" (220).

Since the early modern period (which saw the "enclosure" and privatization of the public commons across England and other parts of Europe), capital has found in the grid a useful mechanism for commodifying land and "opening up" new areas for commercial exploitation. This was particularly true in the United States, where, in the nineteenth century, the grid was extended westward across the country as an aid to expansion and speculation. When the first grid was created in Manhattan by the Commissioners' Plan of 1811, the commissioners rejected the "supposed improvements . . . [of] circles, ovals and stars" that graced L'Enfant's 1791 plan for the nation's capital and instead opted for a pure grid on economic and practical grounds. "A city is composed of the habitations of men, and that strait sided," they pointed out, "and right angled houses are the most cheap to build, and the most convenient to live in." For the commissioners, the glaring lack of public and recreational spaces in the Plan was justified by "the price of land [which] is so uncommonly great, it seemed proper to admit the principles of economy to greater influence than might, under circumstances of a different kind, have consisted with the dictates of prudence and the sense of duty" (qtd. in Marcuse, "Grid" 298). Even though the Plan extended only over the undeveloped land north of Washington Square to 155th Street, the commissioners found themselves juggling the conflicting demands of multiple present and future stakeholders, a situation that recurred when the grid was extended further north in 1870.[9]

Few cities are planned by one isolated individual or a single group of individuals from the ground up, so that it is doubtless generally true that, as Peter Marcuse argues, "city form is a residual. It results from clashes of diverse interests and reflects the compromises and accommodations worked out as a result of those clashes" ("Grid" 289). Nonetheless, Grant asserts that "the historical record refutes Marcuse's suggestion that 'there is a "democratic" aspect to the grid, in which all parcels are created equal and alike. Thus cities where the display of power to the local population is of importance are least likely to be laid out in a grid plan' [294; pagination corrected]" (221). Grant instead argues that "evidence shows that some of the most tyrannical regimes in history, committed to monopolizing power, have used the grid to establish their mark on the landscape" (221).

As an instrument of imperialism and colonization, the grid has a long history. As Mumford notes in *The City in History*, "the standard gridiron plan in fact was an essential part of the kit of tools a colonist brought with him for immediate use" (192). By instituting spatial separations and various types of *cordons sanitaires*, city grids striate urban spaces and facilitate both the visual surveillance and supervision of populations. In their colonial cities, the ancient Greeks "imposed the grid even on quite rough terrain, as the rationality of math and science triumphed over topography" (Grant 230). The occupying powers of ancient Rome used the grid, which was "based on the model of the military camp and reflect[ed] its discipline," in its colonial towns across the Empire: "Subjugated peoples in the colonies were often moved into towns, both for control and for assimilation. . . . [and] the grid plan, rigorously executed from Africa to Britain, made the global authority of Rome physically manifest" (Grant 231). Surveillance, control, and assimilation of subject populations were equally, and explicitly, part of numerous modernist proposals for newly colonized cities, among them Le Corbusier's unbuilt Obus project for Algiers, which was intended to "rationalize" the tangled, imbricated alleyways of the ancient Casbah, which served as both a source of and refuge for resistance to the French colonial powers.[10]

With modernity, from at least the eighteenth century on, the urban grid became part of the state's bureaucratic apparatus of social control within what Foucault has termed "disciplinary societies." Inscribed upon the urban landscape, the grid is related to the "cells," "places," and "ranks" through which, as Foucault observes in *Discipline and Punish*, "the disciplines create complex spaces that are at once architectural, functional and hierarchical" (148). Like the drawing up of tables, this ordering of the space of the city is "both a technique of power and a procedure of knowledge" (148). It remains "a question of organizing the multiple, of providing oneself with an instrument to cover it and to master it . . . a question of imposing upon it an 'order'" (148). This order is, in its essence, *totalizing*: it governs not only physical space but also conceptual and social space. Like the disciplines themselves, the grid creates what Foucault refers to as "mixed spaces: real because [it] govern[s] the disposition of buildings, rooms, furniture, but also ideas, because [it is] projected over this arrangement of characterizations, assessments, hierarchies" (148). It can constitute, therefore, a total and totalizing regime of power/knowledge.

This regime also involves, as Michel de Certeau points out, processes of purification and repression, standardization and homogenization, synchronization and assimilation. "The 'city' founded by utopian and urbanistic discourse," he writes, "is defined by the possibility of a threefold operation":

1. The production of its *own* space (*un espace propre*): rational organization must thus repress all the physical, mental and political pollutions that would compromise it;
2. the substitution of a nowhen, or of a synchronic system, for the indeterminable and stubborn resistances offered by traditions; univocal scientific strategies . . . must replace the tactics of users who take

advantage of 'opportunities' and who, through these trap-events, these lapses in visibility, reproduce the opacities of history everywhere;

3. finally, the creation of a *universal* and anonymous *subject* which is the city itself: it gradually becomes possible to attribute to it . . . all the functions and predicates that were previously scattered and assigned to many different real subjects—groups, associations, or individuals. 'The city,' like a proper name, thus provides a way of conceiving and constructing space on the basis of a finite number of stable, isolatable, and interconnected properties. (94; de Certeau's emphasis)

This coordinate dream of the ordered and orderly city (whose disciplinary functions I examine in more detail in Chapter 3) is a fantasy of life, as Le Corbusier expressed it, "brought to perfection, not something botched. It is mastery, not an abortive chaos. It is fecundity (the total splendor of a lucid conception) and not sterility (the dungheap into which we have been plunged by all those thoughtless admirers of the miseries now existing in our great cities)" (*The Radiant City* 134). But it is not life as it is lived and experienced by real people in real places. Nor is it life as it is actually lived in the places into which projects of the kind Le Corbusier and his followers envisioned are, it appears, unavoidably converted once they are built (Chicago's infamous Cabrini-Green housing project, for example). Despite Le Corbusier's claims, there is such a thing as too much order, or at least too much Cartesian order, such as that envisioned by Le Corbusier, and too much of this order appears to be inimical to city life.

The history of urban spaces from modernity into postmodernity is also that of the transition from modern to postmodern forces and structures of control. Yet, as we move from the "disciplinary society" to the "societies of control," the older disciplinary structures still persist, even in our newest spaces: the virtual spaces and cities of cyberspace. As the images and descriptions of cyberspace given earlier suggest, there are striking resemblances between the Cartesian grid upon which so much modernist and now postmodernist urban design depends and the grids of cyberspace. Indeed, these representations might equally be seen to resemble nothing so much as the great modernist "Futuramas" and "Cities of Tomorrow," including the designs of Le Corbusier and Oscar Niemeyer and their many imitators. In *Neuromancer*'s cyberspace, the chessboard grids between the corporate and governmental data holds are as empty and devoid of street life as the unhappy green voids separating the massive edifices of Le Corbusier's Cartesian cities and, not incidentally, as the windswept glacis that surround the governmental and corporate citadels of present-day cities. It is as if many of the architects of both fictional and actual cyberspace were driven by the same utopian imagination, which, having failed in so many of its real-world incarnations, now sought "realization" in the ethereal realm of virtual reality.

As indicated earlier, the cyberspace of *Tron* is rendered (through, then revolutionary, computer-generated special effects) as a grid composed of intersecting, gleaming lines of light laid out across a black void suspended in space. Arranged on this grid are various geometrical structures that function as barriers, obstacles, and traps, with the "Master Control" (in the form of a high-modernist edifice) at its center. Similarly, the field on which *Neuromancer's* cyberspace data banks are arrayed is decidedly Cartesian—geometrical, abstract, transcendent. The realm of pure information is composed of "bright lattices of logic unfolding across that colorless void" (4), forming a "transparent 3-D chessboard extending to infinity" (52), "lines of light ranged in the nonspace of the mind" (51). The Cartesian (street) grid is equally ubiquitous in actual plans or achieved designs for cyberspaces, including Silicon Graphic's 3-D Fusion Information Landscape Prototype (Wexelblat 69), Michael Benedikt's cybercity (Benedikt 119–224), Apple's e-World, and the cyberspace renderings of Daniel Wise and Stan George (Benedikt, Plates 1–6).

It is perhaps unsurprising that this new realm of information—of knowledge and power—should have first and subsequently, with such frequency, been imagined on the model of this Cartesian "data map" (the coordinate grid), this Foucauldian system of ranks and files, of discipline and order. And yet, as already noted and as will be seen in more detail in the next section, it is, ironically, cyberspace that more than any other technological or conceptual development appears to be taking us beyond the grid, from the Foucauldian "disciplinary society" to the cybertech "society of control," envisioned by Deleuze and Guattari, which is based on a new cybertech model of knowledge and power.

This new model is much more than an "electrification" or digitalization of the grid. It is and will perhaps remain a hybrid of sorts. It incorporates the earlier disciplinary model (which still continues to operate in many of the same spaces Foucault described—from the prison to schools, hospitals, barracks, factories, and offices), but, at the same time, synergistically intensifies it and yet is supplemented (or perhaps is in the process of being replaced) by something quite new. Thus, what makes the various technologies of surveillance depicted in the opening of Tony Scott's 1998 film *Enemy of the State* (satellites, CCTV, and so forth) most frightening is the demonstration of how effective they become when they are interlinked, when the networks become one, and when they are joined by what one might call "the tyranny of the (electronic) archive," the seemingly eternal nature of "data" and, for powerful forces like the state, its seemingly unlimited accessibility and manipulability. Now, as Pynchon's Oedipa feared in *The Crying of Lot 49*, "the tower is everywhere" and largely invisible (11). Deleuze speaks of control as "continuous and without limit" in our culture, as it moves beyond the disciplinary society and its institutions. In the Foucauldian model, the web of power was uneven, far tighter in some places than in others, and it had blind spots. There were still places where one might escape the gaze of power, places to hide, places in which and from which one might resist. Now, however, such zones seem fewer and largely limited to spaces "off the grid"—a position that is nearly impossible for the population of the First World to assume or maintain.

3. DE-COORDINATIONS, MODERNIST AND POSTMODERNIST

To counteract the new forces and structures of "power" in the cybertech societies of control, alternative tactics and technologies of resistance must be developed from within these networks and from within other networks of forces, conceptual and cultural, that have, in fact, long subsisted alongside them. For, as indicated earlier, some doubts concerning the Cartesian way of thinking about nature or culture emerged immediately in its wake and persisted throughout its history, and even took the form of a radical critique of it, as in Nietzsche, for example. These doubts and critiques, however, were at best only able to exist on the margins of modernity and the Enlightenment. Their general impact and specific effects were, we might say with Derrida, deferred—mostly into postmodernity. By early in the twentieth century, however, the Cartesian way of thinking was not merely in doubt; it was in fact under siege from where the attack might have been least expected, from inside the greatest Cartesian bastions of all, mathematics and science. The discovery of non-Euclidean geometry and other radical developments in nineteenth-century mathematics, the rise of thermodynamics in physics (which complicated the idea of causality), and the introduction of the theory of evolution by Darwin were earlier signs of trouble, but they, at least, appeared to allow space for the hope that they could eventually be brought into the Cartesian fold. The great twentieth-century physical assault on Cartesianism in physics came with Einstein's relativity and quantum theory. Einstein's special theory of relativity (1905) and then, more radically, general theory of relativity (1916), a non-Newtonian theory of gravity, were based mathematically on Riemannian spaces. The latter, as discussed earlier, are defined by the multiplicity of potentially Cartesian local neighborhoods and hence by local grids, but disallow any overall coordination. As also noted earlier, Einstein's ideas have a Leibnizian genealogy as well, and thus become part of the longer history during which non-Cartesian thought gradually developed alongside Cartesian thought and eventually came into the forefront of science and culture. Einstein's general relativity also has major cosmological implications, whose significance only became apparent gradually, from the discovery of the fact that the universe is expanding to the fact that this expansion originated in the catastrophic singularity of the explosion known as the Big Bang to the most recent cosmological theories. Most crucial in the present context are the new forms of spatiality defined by Riemann and then Einstein, and given their postmodern philosophical conceptualization, via the relationships between the smooth and the striated by Deleuze and Guattari.

Quantum mechanics (sometimes seen as the first truly "postmodern" theory, at least in science) has since brought this impossibility to its ultimate limit by denying, in view of Heisenberg's uncertainty relations, a classical-like mapping even to any single event, which now could only be partially mapped—that is, if one sees this mapping on the classical model.[11] The ultimate implication of quantum mechanics was that this Cartesian or even Riemannian mapping was no longer applicable to the ultimate constitution of nature, but was only applicable, now strictly partially, to our *observations* concerning nature: we can, as it were, only see half of the classical Cartesian picture. By the same token, at the subatomic level causality was no longer possible and all our predictions could at best amount to estimating the probabilities of the results of the experiments we could stage. As a result, the epistemological architecture of quantum mechanics entailed a number of features that brought it close to postmodern epistemology.[12] This proximity was later amplified by higher-level quantum theories dealing with high-energy processes, which added even more radical aspects to quantum physics, especially those aspects related to the multiplicities that these theories entailed. For, as against the original form of quantum mechanics, it was no longer possible to maintain the identity of elementary particles in physical processes: a given particle, such as an electron, could transform itself into another particle, say, a photon, or even into several particles.

The collapse of Newtonian physics on the "small" or "extra-small" scale of the atom and on the "large" or "extra-large" scale of the universe had a major impact on postmodern knowledge and culture, including on our conceptions of postmodern spatiality, particularly in considerations of postmodern cities and virtual spaces, such as cyberspace. So had other radical, "postmodern" developments in modern mathematics and science, such as Gödel's incompleteness theorems in mathematical logic (which deprive us of our capacity to demonstrate the logically consistent nature of mathematics itself); several major advances in genetics, molecular biology, and neuroscience; and of course the advent of computer technologies, including those leading to the creation of cyberspace.[13] As Lyotard argues in *The Postmodern Condition*, mathematics and science themselves became part of postmodern knowledge and culture, part, to use the subtitle of his book, of the postmodern condition and of postmodern practice, sometimes with science being ahead of philosophy or culture. Accordingly, if we want to accept the first axiom of the Enlightenment, which tells us to be guided by how nature or mathematics work in our models of humanity and culture, then nature and mathematics, as they appear now, seem to direct us away from other Enlightenment axioms, such as those of Cartesianism. This new, non-Cartesian thinking about our cultural, including urban, spaces is possible by virtue of alternative mathematical and physical conceptions of space available to us, in particular those of the Riemannian-Deleuzean type, defined by the heterogeneous yet interactive multiplicity of the smooth and the striated.

One can also link these postmodern spaces of multiple and multiply interactive forms of smoothness and striation to Lyotard's view of the postmodern heterogeneity and plurality of narratives, as against the "grand" and meta-narratives of the Enlightenment, since each striation or grid carries a narrative with it, and vice versa. There are also smooth-space narratives, such as those of "minor" or "nomadic" types, as against those of "major" or "state" types (which are always linked to global, Cartesian grids and Euclidean spaces), as considered by Deleuze and Guattari in *A Thousand Plateaus* (351–423). These are narratives of becoming, of multiple becoming, such as those of Virginia Woolf in *The Waves*, invoked by Deleuze and Guattari and discussed in Chapter 1: "all kinds of becomings between ages, sexes, elements, and kingdoms," in which any "individuality . . . designates a multiplicity," a wave-like moving front of multiplicities, overflowing grids (252).

Indeed, although the undermining of Cartesianism within mathematics and science has a special significance and while alternative philosophical thinking helps in our articulation of non-Cartesian conceptualities, the earliest and the most radical critique of Cartesianism and its scientific, philosophical, and ideological avatars has been undertaken in literature and art. One can think of earlier examples, such as Cervantes, a great literary nomadologist, or, between literature and philosophy, Montaigne. His essays fragment philosophical grids and create smooth literary and philosophical movements; and as such these essays are already quite "postmodern," according to Lyotard (*The Postmodern Condition* 81). By the time Cartesianism reaches its dominance in the Enlightenment, a powerful critique undertaken by literature is underway, especially as part of the Romantic movement that emerged in the end of the eighteenth century. Kleist, one of the most intriguing and most radical Romantic authors, is a crucial literary figure in *A Thousand Plateaus*, which juxtaposes him to both Goethe and Hegel, who are seen as "State thinkers" (*A Thousand Plateaus* 356). Kleist is a thinker and poet of nomadic becoming(s), and "*the most uncanny modernity* lies with him" (356; emphasis added). A brilliant choice of phrase, "uncanny modernity": this is the modernity that has always existed alongside the modernity that aimed at the coordinated "residential development" for humanity and promised us a safe home in this abode of the rational.

The literary and artistic modernism of the twentieth century may be seen as an extension of this uncanny modernity as well, and it arguably pursues a critique of Cartesian modernity more persistently than its affirmation, to some degree even in modernist architecture, dominated as it might have been by Le Corbusier's and related visions and ideologies. Some of Le Corbusier's own projects, usually his separate buildings (such as the Villa Savoye, his most famous building, or Notre-Dame-du-Haut at Ronchamp), are marked by a kind of deconstruction in practice of his Cartesianism.[14] Similar, although more radical, deconstructions and self-deconstructions of the grid are deployed in Mondrian's paintings, sometimes associated (for example, by the Situationists) with Cartesianism and the celebration of the grid. This view is, as I would argue (the argument has of course been made before), quite mistaken.[15] Just about all of Mondrian's "grid" paintings enact subtle and yet radical deconstructions of Cartesianism, a strategy that appears especially impossible to miss (although it has been missed) in his last painting, "Broadway Boogie Woogie" (1942–43). Fittingly using New York City (to which Le Corbusier especially juxtaposed his Cartesian city), New York City portrayed in smooth motion, the painting made the grid dissolve to reveal the staccato or smooth-staccato space beneath it. One can speak here, somewhat paradoxically, of a "smooth-staccato" space because of the uninhibited movement this jazzy staccato rhythm creates, an idea in fact found in Deleuze and Guattari as well, and associated by them with Kleist (*A Thousand Plateaus* 356).

Arguably, however, it is modernist literature, as "minor literature" in Deleuze and Guattari's sense (the subtitle of their book on Kafka), where modernism's fight against Cartesian modernity or Cartesian modernism is waged most passionately and most successfully. Apart from giving him a central role in *A Thousand Plateaus*, Deleuze and Guattari devote to Kafka their important *Kafka: Toward a Minor Literature*, which presents his work as a literary enactment of the program of nomadic, minoritarian resistance to the state apparatuses of capitalism. Lyotard similarly sees key modernist literature, most especially that of Joyce, as a literary enactment of the epistemology and, concomitantly, narrative strategies of postmodernity: "Joyce allows the un[re]presentable to become perceptible in his writing itself, in the signifier. The whole range of available narrative and even stylistic operators is put into play without concern for the unity of the whole, and new operators are tried" (*The Postmodern Condition* 80).

It is, accordingly, not surprising that the urban spaces—the cities—created by modernist literary works (at least of this "postmodernist" kind) give us, and our urban imaginary, some of the best means of conceiving of a different, non-Cartesian city. Dos Passos's New York and Woolf's London, discussed in Chapter 1, Joyce's Dublin, and Musil's Vienna (in *The Man Without Qualities*) are among the greatest examples of such alternative cities in literary modernism. As the discussion in Chapter 1 shows and as will be seen later in this chapter and throughout this study, the postmodernist urban imaginary is not only a break from some, especially Cartesian, forms of modernist or modern urban imaginary, it is also a continuation of non-Cartesian modernism and modernity. It is a continuation of artistic, philosophical, scientific, and cultural, including political, urban thinking that was at work throughout the history of modernity.

More generally, as Deleuze and Guattari argue, minor or nomadic forces of resistance have always existed alongside major or state forces of the Cartesian logic and culture of modernity, and indeed alongside preceding dominant formations of power, perhaps inevitably defined by some form of globalizing or totalizing coordinated striations and grids. Both types of forces (minor and major, nomadic and state) and the respective types of desiring-machines that arise from them use as their resource the same field of energy, which Deleuze and Guattari define as "the body without organs" (a concept that is correlative although not identical to Foucault's concept of "power"). The same reservoir of energy, the same body without organs, which was reshaped by the history of modernity extending into postmodernity, can also provide resources for the postmodern resistance to the forces and global Cartesian striations aimed at by the *state* apparatuses (in both Althusser's and Deleuze and Guattari's sense) developed throughout modernity and now extending into postmodernity.

In "Postscript on the Societies of Control," Deleuze suggests as forms of resistance jamming, piracy, viruses—variations on "hacking." It is true that such tactics might sometimes, at least temporarily, be effective (as was, for example, the digg.com publication of the Sony copy-protection software code that, after Sony forced them to remove it from the website, was independently posted and re-posted thousands of times across the Web, and even inscribed in the lyrics of a song posted on YouTube). In Nadia El Fani's 2003 film *Bedwin Hacker*, a Tunisian hacker interrupts French satellite television transmissions with messages that make visible the existence of France's former colonial subjects in Tunisia and Algeria, and insist that they "are not a mirage."[16] At the same time, Bedwin's reminder that "in the third millennium, there are other epochs, other places, other lives" does not really constitute a very effective critique. For the problem is precisely that, for the French, their former colonial subjects are indeed "the other," inhabiting the "other" epoch of "the primitive past," in places that no longer seem of much concern (except as potential export sources of terrorism). Effective resistance to the forces and structures of control, those of the fortress and those of the scanscape, clearly require a more complex and sophisticated array of strategies and tactics, as Deleuze and Guattari's own deeper philosophical reflections, such as those on smooth and striated spaces and their relationships, suggest. The grid, which, as I argue here, is part of both economies, that of control and that of resistance, may and even must still be used in this resistance, but, it also follows, it is not sufficient. What we need, what we seek, is an open-ended order. Perhaps in order to move to smooth urban (or other) spaces, actual and virtual, or interactively both, we need to start by creating a smooth space, in the manner of parkour, which also involves and makes possible the creation of more resistant and (which is the ultimate aim of the process) more productive striations and grids.

4. CYBERCITY AND URBAN IMAGINARY

To create this smooth space and this new open-ended order (which may often resemble or even necessarily involve disorder) will undoubtedly require a massive deployment of our urban and cyberspace imaginaries, which gave us the city and the cyberspace grids and their transpositions, but which need to give us much more. Part of the difficulty of the task is of course the very nature of urban space (or cyberspace), made more apparent by postmodernist thought in science, philosophy, literature, and elsewhere. As Doreen Massey argues in her "Politics and Space/Time": "'Space' is created out of the vast intricacies, the incredible complexities, of the interlocking and the non-interlocking, and the networks of relations at every scale from local to global. . . . [A]s a result of the fact that [space] is conceptualized as created out of social relations, space is by its very nature full of power and symbolism, a complex web of relations of domination and subordination, of solidarity and cooperation" (79–80). It is quite clear that thus understood, "space" is also an embodiment of the urban imaginary, and any transformation of the structures or architectures of space requires a massive mobilization of the forces and energies of this imaginary. I would like, accordingly, to close this chapter by a discussion of this imaginary. The role of the urban imaginary (as it is developed through literature, film, and art) in illuminating and shaping both the material city and our experience of it is one of my main themes throughout this book—from early literary anticipations to postmodernist literature and film to the multiple interactions between visual art and the urban environment. My focus here, in accordance with the main argument of this chapter, which deals with the relationships between the material city and the cybercity, is on the depictions of futuristic cities and cyberspaces appearing in science-fiction novels and films (and, increasingly, in corporate and consumer advertising).

It may be noted, first, that these depictions inevitably raise questions of whether they should be viewed as plausible forecasts of the future, or whether they are actually best understood as narrative symbolizations of or "figure[s] for our experience of the present" (Fitting 300), as most critics argue. In this regard, the critical reception of cyberpunk, the form of science fiction with which I shall be primarily concerned here, has largely followed the established critical paradigm of reading works of science fiction as thinly veiled commentaries on contemporary trends that are extrapolated (and exaggerated) by their authors for effect. The cyberpunk writers themselves have tended to reinforce this view. In his preface to Gibson's *Burning Chrome*, fellow cyberpunk author Bruce Sterling argues that "these stories paint an instantly recognizable portrait of the modern predicament. Gibson's extrapolations show, with exaggerated clarity, the hidden bulk of an iceberg of social change. This iceberg now glides with sinister majesty across the surface of the late 20th century, but its proportions are vast and dark" (xi). Gibson has himself insisted that this is the impetus behind his own work: "What's most important to me is that it's about the present," he said in a 1989 interview. "It's not really about an imagined future. It's a way of trying to come to terms with the awe and terror inspired in me by the world in which we live" ("High Tech").[17]

Gibson conceived of "cyberspace" prior to the development of any large-scale graphic interface for the Internet or World Wide Web, so his representations of it posed particular interpretive dilemmas, unlike his depictions of Chiba City or the Boston-Atlanta "Sprawl," which correlated fairly easily with the emerging postmodern character of those real-world urban agglomerations. It is, therefore, not surprising that, responding largely to this earlier stage of the history of cyberspace, many literary and cultural critics have considered cyberspace in broadly metaphorical terms as a manifestation of the invisible economic flows or technological systems of the postmodern world. Thus, Jameson views cyberpunk as "the supreme literary expression if not of postmodernism, then of late capitalism itself," which he sees as "a network of power and control even more difficult for our minds and imaginations to grasp: the whole new decentered global network of the third stage of capital itself" (419 n1, 37). Peter Fitting similarly suggests that we "make ourselves see Gibson's concept of cyberspace as an attempt to grasp the complexity of the whole world system through a concrete representation of its unseen networks and structures, of its invisible data transfers and capital flows. . . . Gibson's cyberspace is an image of a way of making the abstract and unseen comprehensible, a visualization of the notion of cognitive mapping" (308).[18] Scott Bukatman's interpretation, while in part influenced by Jameson, is less expansive than Jameson's or Fitting's, but it shares their sense that cyberspace is an attempt to render the invisible visible, the imperceptible perceptible. As depicted in works of science fiction, cyberspace might be seen, he argues, as the genre's "attempt to redefine the imperceptible (and therefore absent to consciousness) realms of the electronic era in terms of the physically and perceptually familiar. . . . to render the electronic fields present to consciousness—to turn them into phenomena—and therefore susceptible to human intention" (Bukatman 117). Thus, cyberspace functions as an allegory or metaphor for "a new and decentered spatiality . . . that exists parallel to, but outside of, the geographic topography of experiential reality," a spatiality that Bukatman calls "terminal space" (105).

Further corresponding to the main trends of postmodernist literary and cultural criticism of the 1980s and 1990s, the literary and cinematic depictions of cyberspace as a "city of text" have made more narrowly focused analyses of the resemblances between cyberspace and the contemporary city irresistible to critics (including me). In such analyses, cyberspace is generally understood as a symbolic landscape or conceptual (or, more broadly, in Jameson's terms, "cognitive") map of the logics and tendencies of the postmodern city. Such mapping is itself an important part of the urban imaginary of postmodernity. In 1999, *New York Times* architecture critic Herbert Muschamp pointed out that *The Matrix* was the latest in a long line of science-fiction films (stretching back through *Blade Runner*, *The Tenth Victim*, *Alphaville*, and *Metropolis*) remarkable for their ability "to crystallize moments of urban sensibility" ("If the Cityscape" 25). To a great extent, then, the "cyberspace imaginary," as it emerges in media representations, has been understood as a reiteration or special species of the urban imaginary.

Observing that "cyberspace arises at precisely the moment when the topos of the traditional city has been superseded" by the "city of simulations," Bukatman explicitly links cyberspace to the postmodern city (122). He also suggests, however, that "perhaps we can begin to learn about Gibson's cyberspace by learning from Las Vegas or Times Square or Tokyo for, on one level, cyberspace only represents an extension of the urban sector located at the intersection of postmodernism and science fiction" (Bukatman 121). Although he doesn't pursue this particular line of inquiry very far, Bukatman's observation that "we can begin to learn about Gibson's cyberspace by learning from Las Vegas" is astute. In particular, it suggests, in accordance with my argument in this chapter, that, like the recurring city/cyberspace dissolves and Gibson's depictions of cyberspace as city and city as "a field of data" (16), the conceptual "traffic" between city and cyberspace goes both ways. In other words, we might look at cyberspace to help us understand our postmodern cities and, conversely, look at our postmodern cities to help us understand cyberspace. It is certainly true that the cyberspace imaginary has been shaped not just by the urban imaginary (as an invention of new urban forms) of those who created and developed it, but also by the material forms of existing cities like Las Vegas. In Neal Stephenson's *Snow Crash*, this role of Las Vegas is made explicit: "it is always nighttime in the Metaverse, and the Street is always garish and brilliant, like Las Vegas freed from constraints of physics and finance" (26).[19]

The approaches to understanding cyberspace just outlined are productive (and I will deploy them throughout this study as well). They tend, however, to shift the focus from the future (even if it's the just-a-moment-from-now future, where the texts themselves situate these forms) to the present. In the process, they risk losing sight of the ways in which these fictions can be powerfully influential and, therefore, proleptic—an aspect of these works that has generally been either preemptively dismissed out of hand or simply neglected. Yet, as I suggested at the outset of this chapter, we not only build cyberspaces partly from the forms offered by "real" cities; we also build the cities (and cyberspaces) that we, first, imagine. The cyberspace imaginary, as it emerges in representations of cyberspace in films and fictions such as *Neuromancer* and *Snow Crash*, and theoretical conceptions like those articulated by Michael Benedikt in "Cyberspace: Some Proposals" have demonstrably influenced the creation of actual, existing forms of cyberspace, and they will doubtless continue to do so in the future.

Neuromancer's impact on the theoretical designs of early cyberspace was already the subject of discussion by the time of the First Conference on Cyberspace held at the University of Texas, Austin in 1990. There, the anthropologist David Tomas noted that "Gibson's powerful vision is now beginning to influence the way virtual reality and cyberspace researchers are structuring their research agendas and problematics" (46).[20] Benedikt's own "Cyberspace: Some Proposals," which has helped to set the terms for cyberspace research and design, is likely an example of this influence. His vision of cyberspace as a "gigantic . . . and spatially navigable database," in which "the immense traffic of information that constitutes human enterprise in science, art, business, and culture," and "information-intensive institutions and businesses [will] have a form, identity, and working reality . . . quite literally an *architecture*" resembles Gibson's depiction of cyberspace in *Neuromancer* (Benedikt 149, 123).[21]

Unlike Gibson's austere and even desolate cybercity, however, the vision of cyberspace proposed by Benedikt (arguably the most engaging and exuberant of the early cyberspace conceptions) imagines it as a roofless city with a rich street life, a "three-dimensional field of action and interaction: with recorded and live data, with machines . . . and with other people" (129). Like a good urban planner, Benedikt (who is also the director of the Center for American Architecture and Design at the University of Texas, Austin) pays careful attention to access, both internal and external. "Once in cyberspace," he writes, "there may be many ways of getting around, from walking and crawling, to leaping through worm holes, from 'bareback' riding or cyberBuick cruising, to floating and flying unencumbered" (130). His cybercity comes equipped with ports, transit stations, and gateways. On the outside, "cyberspace processing should be distributed," he suggests, "and its communication channels [should be] many and alternative: phone lines, satellite, HDTV, cables, even radio and power lines" (218n50). Benedikt is well aware of the obstacles: "The technical aspects of this are daunting. . . And, of course, there are myriad political, economic, and power-related questions involved in this notion of decentralization and redundancy" (218n50). The main point here, however, is his thinking of cyberspace on the model of urban space.

One might, of course, ask why databases should have an "architecture" (organization) modeled on that of urban spaces (see, for example, the proposed MapNet and "City of News" interfaces in Figures 2.3 and 2.4 below) or even why they should be represented as a physical space at all. Numerous theorists and designers argue for the necessity or at least desirability of creating a sort of informational "mirror world" (as in David Gelernter's *Mirror Worlds*) of the one we already know. Benedikt is among them. In his introduction to *Cyberspace: First Steps*, he asserts: "We are contemplating the arising shape of a new world, a world that must, in a multitude of ways, *begin*, at least, as both an extension and a transcription of the world as we know it and have built it thus far" (23). Such designs build upon our innate conceptual familiarity with "spatiality," and so are seen as "anthropic," to use Peter Anders's term, as inherently suited to our thought processes. "We think with space," Anders explains: "Using our mind's ability to dimensionalize information, we reduce complexity to manageable units—objects—of information. . . . Spatial, anthropic cyberspace links to

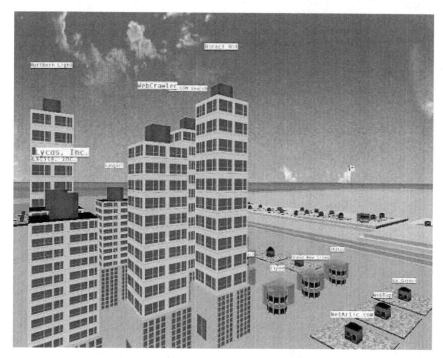

Figure 2.3 Map.net 3D cityscape view of the Web (Dodge and Kitchin 147).

a pre-linguistic knowledge of the world, a knowledge crucial to our navigation, operation, and communication" (9–10). Thus, cyberspace, *as* space, is thought to be more "human."

So far, most of the existing three-dimensional spatial interfaces on the World Wide Web have been in on-line games such as SimCity and interactive communities like Second Life. If the Web itself is eventually to become a three-dimensional cyberspace environment resembling the various "mirror world" conceptions of cyberspace theorists, such as Gelernter and Benedikt, and cyberpunk novelists, such as Gibson and Stephenson, it appears that it is likely to emerge out of the development of Microsoft's Virtual Earth 3D or the much more extensive Google Earth, the navigable (and zoomable) virtual globe constituted from high-resolution satellite imagery, aerial photographs, and Geographic Information System (GIS) data. Launched in 2005, Google Earth had image-overlay capability that made it possible to see, for instance, the National Geospatial Agency's preliminary post-Hurricane Katrina damage assessment map and the National Oceanic and Atmospheric Agency's images of the hurricane's impact superimposed upon a pre-Katrina satellite image of New Orleans.[22] Similar to earlier transparent celluloid overlay maps that allowed one to superimpose different types

Figure 2.4   "City of News," 1997, a dynamically growing three-dimensional Web browser created by Flavia Sparacino at MIT.

of data (e.g., topographical features or rainfall statistics) on top of a base map, the Google Earth overlays can be moved aside to reveal those beneath or above. In 2006, this two-dimensional overlay capability was extended to three dimensions with the release of SketchUp, a program that makes it possible for users to layer three-dimensional structures on top of Google's interactive virtual Earth.

Google Earth originated in a product called "Earth Viewer," developed by Keyhole Inc. prior to the company's acquisition by Google. In his narrative of the origins of Google Earth, former Keyhole CEO John Hanke cited the influence of *Snow Crash*:

> In terms of . . . where this thing came from . . . I met some guys from Silicon Graphics several ago, and they said, 'You know, you've probably read *Snow Crash*,' and I said, 'yeah, I had,' and they said, 'well, you know that thing that the character uses, that Earth thing where it's there in 3-D [i.e., the Metaverse], and you can just dive in and get information?' They said, 'We can build that.' . . . And that was our starting point, and it really was that idea that you could build a whole world and represent it truly and three-dimensional, not to sort of suggest that you could fly down to an area, but that you could use 3-D graphics and stream the data and really literally fly in and have it be like a video game. So that's the kind of thing that we're trying to build.

Hanke went on to explain: "Google's larger mission is to organize the world's information and make it universally accessible and useful. And we're really looking at it from the perspective of organizing all of the information on the Web that has a geographic component to it . . . places of business . . . history, news, other kinds of data that is definitely geographically tagged." This description, in turn, bears a strong resemblance to Stephenson's description in *Snow Crash* of a "rendition of Planet Earth" encountered by Hiro in the Metaverse, generated by a software program that "is the user interface that CIC [the Central Intelligence Corporation, a privatized amalgam of the Library of Congress and the Central Intelligence Agency] uses to keep track of every bit of spatial information that it owns—all the maps, weather data, architectural plans, and satellite surveillance stuff" (106).

A 2006 article by Chris Taylor in CNNMoney.com seeking to explain the importance of the Google Earth SketchUp launch also drew heavily upon *Snow Crash*: "The notion that you can create objects and buildings and place them in a virtual world makes Google Earth sound less like a mapping tool and more like a metaverse." Taylor suggested that "the result" of Google Earth's innovation "could be that we'll soon populate a virtual version of planet Earth instead of the made-from-scratch metaverses like on-line games or Second Life." The article also reported on "the Metaverse Roadmap Summit, a gathering of programmers of virtual worlds," whose agenda "was to outline how we're going to get from here to the metaverse in ten years."[23]

The question is, however, what kind of Metaverse we will create, one dominated by the forces and architectures of control, the fortress and the scanscape, and their grids, or one that will be defined by ever-widening gaps in the networks of control and by the polis and its smooth spaces. Our urban/cyberspace imaginary and our theoretical, including mathematical and scientific, thinking appear to be powerful enough to imagine and design such a polis Metaverse. The challenge will be finding the means to implement it in practice, given the persistence and power of forces, the forces of control, which, for now, appear to have the upper hand.

3   The City of Control and the Polis

This chapter argues that the city and cyberspace are both subject to the same two competing urban models, which I shall call the "control" and the "polis" models. The first may also be seen as a "police" model, and the second as a "freedom" model, accordingly also allowing for the control/freedom or the police/polis opposition. The "control" terminology is in part courtesy of Gilles Deleuze's concept of "the society of control" (mentioned in Chapter 2 and to be discussed later in this chapter). Each of these models is defined by its own distinctive spatial logics—the principles governing the organization of space and the strategic, material forms that economic and political power assumes in them.

In the first, the control model, the spatial logics are those of control, containment, exclusion, and surveillance, all of which relate to the deeper logic of the grid discussed in the preceding chapter. The control model is in turn defined by two primary forms of control or policing, the "fortress" and the "scanscape." The fortress city is manifest in the architecture of security-hardened buildings and the proliferation of gated communities, the scanscape in the closed-circuit TV cameras and other surveillance mechanisms that are increasingly being woven into the fabric of our cities. In cyberspace, the fortress and the scanscape take the form of censorship and website blocks, and various types of Internet surveillance mechanisms and spyware.

In the second spatial model, that of the polis, the logics are those of freedom, access, equality, and interchange. The polis emerges in spaces built to foster interaction and civic participation, from the piazzas of Italian cities to the public parks and brownstone stoops of New York and Chicago. The cyberpolis is found in the accessible, open spaces of the Web—the listservs, newsgroups, chat rooms, "town halls," and simulated worlds like Second Life. Whether we deal with the control or the polis model, however, the construction of virtual cities, as Alessandro Aurigi and Stephen Graham observe more generally, "necessarily [has] to engage with many of the key issues of social divisions, citizenship, civic culture, and urban policy and planning" (492).

The ongoing evolutions of cities and cyberspace are being determined by many of the same conceptual and material forces, which in part accounts for this mutual mirroring of spatial logics, but also reveals the more extensive and more complex nature of the relationships between the city and cyberspace. Among these forces is, first of all, our urban imaginary, our conceptions of what the city is and should be, some aspects of which were discussed in Chapter 2. Derived from our literary and visual representations of the city as much as from the material city itself, the urban imaginary extends to the historical and theoretical conceptions developed by those—such as fiction writers, scholars, architects, Web designers, and others—who envision, often futurally, the city and cyberspace.[1] The urban imaginary also encompasses our subjective mental images of the city, which have been shaped by those representations and conceptions of the city we've encountered and by our own particular experiences of it, and they are far more difficult to assess. These conceptions, however, inevitably influence the construction of both our material and cyberspace cities. In sum, as discussed in Chapter 2, we build the cities we imagine, both in actual space (physical and cultural) and in cyberspace.

Urban habitats and cyberspace, and their relationships, are also shaped by powerful economic and politico-economic forces, including the immense flows and exigencies of global capital. The "on the ground" effects of massive movements of capital either into or away from cities have been well documented and examined in many studies, and the subject is also discussed in more detail in Chapters 1 and 5 of this study. Major corporations such as Microsoft, Network Solutions, Cisco, Google, and Yahoo have played and will continue to play a decisive role in determining the growth and form of the Internet and World Wide Web. Of course, governments are also important forces in the ongoing development of the city and cyberspace. As will be seen, however, they often respond more to the demands of corporate power than to those of their citizens, and thus become complicit with corporate influence in the political economy of the city and cyberspace. Capital, moreover, not only shapes the material form and nature of the city and cyberspace, but also links them to one another. Contemporary concentrations and movements of economic and political power can be traced across the urban landscape by charting the electronic flow of information. William Gibson's *Neuromancer*, one of the great contributors to our visions of cyberspace as cybercity, proposes a type of "mapping by megabyte" that makes these flows legible: "Program a map to display frequency of data exchange, every thousand megabytes a single pixel on a very large screen. Manhattan and Atlanta burn solid white. . . . At a hundred million megabytes per second, you begin to make out certain blocks in midtown Manhattan" (43).[2] Digital networks tend, unsurprisingly, to retrace and strengthen already existing connections among urban power centers.

Functioning as the "command and control" hub for global capital, global cities like New York, London, and Tokyo are the principal sites of the technology-intensive communications, information-processing, and financial services required for these operations.[3] The dense networks of talent and technologies created within such cities, in turn, drive technological innovation. Computer technologies (and cyberspace) are thus both determining and increasingly determined by the economic structure of the city.[4]

This tech-heavy service economy is, reciprocally, reshaping the built space of the city through the creation of the telecommunications infrastructure required by these industries and by the consumer demand concentrated there. This developing infrastructure includes wireless access to the Internet in public spaces, a utility that affects our experience of material urban spaces and our sense of self as we shift between city space and cyberspace, or occupy them simultaneously, when, for example, sitting in a park or café and surfing the Web. The changes brought about by the tech-heavy urban service economy go far beyond the telecommunications infrastructure, however. With this economy comes a rising demand for upscale housing and amenities (restaurants, boutiques, and so forth) for the legions of white-collar workers employed in these service industries, a demand that frequently results in the gentrification of neighborhoods, particularly near city centers, and the displacement and relocation of blue-collar workers and the poor to the expanding periphery of the city.

Cyberspace plays a key role in determining the character of the postmodern city well beyond its role in the city's economic structure, however. As part of a vast and expanding network of surveillance technologies, cyberspace is helping to create the fortress city and urban scanscape. Yet, as an augmentation of the public sphere, cyberspace is also simultaneously helping to create the city as polis (a formation that, it should be noted, is also required for capital to function most effectively). Both of these spatial logics (the fortress and the polis) are ancient, but the particular forms they take in the contemporary city and, obviously, in cyberspace are specific to our time.

In this chapter I shall look more closely at these forms and, more broadly, at the ways in which conceptions of the modern and postmodern city are shaping cyberspace design, and how, reciprocally, cyberspace is shaping the material and imaginary spaces of the postmodern city and our experiences of them. I would like to stress that I will be dealing not only with empirical description (how the physical and economic spaces of the city and cyberspace are developing), but also with epistemological description (how the postmodern city and cyberspace are transforming our ways of knowing and perceiving the world and ourselves as subjects in it).

The chapter will proceed as follows. Section 1 discusses the fortress part of the control logics of the city. Section 2 moves, via Neal Stephenson's *Snow Crash*, to cyberspace and then to the material, corporate world of cyber industries. Section 3 addresses "the past, present, and future of the

Internet," as a polis and a control economy. Section 4 extends this discussion to a broader analysis of the "capital of the information age." Section 5 is devoted to the scanscape. Section 6 leaves the city and cyberspace economies of control and moves to the polis.

1. FORTRESS CITIES AND STREETS

Among the most important (and most discussed) urban trends of the late twentieth and early twenty-first centuries has been the emergence of the postmodern "fortress city." It is characterized by, in the words of Michael Dear and Steven Flusty, "the omnipresent application of high-tech policing methods to the high-rent security of gated residential developments [and] panopticon malls" and the conversion of public space into "interdictory space" characterized by, for example, "jittery space ostentatiously saturated with surveillance devices" (57). "The city of the future" predicted by the 1969 report of the National Commission on the Causes and Prevention of Violence was the fortress city: a city "in which the affluent would escape to gated communities and more distant suburbs. The suburbs would be connected by 'sanitized corridors' to high rise office buildings protected by high technology in central business districts that would become deserted at night. The corridors would run over or bypass 'ghetto slum' neighborhoods—places of 'terror and widespread crime'" (Milton S. Eisenhower Foundation).

A follow-up study conducted by the Milton S. Eisenhower Foundation in 1999 found that many of the 1969 "Commission's predictions were chillingly accurate," including the proliferation of "fortified" high-rises and walled communities with private security guards, "the American withdrawal from shared space," the intensifying isolation of the inner-city poor, the dramatic rise in urban crime since the late 1960s (even with the improvements in the late 1990s—which continued into the early 2000s), and the unhappy fact "that a city based on the principle of flight to safety would only deepen social divisions." The Foundation report also took note of the subsequent developments that the Commission had not foreseen, including "that the spiral of decay would spill over from the central cities into the suburbs." The study, thus, corroborated Edward Soja's assessment of the situation: "The new topography of race, class, gender, age, income and ethnicity has produced an incendiary urban geography in Los Angeles, a landscape filled with violent edges, colliding turfs, unstable boundaries, peculiarly juxtaposed lifespaces, and enclaves of outrageous wealth and despair" ("Postmodern Urbanization" 134).[5]

Looking back over the past three or four decades, it is not difficult to trace the underlying causes of the development of the fortress cities and suburbs and their attendant pathologies. The postindustrial restructuring of the economy has fundamentally altered or eroded the economic base of many older urban centers in the U.S. and spurred the exurban developments variously referred to as "exopolis," "edge city," "metroplex," "technoburb," or "technopolis." As their economic base eroded, "rust belt" cities caught on the wrong side of this economic shift saw their centers deteriorate as citizens with the economic means (the middle and upper classes) moved farther and farther out into the "burbs" (the deterioration of many of these cities has now spread outward to encompass the "first-ring" suburbs as well), and much of the remaining population found itself with few employment options beyond low-wage service jobs. To some extent, this restructuring might be argued to have completed a trend toward suburbanization that had been underway for several decades.[6] The older cities spared this fate (New York is the best example) have by and large been those that function as command-and-control and service centers for global corporations, a formation Chapter 5 deals with in more detail.

In conjunction with dramatic shifts in federal tax policies beginning with the "supply-side economics" of the Reagan era, this economic restructuring in America has brought about a staggering rise in inequality in wealth, income, and wages over the past three decades. In 2004, the wealthiest 1% of the American population was in possession of 34.3% of the nation's wealth (total net worth) and the top 10% held 71.2%, while the bottom 90% accounted for 28.7%, a degree of disparity unseen since just prior to the Great Depression.[7] As income has risen for the upper class and stagnated or fallen for the middle and lower classes over the past 30 years, income inequality has also reached a level unmatched since the late 1920s: In 2005, the top 1% of Americans received 21.8% of the nation's income and the top 10% received 48.5%, leaving the bottom 90% to divide the remaining 51.5%.[8] This immense economic divide has spawned a culture of "privatization" and what is sometimes referred to as "civic secession"—a withdrawal from the public sphere and its concerns and responsibilities on the part of the wealthy and, increasingly, the middle class. Thus, both cultural and economic forces are driving the progressive fortressification of American cities and suburbs.

Among the most important manifestations of this fortressification is the privatization of public spaces that is apparent in the privatized agoras of shopping malls (including those in city centers), and the building of systems of tunnels and skyways that make it possible for some pedestrians to bypass sidewalks and streets in such cities as Charlotte, Dallas, Detroit, Minneapolis, Philadelphia, and New York. These "surrogate streets" are components or continuations of the fortress city, and, as Trevor Boddy points out, "they accelerate a stratification of race and class, and paradoxically degrade the very conditions they supposedly remedy—the amenity, safety, and environmental conditions of the public realm" (124).[9] The less we see of one another, the more likely we are to fear one another; and as Jane Jacobs argued long ago, taking increasing numbers of people off the streets makes them more—not less—dangerous.

A particularly hostile form of privatization is what Mike Davis describes in *City of Quartz* as the "hardening" of public spaces (mostly against the poor and homeless), a "tendency to merge urban design, architecture, and the police apparatus into a single, comprehensive security effort" (324).[10] This merging takes myriad forms, from architectural designs that evoke upended or underground bunkers, medieval citadels, and military forts to the presence of intimidating signage, surveillance cameras, and security guards to the unfriendly design of spiked ledges, barrel-shaped benches, and vast, empty, windswept plazas.[11] The subtitle of *City of Quartz* is "Excavating the Future in Los Angeles," and, indeed, in the nearly two decades since it was published, the militarization of urban space Davis surveyed in Los Angeles has spread across America. Building on his work, Peter Marcuse and Steven Flusty have developed elaborate taxonomies of walls and of "interdictory spaces"—design elements that seek to exclude or inhibit through the use of physical barriers and hostile "cognitive signals."[12] Such spatial forms and elements are material manifestations (and sometimes deliberate obfuscations) of economic and social divisions in the polity—divisions that they simultaneously reflect and help to perpetuate.

Civic secession takes the form of the withdrawal of the upper and middle classes into gated enclaves and, on a larger scale, the secession of affluent "break-away" communities from mixed-income cities and counties.[13] In 2005, Evan McKenzie, the author of *Privatopia*, estimated that gated communities accounted for approximately 18% of America's total housing but 60% of all new housing.[14] Gated communities generally include private streets and recreational spaces such as parks, playgrounds, tennis courts and pools that residents pay to maintain and police (via private security services). These communities are also managed by paid staff and governed by the "quasi-constitutions" known as CC&Rs (conditions, covenants, and restrictions), the primary aim of which is the protection of property values.

As more and more people have moved into gated communities and as their sense of outrage over being "taxed twice" has grown, they have been increasingly wielding their well-financed political power to lobby state legislators to make homeowner dues tax deductible and to compel municipalities to rebate property taxes paid by gated-community residents. This sense of no longer being a part of the polity also underlies a host of other political movements and initiatives like California's infamous "Proposition 13" (officially, "The People's Initiative to Limit Property Taxation") that decimate municipal tax bases and lead to the slashing of public education and health and other services; campaigns against affirmative action and bilingual education; and prohibitions by planning and zoning commissions against the creation of low-income housing.[15] Meanwhile, the inhabitants of mixed- and low-income neighborhoods have also increasingly turned to (or, in some cases, had forced upon them) strategies of enclosure, fragmentation, and self-segregation. At the urging of the local police and based on urban planning concepts developed by Oscar Newman, author of *Defensible Space: Crime Prevention through Urban Design*, middle-class communities such as the Five Oaks neighborhood of Dayton, Ohio have divided their neighborhoods into multiple "mini-neighborhoods" and installed "speed bumps and barriers, closed streets and alleys and put up brick and metal gates tastefully decorated with plaques bearing the neighborhood logo" (Cose 57). Seeking a low-cost way to reduce crime, neighborhoods across the country have followed Five Oaks' example.[16] Others have had the model imposed on them: by the mid-1990s, the U.S. Department of Housing and Urban Renewal was adopting (virtually by fiat) Newman's strategies throughout all of its new low-income housing projects. In 1996, HUD even published a do-it-yourself guide to self-segregation by Newman entitled *Creating Defensible Space*.

The cover of *Creating Defensible Space* (Figure 3.1) features a remarkable photograph of three young African-American boys, perhaps seven or eight years old, playing catch on a street that is divided by a locked iron gate set between brick pillars. The gate looms behind the children, and beyond the gate is a tree-lined street of well-kept, modest houses. It is unclear whether the children are walled in or out: my first impression was the latter, since the sidewalks on the other side appear to stop at the gate and the pavement on which the boys are playing is littered and in bad repair. Upon reflection, however, since the book touts the benefits of "defensible spaces," it seems more likely that we are intended to see the boys as safely enclosed, protected from traffic and whatever other dangers might be lurking in that leafy neighborhood beyond the gates.

The point here, which seems to completely escape Newman and his adherents, is that the meaning and effect of these gates goes far beyond and is far more complex than the "safety behind walls" that is generally assumed by those who advocate and build them. It is not just a matter of which side one finds oneself on: the residents of the ultra-exclusive "sanctuary" might feel safely enclosed, while residents of HUD's Newmanesque developments might well feel more imprisoned than protected. Even in Five Oaks, where many residents *chose* to erect the walls around them, other residents of the community see them "as barricades designed to encourage segregation. 'This is just like South Africa, caging people in like this,' said Curtis Print, a black resident who works in a manufacturing plant'" (qtd. in Owens).

The pernicious effects of the fortressification of the city and suburbs are not limited, however, to the alienation of America's less affluent citizens and the collapse of tax bases and funding for public services (including schools and hospitals) and infrastructure. For, as numerous studies have shown (and common knowledge of human psychology might suggest), those who shut themselves off from all contact with others who are different from them are likely to forget or discount those others, along with their perspectives and interests, or, if they think of them at all, are much more likely to view them as both alien and threatening. It is also true that the

Figure 3.1 Creating Defensible Space (cover). (Originally published by the U.S. Department of Housing and Urban Development, Office of Policy Development and Research. Reproduced here with the department's permission.)

involuntarily ghettoized are also likely to view more privileged others (or their agents, such as private security guards) as more alien and threatening. The walls themselves, therefore, establish and perpetuate the threat (or at least the sense of threat) on both sides of the divide.

These walls must also be seen in the context of the scanscape. Samuel Nunn relates the origins of modern surveillance to "seeking an enemy, an 'other.'" He writes:

> Surveillance technologies highlight differences, because it is through some form of difference that persons or groups stand out, are identified, and selected by watchers via surveillance. Considering the video gaze, if all is the same or if all activity is routine, the camera cannot focus on a subject of difference—there is nothing to create contrast, no figure against ground. It is difference that surveillance systems seek. The identification and exclusion of difference, then, becomes the objective of surveilled space. Find what does not fit, then take action against it (earmark it, arrest it, eject it, exclude it, refuse it, repel it). (273)

All of these formations of surveillance and enclosure, then, constitute strategies and tactics of a war against difference. They seek not only to privatize formerly public spaces, but also to "purify" them by expelling those who are "different" in some way. Yet such purifications can only serve to increase our fear of "the other." When we lose our daily contact with one another—when we no longer pass one another on the street, see each other strolling through the park and our children playing together on the playground, sit next to one another on the train or bus, and file into the voting booth one after another—we also lose our ease with the unfamiliar and our tolerance for it. To have a vital public culture, we must have some degree of familiarity with the unfamiliar.

2. STREET: TOLL ROADS AND CYBERSPACE

While "the street" and even more so its fraternal twin "the road" have long carried connotations of freedom and opportunity, throughout history both have equally been the markers—and their designators' means—of conquest and control. States have historically extended their power over populations in part through the creation and regulation of what Paul Virilio terms "transportation vectors," along which travel not just individuals and commercial goods but also governmental services (including the tax collector) and the forces of state security.[17] The Persian Royal Road, built in the fifth century BCE and stretching from Sardis in the west across Asia Minor and Persia to Susa in the east and Persepolis in the south (over 1,500 miles), made possible the movement of troops, trade, and messages that enabled Darius to govern one of greatest kingdoms of the ancient world. So, too, centuries later, the Romans' vast system of roads (over 53,000 miles) was essential to the governance of the Empire. In his analysis of the disciplinary and symbolic functions of the Roman road, Henri Lefebvre observes that it "links the *urbs* to the countryside over which [Rome] exercises dominion. The road allows the city, as people and as Senate, to assert its political centrality at the core of the *orbis terrarum*. The gate, through which the imperial way proceeds from *urbs* to *orbis*, marks the sacrosanct enceinte off from its subject territories" (*Production* 245). The road's spatial logics of freedom, commerce, and control continue through the twentieth century: begun in 1956, the more than 46,000-mile-long American interstate highway system (officially, the Dwight D. Eisenhower National System of Interstate and Defense Highways) was designed not only for automobile and truck traffic, but also to facilitate the rapid deployment of troops and equipment for military and civil defense operations. The orthogonally intersecting streets of the urban grid similarly serve not just the purposes of navigation and the parceling of property, but also help to regulate the circulation of populations, goods, and, not incidentally, troops and military matériel. The broad boulevards of Baron von Haussmann's reconstructed mid-nineteenth-century Paris were not only meant to lend a grandeur suitable to the capital of the Second Empire; they were also intended to allow for the swift deployment of troops in the event of civil unrest and to thwart the barricading of or escape through the narrow streets and alleys they erased.

In mid-twentieth-century American culture, from Stanley Kramer's *The Wild One* and Jack Kerouac's *On the Road* through the Merry Pranksters and the Beach Boys' "I Get Around," the road still maintained its mythic aura of freedom, mobility, and self-determination (and for many, it still does). "Autotopia" is an essential part of L.A.'s "ecologies," according to Reyner Banham, who argues that, "[the] freeways system in its totality is now a single comprehensible place, a coherent state of mind, a complete way of life" (213). Yet one can also discern an undercurrent of disillusionment in popular culture depictions of this "way of life," from Burt Bacharach's "Do You Know the Way to San Jose?" to Thomas Pynchon's *The Crying of Lot 49*, in which the freeway's "speed, freedom, wind in your hair, unreeling landscape"—are soon revealed to be only "illusions," the road a kind of "fix": "What the road really was, she [Oedipa] fancied, was this hypodermic needle, inserted somewhere ahead into the vein of a freeway, a vein nourishing the mainliner L.A., keeping it happy, coherent, protected from pain, or whatever passes, with a city, for pain" (14). The freeway is also a "fix" in the sense of a set-up, an illusion of freedom overlaying the machine of domination. (In *The Crying of Lot 49*, the outsider status of all those who use the WASTE mail system is emphasized by the location of its clandestine drop boxes *under* the freeway, beneath the surface of legitimate circulation.)

Nearly twenty-five years later, in *Snow Crash*'s 1990 just-a-moment-from-now rendition of the future, commerce has overtaken citizenship on the road, and, in a reversion to the medieval practice of the "toll," all the freeways have been privatized and are being maintained and built by companies with names like Fairlanes, Inc. and Cruiseways, Inc. In this regard, too, we are fast approaching Stephenson's future, as our previously public, toll-free American highways are increasingly privatized and metered for tolls. In a related trend, London, Singapore, Hong Kong, and other cities around the world have begun imposing "congestion pricing" charges for driving into city centers on weekdays. In London, ubiquitous surveillance cameras photograph and record license plate numbers of all vehicles entering the central-city congestion zone, matching the identity of their drivers with payment records and imposing fines on those who have not paid. While not a privatization of public space like the pay-as-you-go highways, this development has the effect of creating a two-tier class system of access to and movement within the city. The incidental surveillance and tracking of individuals' movements through the city accompanying this system have their own troubling implications, as they extend the urban scanscape.

Now, in the beginning of the twenty-first century, we can see these competing logics of freedom, commerce, and control being replicated in the ever-expanding territory of cyberspace—the "Information Superhighway," as American politicians are fond of calling it. The overlap here is both conceptual and material, geographical: as Goldsmith and Wu point out, "they lay the fiber-optic cables that make up the Internet's most powerful interconnections along the same routes that link cities by train and phone" (56). In contrast to *Neuromancer*'s largely dystopian depiction of cyberspace, the early days of the Internet and World Wide Web were marked by a utopian rhetoric of freedom. Internet pioneers were among the most articulate, from WELL-founder Stewart Brand's much-quoted assertion that "Information wants to be free" to MIT's Media Lab director Nicholas Negroponte's claim that "the Internet cannot be regulated" (qtd. in Andrew Higgins and Azeem Azhar) to Michael Benedikt's oracular declaration that "through its [the Internet's] myriad, unblinking video eyes, distant places and faces, real or unreal, actual or long gone, can be summoned to presence. From vast databases that constitute the culture's deposited wealth, every document is available, every recording is playable, and every picture is viewable" (2).[18] The Internet, it was suggested, would cause enormous power shifts, moving power away from national governments and corporate hegemons and dispersing it more evenly among individuals. It would also shift power geographically, away from First World urban areas and toward new, worldwide virtual communities. Theorists such as William J. Mitchell even predicted that the new information and communications technologies would, in many ways, make the city obsolete.[19]

By the early 1990s, the mainstream media, too, were discussing the Internet in decidedly utopian terms. In a 1994 *Nation* article, "Free Speech on the Internet," Jon Wiener surveyed the most recent press coverage of the development of the Internet:

> It's "the most universal and indispensable network on the planet," *The New York Times Magazine* recently proclaimed, because, at a time

when the "giant information empires own everything else," the Internet is "anarchic, but also democratic." *Harper's Magazine* joined the utopian talk: The Internet marks "not the beginning of authority, but its end." . . . *U.S. News & World Report* declared in January that, on the Internet, "everyone has a virtually unlimited right to express and seek information on any subject." (825)

Corporate white papers, mission statements, and advertising, particularly by information and communication technology companies, have also been among the leading disseminators of utopian visions of the Internet and the future it will create for us. IBM's corporate statement on "The Future of Computing" is typical: "IBM's view of a 'network centric' future is driven by the desire of people and enterprises to connect to other people and enterprises around the world and leverage information using powerful new technologies that transcend distance and time, lower boundaries between markets, cultures and individuals and actually deliver solutions that fulfill the promise of universal connectivity."

Several key themes and images recur in these corporate texts: a world without borders, the future is now (ready or not), the compression of time and space, infinite opportunity, unlimited communication, universal harmony among men.[20] "Welcome," a 2007 Cisco ad begins, "Welcome to a brand new day. Welcome to a place where books rewrite themselves . . . Where maps are rewritten. And anyone can be famous. Where we're more powerful together than we could ever be apart. Welcome to the human network. Cisco" (www.cisco.com). Information and communication technologies, such ads suggest, will make national borders irrelevant and lead us to a cosmopolitan, post-national future: "You know who makes the best poppedum in Kensington. You know where to find a puppet show in Rome, every afternoon except Wednesday. You know rugby, cricket, football, bocci, and baseball, and now you know how to get clear, fast connections virtually anywhere there is a phone. . . . everywhere you want to call. MCI World. For citizens of the world." The Information Revolution, a 1998 Oracle ad predicts, will liberate us from history, from violence, ideology, and conflicts among nations: "A revolution is in our destiny. This revolution however will not be fought with guns or soldiers. It will not be a war of words or of countries. For this revolution will be about knowledge and access. About progress and opportunity. . . . We make the software that manages information. That will enable anyone, anywhere, to sit at the seat of knowledge. Oracle. Enabling the information age." Nor, apparently, will we be subject to economic constraints. Thus, a 2001 NASDAQ ad asserts, "One day everyone in the world will be able to invest in any company in the world. Trading across international borders with an ease and speed and economy that can only be imagined today. There is a place where this technology is now taking shape, laying the groundwork that will open the wonders of the Internet to investors all over the world. NASDAQ, Stock

Market for the digital world" (Goldman 1998–2003). Yet, beneath these technotopian dreams lie very real structures of governments and laws and of transnational corporations and global markets.

3. THE PAST, PRESENT, AND FUTURE OF CYBERSPACE: FROM CYBERPOLIS TO CONTROL SPACE

The development of the Internet and World Wide Web has been brought about by an array of powerful interests, with key roles being played by the U.S. government (and, subsequently, other governments) and major corporations, so that the reality of cyberspace has turned out to be quite different from the virtual worldwide polis anticipated by many early visionaries and commentators. The Internet, likely the most important communication vector of the twenty-first century, might be seen to be analogous to the transportation vectors—from roads and sea routes to railroads and flight airspace—that have always been so essential to governmental rule and commercial development. Like the roads of the ancient Roman Empire, the "Information Superhighway" of the Internet was originally created to ensure national security and serve national interests. In the past decade, however, commercial interests have come to play an increasingly important role in its development and functioning. As with the proliferating pay-as-you-go highways and "congestion zones" of our cities, access to cyberspace is, for many, contingent upon one's ability to pay, which significantly complicates and often inhibits the polis-potential of the Internet. Even more disturbing, the carceral logics of our emerging postmodern urban scanscapes and fortress cities, or indeed of contemporary countries and the overall global, and globalized, geopolitical landscape, have migrated to cyberspace. Overtly and covertly surveilled by governments and corporations around the world, the Internet has become our newest scanscape. Across Asia, the Middle East, and elsewhere (for example, in the territories of the former Soviet Union), repressive regimes are erecting nearly impenetrable firewalls to create nationwide cyberfortresses. The ideal of the cyberpolis, while still championed by many, is receding into the distance as a realizable possibility. In order to understand the present form and competing logics of the Internet and why some visions of it are prevailing over others, it is necessary to briefly retrace its origins and development over the past forty or so years.

The U.S. government funded virtually every stage of the Internet's early development, and even as the Internet has become a global communication network vital to the cultural, educational, economic, commercial, and political functioning of over a billion individuals and dozens of nations, it has retained either direct or proxy control over several of its vital functions.[21] Principal among these is "root authority"—control over the Internet's domain naming and numbering (IP addresses that identify computers on the Internet) system, and the DNS root-server administration.[22] "The root authority," Goldsmith and Wu observe, "is very close to a truly global authority for the Internet—the ultimate intermediary on which everyone depends" (168). With this control comes the capacity (however rarely deployed) to withhold, divert, or withdraw Internet domain names and numbers. Thus, if the U.S. government chose, "individuals, institutions, or even whole countries could lose domain names, IP addresses, or even Internet membership" (Goldsmith and Wu 32).

Beyond control of "the root," there are an array of other ways in which the U.S. and other governments have sought—and succeeded in exerting—control not only over the technological architecture but also over the use and content of the Internet, both within and far beyond their national borders. As Goldsmith and Wu note, recent decades have seen the emergence of "a new kind of Internet—a bordered network where territorial law, government power, and international relations matter as much as technological invention" (vii). The geographical boundaries, the ideological fault lines, and the economic divides of the world are being reinscribed in cyberspace. In some ways, the fragmenting or "bordering" of the Internet is, they explain, a reflection of "bottom-up pressures from individuals in different places who demand an Internet that corresponds to local preferences, and from the web-page operators and other content providers who shape the Internet experience to satisfy these demands" (Goldsmith and Wu viii).

Chief among these "local preferences" is, doubtless, language. As of 2007, the top languages on the Internet were English (with 329 million users), Chinese (Mandarin and Cantonese—159 million), Spanish (89 million), Japanese (86 million), and German (59 million).[23] The English-language dominance of the Internet has been rapidly diminishing as more and more speakers of other languages come online. As a world language, English is second (behind Chinese), with an estimated 1.14 billion speakers, including those who speak it as a second language. Many of the Spanish-, Japanese-, and German-speaking users of the Internet, therefore, also have linguistic access to its English-language sites, particularly since the majority of them live in countries that have relatively few governmental restrictions on Internet usage. This is also true of many of the speakers of other major languages, such as Bengali, Hindi, and Russian, that will likely be increasingly well represented on the Internet in the future.

Yet, as in the material world, this linguistic Babel has resulted in a fragmentation and division of the Internet into what are effectively multiple, language-specific Internets. In this context, the position of Chinese as the second-most-spoken language on the Internet is of particular importance. Worldwide, Chinese is the language spoken by the largest number of people. By early 2007, only 11.8% of the world's estimated 1.3 billion Chinese speakers had Internet access, but the number of Chinese-speaking users of the Internet was growing at roughly three times the rate of English-speaking users.[24] China's share of and influence over the Internet can, therefore, be expected to continue to increase even more dramatically in the future. Since China currently has the world's most highly developed system of Internet censorship, its rising importance on the Internet has disturbing implications for the future of cyberspace and the ideal of the cyberpolis. The United States, on the other hand, has the distinction of having the world's most highly developed system of Internet surveillance. For better or worse, the United States and China are likely to remain the primary shapers of the Internet in the foreseeable future, with effects that extend, like the Internet itself, far beyond their territorial boundaries.

No country has done more than China to darken visions of the Internet as a force for openness and democracy. The government of the People's Republic of China has, as Reporters Without Borders observes, demonstrated that "the Internet can indeed become a propaganda media. On its own, it will not suffice to support the emergence of democracy in any significant way. And it can be totally controlled by a government that equips itself to do so" ("China"). China has successfully erected a vast, nearly impenetrable firewall around the entire mainland Chinese Internet, ensuring that all Internet communications and content are controlled and censored, that all public-access terminals are equipped with surveillance systems, and that cyberdissidents are swiftly tracked down and imprisoned. It has done so, moreover, with the assistance of major U.S. corporations, including Cisco, Microsoft, Yahoo and Google, thus creating a kind of complicity between capitalism and communism, *a certain form* of communism (to the degree the denomination is applicable) that was unimaginable during the cold war. Yahoo, Google, and Microsoft all have, as a condition of doing business in China, signed a document entitled the "Public Pledge on Self-Discipline for the Chinese Internet Industry," in which they agreed to fulfill the following disciplinary obligations with respect to the Internet services they provide:

1. Refraining from producing, posting or disseminating pernicious information that may jeopardize state security and disrupt social stability, contravene laws and regulations and spread superstition and obscenity. Monitor the information publicized by users on websites according to law and remove the harmful information promptly;
2. Refraining from establishing links to the websites that contain harmful information so as to ensure that the content of the network information is lawful and healthy. (Internet Society of China)

By doing so, these corporations effectively transform themselves into, in the words of Reporters Without Borders, a "Chinese police auxiliary" ("Living Dangerously").[25] Such "pernicious information" apparently includes anything relating to such interdicted terms as "freedom," "democracy," "multi-party elections," "public opinion," or "human rights." In this context at least (but this is far from the only context in which this argument applies), the disconnect between the rhetoric seen in corporate advertisements and "mission statements" and the actions of those corporations is massive. Consider, for example, this statement from the Google corporate website's "Company Overview": "Google's mission is to organize the world's information and make it *universally* accessible and useful" (emphasis added). Several of the "truths" propounded in the section entitled "Our Philosophy—Ten things Google has found to be true" are also noteworthy. *"Democracy on the Web works."* The "democracy" they refer to here, as their explanation makes clear, pertains to their PageRank system, which allows users to "vote" on the usefulness of websites. Not the *other* kind of democracy. Another "truth" is *"You can make money without doing evil."* Significantly, the subsequent explanation of this principle begins, "Google is a business" and goes on to explain that advertising on Google search pages is clearly identified and limited only to ads relevant to the particular search. To do otherwise, it seems to suggest, would be "evil." Censoring the Internet at the behest of the Chinese government and helping them track down political dissidents, apparently, is not.

The "cooperation" of Google and other corporations with the Chinese government's censorship of the Internet justifies MacKinnon and Palfrey's assessment that "The Great Firewall of China isn't the state's only weapon; there is also Censorship Inc." China's massive censorship and surveillance system does not, however, only affect its 1.3 billion citizens. As MacKinnon and Palfrey point out, "China's efforts to keep sensitive information from reaching its citizens is the envy of every authoritarian regime in the world." China's system of Internet control has served as a model for many of the world's most repressive governments. China is, however, more than just inspiration for such repressive regimes. "Censorship," MacKinnon and Palfrey report, "has become a popular Chinese export. Techniques and software for Internet control, developed in China, are now being applied in countries like Vietnam and Iran." Nor is Internet censorship limited to just these countries: some degree of Internet surveillance and censorship (usually justified on the grounds of national security, crime prevention or prosecution, or enforcement of copyright and intellectual property laws) also occurs in most of the world's major democracies.

This surveillance and censorship generally make use of both content analysis and blocking technologies. Content-analysis software screens content requests (e.g., Internet searches) and the actual content of websites, blogs, discussion forums, and e-mail by searching for forbidden keywords, phrases, and even images. For example, in the U.S., a Google Images search for "Tiananmen" yields multiple versions of the famous photograph of the lone man confronting the line of tanks during the Tiananmen Square protests; the same search on Google Images China yields an array of touristic shots of the Square (Sullivan). Like Internet search software, this content-analysis software is increasingly acquiring sophisticated and effective semantic capabilities that go far beyond simple word recognition.[26] At present, however, the Chinese State Security Protection Bureau supplements these capabilities by employing legions of human censors who compile lists of forbidden websites, blogs, and proxy servers and anonymizers (both of which can be used to circumvent blocking technologies) that are then programmed into the various screening and blocking mechanisms.

Such content screening and concomitant content blocking can take place on multiple levels. Individual computers can be equipped with customizable filtering software, which, for example, many repressive governments install on Internet café, library, and other public-access computers (which provide virtually the only access available in many parts of the world). The use of these control devices is, of course, not restricted to China's and other repressive governments, or democratic governments, which can also become repressive with the help of such devices. Private citizens and corporations increasingly use them as well, bringing various forms of control into the polis of the Web. Organizations with local area networks, such as corporations that might wish to curtail their employees' access to parts of the Internet (or ability to surf the Web on company time), can arrange for the filtering to occur at the level of the network or an intermediary "proxy" server. Internet service providers and search companies, too, can provide such filters.

The U.S. government, citing efforts to combat terrorism and on-line crime, has engaged in Internet surveillance on multiple levels. In late 2005, news reports revealed that the U.S. National Security Agency, under the authority of a presidential executive order, had been engaging in extensive warrantless domestic Internet data mining and e-mail surveillance operations since 2002. This surveillance program involved "tapping directly into some of the American telecommunications system's main arteries" (Lichtblau and Risen). Under the USA Patriot Act, the U.S. Justice Department has demanded records of library patrons' Internet use, and, reportedly "as part of its effort to uphold an online pornography law, the Justice Department had asked a federal judge to compel Google to turn over records on millions of its users' search queries" (Hafner). Yahoo, MSN, and America Online had, apparently, already turned over records of their customers' Internet searches (Hafner).

Governments around the world attempting to exert control over the Internet and use it as an instrument of social control over their citizens have, as we have seen, found willing partners among many American corporations. Such controls are not limited to the territorial boundaries of particular nations. Governments wishing to influence and control the behavior of individuals, organizations, or corporations beyond their shores have frequently found ways to do so. Generally, this is done via local intermediaries—everyone from the company that sells you a computer and software to the phone or cable company through which you connect to the Internet to Internet service providers like AOL and Compuserve to search engines like Google and Yahoo to credit card companies, banks, and services like Paypal that enable one to carry out on-line financial transactions to Internet businesses like amazon.com. At any point in this long chain, governments have leverage to influence these corporations and, through them, to control what happens on the Internet.

Thus, for example, governments don't necessarily need to target individual users (though they often do) to control the flow of information on the Internet when ISPs and search engines are willing to do it for them in order to avoid either local prosecution or loss of access to the market. On the other hand, when governments do want to pursue individuals within their territorial boundaries, they can also generally count on the assistance of corporations eager to obtain or maintain business relations with them. Corporate complicity in such cases is, unsurprisingly, bound up with commercial interests, which are among the primary shapers of the Internet and cyberspace. New conceptual, ideological, rhetorical, and material tensions arise and some old ones take new shapes in this new set of contexts. These tensions are part of the developing conflict or set of conflicts between the polis of democracy or, within capitalism itself, the polis of the free market and the control/police forces or new cyber-age mechanisms through which they operate, or in Foucault's idiom, new "technologies of power," in the age of the Internet or, more broadly, the (postmodern) Information Age.

4. THE CAPITAL OF THE INFORMATION AGE

Early in *Snow Crash*, Hiro provides an incisive take on the postindustrial, globalized American economy:

> When it gets down to it—talking trade balances here—once we've brain-drained all our technology into other countries, once things have evened out, they're making cars in Bolivia and microwave ovens in Tadzhikistan and selling them here—once our edge in natural resources has been made irrelevant by giant Hong Kong ships and dirigibles that can ship North Dakota all the way to New Zealand for a nickel—once the Invisible Hand has taken all these historical inequities and smeared them out into a broad global layer of what a Pakistani brickmaker would consider to be prosperity—y'know what? There's only four things we do better than anyone else
> music
> movies
> microcode
> high-speed pizza delivery. (2)

Hyperbole aside, Hiro has a point: America's position in the global economy is increasingly dependent upon its powerful information and communication technologies and the content (music, movies, and so forth) developed and distributed through them. These technologies have made possible and propelled the restructuring of the world's economies over the past three decades. They have been the engine of enormous economic opportunity and growth and, concurrently, no small amount of Schumpeterian "creative destruction." One cannot overestimate, however, to what degree this process was shaped by the logic and interests of advanced capitalism in the realm of cyberspace, which is emerging as the preeminent public sphere and arena of economic development of the twenty-first century.

The interests of global capital, like those of the state, are subject to the competing logics of control and the polis, which are, in turn, played out through corporate actions and influences in cyberspace and our global cities. Gibson's *Neuromancer* offers a meditation that reveals capital's complex dependency upon an (admittedly criminal in this case) version of the polis. (Both the city of control and the polis have their "dark" and "light" sides.) Much of the novel's action takes place in "Night City," an outlaw zone located adjacent to Chiba, Tokyo's industrial backyard. "Synonymous with implants, nerve-splicing, and microbionics," Chiba is the center for the cyborg technologies that dominate the markets, licit and illicit, of the Gibsonian future (6). It is also a magnet for the "techno-criminal subcultures" that thrive on the economic periphery, in the black markets of the borderland "with no official name" known as Night City, where 'biz' is "a constant subliminal hum" (6–7). Night City is Chiba's dark counterpart, essential night to Chiba's day. The most likely explanation for why it was tolerated by the authorities, *Neuromancer*'s protagonist Case muses, lay "in the notion that burgeoning technologies require outlaw zones, that Night City wasn't there for its inhabitants, but as a deliberately unsupervised playground for technology itself" (11).

Whether in the cities or cyberspaces, capital needs the free exchange, the unanticipated synergies, the anarchic inspirations and innovations of the polis. There may be no field in which this is more true than that of new information and communication technologies, where innovation frequently comes not from inside the massively funded corporate research group, but from below and outside—the geeks in the garage assembling the next new thing from off-the-shelf parts, the hacker devising the new code, the hipster developing new applications for existing technologies or demanding new features for the old. Above all, however, capital needs ever-expanding markets, and the polis is among the primary providers of them.

Yet capital is torn between this polis (the corporate advertising and mission rhetoric about freedom, openness, and opportunity is not all factitious) and its attraction to the forces and structures offered by various incarnations of the control space. Corporations' most immediate need for the control space concerns the protection of proprietary code and trade secrets, types of intellectual property (but hardly the only ones with which corporations concern themselves). It is also true, as Goldsmith and Wu argue, that to function on the Internet, businesses rely upon a range of government-provided "public goods," including "a reliable banking and credit environment, . . . criminal law, property rights, and contract enforcement," all of which are ultimately guaranteed through the coercive powers of the state (182, 140). As we have seen, however, the forces and structures of the control space are also profit centers for capital, and they usually benefit capital to the detriment of the citizenry and the polis.

Before moving on to the multiple ways in which the control space as corporate profit center extends beyond the profits gleaned from the creation and implementation of governmental censorship and surveillance systems, it will be useful to briefly examine what one might call the inherent Janus-faced nature of new technologies (or, "how good technologies go bad"). As the Internet developed and the volume of information on it grew apace, so did a demand for mechanisms capable of sorting and selecting content based on users' linguistic or other preferences (relating to interest, culture, geography, currency, and so on). Responding to this demand, companies began developing technologies that made it easy to filter information and to target or match it up with particular users. These technologies made the use of the Internet far easier and more effective, but they also made it possible to censor Internet content and to identify and surveil its users. In the near future of *Snow Crash*, the universal database belongs to the "CIC," the Central Intelligence Corporation, created through a merger of the CIA and the Library of Congress—a transformation that follows a familiar trajectory from public resource to surveillance zone to commercialization and privatization (with the surveillance intact and growing).

In "The Enclosure of Cyberspace," Ronald Bettig argues that the development and deployment of new communication technologies like cyberspace are determined by three primary "structural tendencies": concentration via the "mergers, acquisitions and joint ventures that are driving the process of media convergence," the expansion of intellectual property rights, and "the growing commercialization of information and cultural output" (139–40). Each of these three tendencies has a dramatic effect upon the infrastructure of the Internet and its content. Reminiscent of the early development of film, in which studios controlled not just the production but also the distribution through ownership of the movie theaters, the flow of capital in the Internet and communication industries is shaped by the consolidation of "content providers" and media distribution channels, which now include not just telecommunications companies but also software, ISP, and search engine companies. The series of mergers and acquisitions that brought the agglomeration of AOL-Time-Warner (CNN) is a good example of such consolidation, as is, more recently, Rupert Murdoch's Newscorp/Fox merger with DirecTV, the partnerships of ABC and Disney and of NBC Universal and Microsoft (MSNBC), or Google's acquisition of YouTube and DoubleClick.[27]

These media oligopolies, Bettig points out, "want to be the owners of both the highway and the information that travels over it" (141). There are many obvious dangers in this consolidation and centralization of media, including the erosion of press freedom and the homogenization of the infosphere—and others have written about them at length.[28] Monopolized in this way, the media cannot help but become the servant of the interests of a small, corporate elite—a combination of political/economic propaganda, bread-and-circuses diversionary entertainment, and commercial marketing, or, as Dear and Flusty suggest, a "consent factory" and "disinformation highway [DSH], a mass of info-tain-mercial media" that "disseminates holsteinizing ideologies and incentives, creates wants and dreams, and inflates the symbolic value of commodities" (64). This consolidation of the media takes us in many ways farther from the polis and its democratic foundations as more and more information (or, as they say, content) and distribution channels are controlled by fewer and fewer powerful individuals and corporations.

This corporate control over information has been tightened by recent changes in copyright law, spurred by the development of new media technologies that make it easier to reproduce and distribute music, film and video, visual art, and written texts. These technologies—from Xerox machines and audio-cassette recorders in the 1960s to today's CDs, DVDs, DVRs, MP3 players, and peer-to-peer file sharing software—often result in legal struggles over copyright ownership of media content at their inception. These struggles, however, have generally been resolved in favor of copyright holders, particularly large communication and entertainment corporations, which are continuously expanding their ownership of information and cultural productions.[29] With the backing of powerful corporations like Disney, this copyright ownership was dramatically prolonged, far beyond the lifetime of individual creators or their children, by the passage of the Copyright Term Extension Act of 1998 (a.k.a. "The Mickey Mouse Act"), which lengthened the period of copyright protection by twenty years.[30] In this era of visual, textual, and auditory collage, montage, pastiche, sampling, mash-ups, and mixes, the potential for copyright considerations (and charges) to stifle artistic creation and thwart the progress and circulation of knowledge is considerable. These extensions of copyright protections have been accompanied by parallel developments in patent laws, as the range of "patentable" information (parts of the genetic code, for instance), discoveries, and inventions continues to expand, with demonstrable negative consequences for scientific, medical, and technological research and development. In addition, cyberspace has provided yet another venue in which information, including information that might previously have been free and publicly available, can be bought and sold. Once the Internet moved beyond being the sole province of the U.S. armed forces, scientists, and academics, it quickly became clear that the new information class hierarchy was going to look very much like the old property class hierarchy.

The commercialization and privatization of cyberspace thus go hand in hand with this ever-increasing commodification and corporate control of information, and they raise similar issues: Who has access? For how much? These questions are, of course, interrelated. Michael Benedikt's memorable depiction in his visionary "Cyberspace: Some Proposals" of "unencumbered" movement ("walking," "crawling," "leaping," "'bare-back' riding or cyberBuick cruising," "floating and flying") through the cybercity was, as it were, brought down to earth by his observation (in a footnote) that "the dollar-cost of travel to users may be one of the economic engines that drives cyberspace as a money-making enterprise" (219). Access to the Internet remains highly dependent upon several variables, and income is, as Benedikt's "the dollar-cost of travel" might suggest, one of the most important.

Access to the Internet is, of course, not free—someone must pay for both the computer hardware and, once that investment has been made, the connection (on an ongoing basis). Thus, on our "Information Superhighway" there are different levels of service. For the wealthy, there are the electronic equivalents of congestion-free toll roads: high-speed DSL or Wi-Fi connections. For the poor, there are the go-slow equivalents of the L.A. freeways: slower dial-up connections, Internet cafés, or the limited free access provided by public libraries, schools, and employers. Even in the most affluent and technologically developed countries of the world, the urban social orders are composed, in Dear and Flusty's witty terms, of the inhabitants of "cyburbia (those hooked into the electronic world) and cyberia (those who are not)" (65).

As mentioned earlier, both Internet activity and hardware tend to be most concentrated in major First World cities, where there is both massive demand for information technologies and the capital resources necessary to create and maintain them. In many Third World countries that lack both capital and infrastructure, there may be little or no Internet access outside of the largest cities. Thus, ironically, geography also turns out to be one of the most important determinants of Internet access or the lack thereof. And, as my earlier discussion of Internet censorship demonstrates, geography and income affect not just one's connection to the Internet: they also help to determine what one can access there.

In 1991 Benedikt predicted a Midas-like array of potential "sources of income to the owners and maintainers of the system," and, thus, potential costs to users of the Internet. These sources included "outright purchase of real estate in cyberspace, the leasing of such, advertising time and space, connect-time charges to the system and to individual presences, innumerable hardware purchases and upgrades, cabling systems, satellites and so on, access software, endless enhancements to this, etc.; and all this in addition to the value of the information bought and sold as such within the system" (219n59). While the vast commercial potential of cyberspace was apparent to cyberspace theorists like Benedikt by the beginning of the 1990s, it was not until the mid-1990s that American corporations began to use the Internet as a large-scale site for the marketing and sale of consumer goods and services (amazon.com, which was launched in 1995, was one of the first). In cyberspace, "like any place in Reality," as Stephenson's Hiro coolly notes, "the Street is subject to development" (24). The Metaverse in *Snow Crash* more closely resembles the hypercapitalist terrain of Benedikt's vision than the somewhat more austere (though also capitalist) version of cyberspace in *Neuromancer*. When Hiro enters the Metaverse and surveys the Street, he "sees buildings and signs stretching off into the darkness, disappearing over the curve of the globe" (25). The marketing and sales opportunities in cyberspace, as Stephenson suggests in the novel, are immense: "Put a sign or a building on the Street and the hundred million richest, hippest, best-connected people on earth will see it every day of their lives" (26).

While, to return to our present Internet reality, annual Internet retail sales have been growing at roughly 25% a year, every year, since 2001, as of early 2006, the e-commerce share of total American retail sales was only slightly over 2.5%.[31] The Internet's commercial potential has really only begun to be exploited. In many ways, Internet commerce is obviously advantageous. Thousands of people have launched new businesses on the Web, including many who would not have had the capital or resources necessary to do so in bricks-and-mortar environments. Tens of millions have used the Web to purchase goods and services, some of which they would have had difficulty finding otherwise. And millions are participating in enterprises that could only exist on these scales on the Web, for example, massively multiplayer on-line role-playing games (MMORPGs) like World of Warfare, Lineage, RuneScape, Final Fantasy, and Everquest, or virtual worlds like Second Life (inspired by the Metaverse in *Snow Crash*) and The Sims Online. These cyberspaces are, by and large, profit-making enterprises for the corporations who develop and administer them, and also, increasingly, for many of their subscribers/participants who produce, sell, and buy virtual goods there, often for real-world money.[32] At the same time, they constitute important new forms of community.[33]

The appeal of cyberspace is similar to the appeal of the city and the suburban mall. Businesses generally conceive of these primarily as sites of consumption, and for individuals, too, this is among their most important attractions (with all of the complexities consumption involves). Like the postmodern city, the Metaverse in *Snow Crash* and many of our current cyberspaces, fictional and real, are signscapes, as any Web surfer annoyed by the relentless appearance of pop-up and banner ads is well aware. Yet they are also sites for fantasy and entertainment in both commodified and uncommodified forms.

The seemingly infinite possibility and pageantry of city streets have always been among the city's strongest attractions, attractions that suburban malls endeavor to challenge or even reproduce in various sanitized forms. The Mall of America (presently the largest mall in the U.S.) contains an indoor amusement park, an underground aquarium, a church and wedding chapel, an alternative high school, and a university campus. The West Edmonton Mall in Canada (the largest mall in North America) also contains an indoor amusement park, an indoor water park, an ice palace, a casino, and a hotel. Perhaps most remarkable, the West Edmonton Mall also includes three urban "theme areas": a tidied-up reproduction of New Orleans' famous French Quarter "Bourbon Street," a generically "foreign" "Europa Boulevard," and a commercial "Chinatown." What these malls seek to create is, in Margaret Crawford's words, "essentially a fantasy urbanism devoid of the city's negative aspects: weather, traffic, and poor people" (22). Cyberspace virtual worlds and MMORPGs offer both less and more interesting fantasy environments, if in somewhat attenuated forms, bounded as they are by the perimeter of the computer screen. The Metaverse's main commercial drag, the Street, and its smaller offshoots are spaces that resemble the fantasy-laden spaces of both city streets and suburban malls (also constructed in the familiar multiple hub and spoke pattern), filled with "buildings, parks, signs, as well as things that do not exist in Reality, such as vast hovering overhead light shows [and] special neighborhoods where the rules of three-dimensional space-time are ignored" (Stephenson 25).

People who visit or inhabit all of these spaces, however, are seeking more than just a change of pace (or place). Throughout history, people have been drawn to what Jonathan Raban argues is "one of the most dangerous and essential city freedoms"—the chance to remake one's identity, "to have a platonic conception of oneself, and to make it spring forth, fully clothed, out of one's head" (65). Malls would seem to offer relatively little of this freedom, beyond the fantasies offered by shopping. They are, in a sense, a domesticated "elsewhere" for people who have nowhere to go. Cyberspace, however, offers such opportunities on an unprecedented scale, as individuals, at least temporarily freed from such involuntary markers of identity as gender, race, class, and ethnicity, adopt on-line personas and select virtual stand-ins in the form of avatars. For many, these representations of self are pure fantasy or sometimes calculated deceptions, but for others, they are regarded as revelations of their "true" or truer selves, unencumbered by the material constraints of the body and the unchosen contingencies of "real" life.[34] Escape is, of course, also a common element in both spaces—from the young adults who flock from the country and suburbs to the cities, to the bored suburban housewives, teenagers, and retirees who take refuge in American malls, to the multitudes seeking distraction on the Internet, like Stephenson's Hiro, who vastly prefers the Metaverse to the U-Store-It unit where he lives.

People seek more than freedom in these places, however: they also seek community, the society of the agora. In ancient Greece, the agora was the commercial, political, and social heart of the city. It was a marketplace of goods and ideas, a place of public assembly and of intellectual and cultural exchange. In the Western tradition, the agora is arguably one of the most important origins of modern conceptions of public and civic space: the essence of the city or, on a smaller scale, the town or village square.

Although the agora included commercial space, it was not primarily or exclusively commercial space, unlike suburban malls and most of cyberspace, both of which might be seen to be increasingly displacing or replacing the city streets and town squares that have functioned as the agora for millennia. Malls turn the agora inside out, enclosing, privatizing, and "fortressifying" it—actions that have corollaries in the ongoing commercialization of cyberspace.[35]

While the mall fulfills many of the functions of the city—it is not only a marketplace but also a community center where entertainment events are held, groups like the American Legion sometimes meet, and people gather to socialize—these activities take place in a very different context. The city streets are public space; the mall is a private space, an extension of the "privatopia" logic of the suburbs themselves.[36] Mall owners have repeatedly, therefore, insisted that they are not legally obliged to allow the exercise of free speech within its confines. There have been numerous local, state, and federal court cases in which this claim has been contested by a wide variety of groups, from anti-Vietnam War protesters to picketing union members to defense of civil rights groups to campaign workers soliciting ballot petition signatures. Most of these free-speech arguments are based in the claim that malls function, for all intents and purposes, as public space—a claim that echoes Supreme Court Justice Thurgood Marshall's 1972 argument, in his dissent to Lloyd Corporation, Ltd. v. Tanner, "that since the mall had assumed the role of the traditional town square, as its sponsors continually boasted, it must also assume its public responsibilities" (Crawford 23, her summary). The outcomes of these legal cases have swung both ways, so that the issue seems far from decisively settled. The mall, it appears, will remain a contested space for the foreseeable future.

The semipublic/semiprivate spaces of Internet virtual communities and game worlds are, in terms of free speech issues, similarly contested terrains. Legally, they have been considered private clubs, with the right to censor or expel members who violate club rules against, for example, the use of obscene language. Nearly all of these communities and MMORPGs have nonnegotiable "terms-of-service" agreements that effectively require subscribers to sign away their First Amendment rights; these are businesses, not democracies. Yet, as the numbers of participants in these communities skyrocket, more and more conflicts relating to governance (e.g., subscriber input into the rules of the community) and free speech are arising. Some legal scholars reportedly believe that the courts may come to consider these cyberspaces to be "in the same gray area as shopping malls, which several state courts have ruled can be forced to uphold free speech rights despite being private property" (Harmon). Free speech conflicts within cyberspace, in any event, also seem likely to persist far into the future.

Corporate attempts to control the activities that take place in malls and cyberspaces are underpinned by an array of surveillance and security mechanisms. Malls are surveilled by ubiquitous closed-circuit television monitors and patrolled by highly visible uniformed private security details, creating what Crawford aptly calls "a spectacle of reassurance and deterrence" (27).[37] In cyberspace, corporations also seek to surveil and control user access. They deploy many of the previously discussed surveillance and censorship methods used by governments—including content analysis, data mining, and content blocking, for example—to make their cyberspaces "safe," prevent unauthorized copying of data (such as music or video), and, crucially, to improve their marketing and boost profitability by tracking Internet users' movements and actions. They make extensive use of various forms of spyware (such as spiders and cookies), software programs that gather personal data on users and use their computers' resources without their knowledge or consent. These programs (which often come secretly bundled with legitimate software or are built into the program with which the user is interacting) covertly record Internet browsing and purchasing histories, log users' keystrokes, and scan their hard drives for information that can be used to carry out market research, target advertising, and "suggest" products that might be of interest (cf. Amazon's "recommendations" and "top picks for you," and Netflix's "movies you'll love" listings). Such "features" are generally, as Greg Elmer points out, "framed by the ubiquitous rhetoric of interactivity, freedom and choice," but what lies behind them is "a cynical and all-encompassing desire for consumer profiles, wherein advertising links, and commercial Web pages in general, incorporate strategies, tactics, and, most importantly . . . techniques of demographic and psychographic 'solicitation'" (186). One is "profiled" not just on the basis of age, sex, and income level, but also on values, lifestyles, and belief typologies.[38] Some versions of spyware software not only profile users, they also rewrite search engine results and redirect Web traffic. In the hands of criminal enterprises, the software can be used to gather personal financial data and passwords, to hijack users' computers to disseminate spam and viruses, or to infiltrate hard drives to destroy personal data. Even when the immediate effects of these programs seem relatively benign (as in the case of Amazon's and Netflix's "recommendations"), the covert gathering and archiving of data constitute invasions of privacy with important implications for civil liberties. This was made clear by recent cases in which governments have made use of such commercially gathered data in prosecutions of, along with others, political dissidents.

These sophisticated forms of profiling and persecution might be seen as an indicator of the shift, discussed earlier, from the Foucauldian model of "disciplinary societies" and their grids to the "societies of control," in which power is no longer solely situated in discrete locations (prisons, schools, offices, factories) but dispersed throughout interconnected (and often electronic) networks. Embedded in the abstracted versions of identity produced by the "societies of control" (and mechanisms such as demographic/psychographic profiling) are, as Deleuze argues, a reconception of the "mass/individual pair. Individuals have become '*dividuals*', and masses [in which '*dividuals*' are aggregated], samples, data, markets or '*banks*'" ("Postscript" 311; emphasis in original). While the fortress persists in the "societies of control," the dominant form of policing of the polis becomes the scanscape, which, however, also helps to create new types of fortresses.

5. SCANSCAPE

The commonalities between urban space (or the pseudo-urbanized spaces of the suburban mall) and cyberspaces go far beyond their shared spatial imaginaries or the deployment of similar strategies of control within them. Computer technologies are integral to the expanding network of surveillance technologies that are creating the urban scanscape and fortress city. Indeed, it is the integration of video-surveillance and data-processing technologies that primarily differentiates modern from postmodern surveillance. A good starting point for tracing this difference is provided by the juxtaposition between the world of Francis Ford Coppola's 1974 film *The Conversation* and that of Tony Scott's 1998 *Enemy of the State*. Coppola's film is also especially interesting here because it was made on the brink of the introduction of postmodern surveillance technologies, the development of which (and of information technology in general) was explosive during the late 1970s and early 1980s. By the time of *Enemy of the State*, these new technologies had developed their extraordinary and often menacing power, although they might be seen as nearly child's play by now, merely a decade later. The pace of technological development has remained explosive over the last twenty years, following and often outpacing the remarkably prescient imagination of science fiction writers and futurists.

Both films feature nefarious conspiracies, in part organized around widespread illicit surveillance and recording, and in this respect they are defined by analogous conceptual matrices. They are, however, fundamentally distinguished by the respective power of the two forms and apparatuses of surveillance they depict. These forms and apparatuses also shape the conceptual matrix and even the development of the plot of each film and thus, as noted, make them only analogous rather than strictly parallel. The capabilities of the contemporary National Security Agency (NSA) depicted in *Enemy of the State* far exceed those of the anonymous corporation in *The Conversation* because of the vast computer power it wields—a point that is emphasized by the multiple juxtapositions of computers and video monitors in the film. This difference in capabilities may also account for the narrative shift from the private corporation in the first film to the information-gathering NSA in the second, and why the reclusive surveillance expert played by Gene Hackman in both films worked for a corporation in the first and the NSA in the second.[39]

Many of the advanced surveillance technologies currently being deployed by metropolitan police forces around the world were originally developed by government defense contractors for the use of the military, a point obliquely suggested by the montage of images in the opening credit sequence of *Enemy of the State*.[40] The montage begins with a moving aerial establishing shot that swoops over the Lincoln and Washington Monuments and up the Mall to the Capitol Building—a shot repeated twice to emphasize that it's a recorded image being played and replayed. It is followed by a rapid set of aerial shots on which a tracking grid is soon superimposed, capturing a car as it moves down a street and then, seen from much higher up, as it moves along the Beltway. An aerial shot of the Pentagon (from which, in addition to the earlier shots of the Capitol and monuments, we are probably intended to infer that the surveillance is governmental) is followed by close-ups of swiveling surveillance cameras and more fast-cut aerial shots overlaid with the restless tracking grid. From the air we see police chases and individuals attempting to elude them, and then a cut to a man before an immense circular array of surveillance monitors on which we see, in close up, crimes being committed and criminals being booked. But then, as though to emphasize that *everyone* looks like a criminal in the grainy, low-resolution over-exposure of video images, we see shots of individuals just standing alone in rooms or buying things at the convenience store. Then, the montage reverts to images of criminals committing crimes, running, and being apprehended; fleeing cars and hovering helicopters; surveillance cameras and satellite dishes. Our sense of these chase scenes alters later, however, since in the diegetic world of the film, it's only the good guys who are doing the fleeing.

The proliferation of surveillance cameras, to take just one of the more "visible" manifestations of such technologies, less than a decade after the release of *Enemy of the State*, has been staggering in cities such as New York and London. A 2006 survey of four Manhattan neighborhoods by the New York Civil Liberties Union, for example, found that there were nearly 4200 street-level surveillance cameras in downtown Manhattan alone (below 14th Street)—a fivefold increase since 1998.[41] Surveillance cameras follow us down supermarket and drugstore aisles, through airport terminals and train stations, and along the hallways of offices, schools, hospitals, and apartment buildings. They gaze out at us from ATMs and subway token booths, perch from building facades and roofs, and peer down from lampposts and traffic lights. High overhead, helicopters and satellites keep watch.[42] Camera phones are omnipresent and ever ready, Little Brother emulating Big Brother. Images that used to be monitored but not recorded or that were recorded only on videotapes that were erased and reused are now being digitally recorded and stored, often on the Internet.

Cameras are not, however, the only means of widespread surveillance. In his survey of surveillance technologies, Nunn draws a distinction between "stationary" surveillors (like CCTV cameras) and "roving" surveillors, which are far more difficult to avoid. Mass transit fare cards with magnetized strips, for example, remember where you have been and when. Our cars' GPS systems, LoJack radio transmitters, and E-Z Pass transponders also register and broadcast our movements.[43] Every use of a credit or debit card generates a record—date, time, place—and now they can be scanned without being removed from your wallet. In present-day America, it is virtually impossible not to leave traces behind in most of the things you do and places you go. Identity cards (including the national identity cards recently proposed for American citizens) and passports all over the world are equipped with similar magnetized strips that could contain far more data than just name, address, sex, and citizenship, and there is no reason to assume that only governments will scan and make use of this data.

We need not, however, necessarily carry such data in the form of cards or bar codes around with us: in a very real sense, we *are* the data. Biometric technologies that measure and analyze unique physical characteristics—facial features, the patterns of retinas and irises, and fingerprints—are growing increasingly precise and effective. There are also scanners that can recognize certain characteristic physical movements—how one walks, types, moves a mouse, signs one's name. Voice recognition software can incorporate programs that measure the level of stress in one's voice—functioning, in effect, as a form of lie detector. Once used only in high-security governmental and corporate sites, biometric data is now being incorporated into identity cards, passports, and an array of consumer goods, including automobiles (replacing keys) and computers (replacing passwords).[44] Biometric readers are being deployed in a rapidly expanding variety of public spaces, including airports, train stations, libraries, and even Disney World (which uses them to make certain that multiday tickets are used by the same person).

Very little of the data that is being gathered about us—videotapes and records of our movements, our purchases, our legal and medical records—is ephemeral: more and more of it is being digitally recorded and permanently stored, indexed, and correlated on Internet-accessible government, commercial, and private databases that are themselves increasingly interlinked. Indeed, as Nunn points out, "a biometric system is largely useless without a broad and deep infrastructure of databases containing catalogs of individual subjects and their biometric parameters" (274). Thus synergistically linked together, the reach and effectiveness of these instruments of surveillance are enormously amplified. Each connection extends and strengthens the web of surveillance suspended above and around us.

One might think that the accumulation of such enormous quantities of information would itself pose considerable difficulties: how to find the needle in the digital haystack? But technologies for handling and sifting through and correlating data are growing more sophisticated and efficient, as the Internet filtering and censoring mechanisms discussed earlier demonstrate. Those CCTV monitors, for example, will soon no longer require human watchers to identify individuals or to scrutinize their actions: those functions may largely be taken over by sophisticated motion-analysis technologies that would detect suspicious patterns of movement (lingering too long in one place and paying too much attention to the position of surveillance cameras, or walking away from a package or suitcase, for instance). Such technologies are currently being developed and some have already been deployed by both governments and private corporations. Security is not the sole motivation: marketers and retailers are very interested in how long you pause in front of particular product displays or linger in certain departments.

These technologies obviously provide a material basis for imagining, as Case, the protagonist of Gibson's *Neuromancer*, does, the city as a field of data. It is more likely, however, to be computers reading and making sense of it than individual human beings, whose conscious ability to synthesize vast quantities of information may turn out to be relatively limited compared to those of our information technologies (our unconscious ability, part of which we sometimes refer to as intuition, might be a different matter).

We are already well on our way to such prescient technologies. Even now, it is astounding how complete a profile of an individual can be assembled on the basis of publicly available Internet sources (and our government clearly has access to far more). This "efficacy" of the virtual world within the real can only be further extended as "Internet-enabled" computing devices are embedded in everything from camera phones and PDAs to "smart" household appliances, buildings, cars, and clothing. In the future, the Internet will no longer be a place we visit, but rather an "always-on" web of connections that pervades the world around us and enmeshes us within it. Yet there is no denying that, whatever the practical benefits of many of these technologies, they also inevitably constitute an immense, largely invisible swarming of disciplinary mechanisms. Were they suddenly made visible—the flights of data, the churning of indexes, the lines of sight, the fields of forces and, behind them all, the physical power of the state— the image might resemble Piranesi's dark Carceri, nightmares of elaborately entangled machines surrounding us amid perspectivally confused stone arches and walls from which there is no escape.

It seems fair to say that security and profit are the two primary motivations for the development and implementation of all these surveillance technologies by governments and private industry. And these two are clearly intertwined—if the government and private sector were not generating demand for these technologies, there would be little profit in them. That said, the most important one is clearly security, which raises a number of questions. Do such technologies indeed make us safer? From whom? At what cost? These subjects have been and will undoubtedly continue to be debated at length. Given the limits of this study, I cannot address them in any detail here. A few observations suffice, however, to convey the most essential points at stake. In 2006, the international civil liberties group Privacy International ranked Britain with Russia, Malaysia, and Singapore as the world's most "endemic surveillance societies." The United States,

Thailand, and the Philippines were just behind them, as the world's most "extensive surveillance societies." Britain is presently the most visually surveilled country in the world.[45] Yet, a comprehensive 2005 British Home Office study of the use and effectiveness of CCTV surveillance in Britain concluded that "the majority of the schemes evaluated did not reduce crime and even where there was a reduction this was mostly not due to CCTV; nor did CCTV schemes make people feel safer, much less change their behaviour" ("Community Cohesion"). Nonetheless, the cameras continue to proliferate without much opposition.

Even in the world's "liberal democracies" (among which Britain and the U.S. number themselves), many people believe that those with nothing to hide have nothing to fear from the expanding invasions of citizens' privacy on every front. Many view this surveillance as a necessary evil. The NSA villain Thomas Reynolds in *Enemy of the State* exemplifies this view when he declares, "Privacy's been dead for thirty years because we can't risk it. Maybe the only privacy that's left is inside your head and maybe that's enough." It may be that these attitudes are particularly prevalent in liberal democracies because their citizens, by and large, trust their governments and do not envision their countries being transformed into totalitarian states.[46] Many are more concerned not only about the dangers posed by terrorists, which is, at least, understandable, and about garden-variety criminals than they are about those posed by governments in possession of unprecedented surveillance capabilities that are directed primarily at their own citizens. This is remarkable, in view of the well-known persistent abuses of the surveillance capabilities or other governmental power even in Western democracies, let alone given the twentieth-century's horrific demonstrations of the dangers of police states of various ideological leanings, from Nazi Germany and the Stalinist Soviet Union (who together killed tens of millions) to smaller-scale but similarly frightening regimes. In the long run, of course, we too might experience a government unworthy of such confidence. Oppression has arrived more than once under the guise of protection in the past, and there is no special reason to think that it cannot happen in the future, even in democratic societies. Democracy and the polis (they are perhaps indissociable, at least in the postmodern world) sometimes make us forget that they need protection and vigilance, if not surveillance, including against the agencies and technologies of surveillance they create. *Enemy of the State* contains an apt commentary on this problem. Toward the end of the film, Carla Dean and Robert Clayton Dean watch the television interview of Congressman Sam Albert in which he states, "We knew that we had to monitor our enemies. We've also come to realize that we need to monitor the people who are monitoring them." Instantly perceiving that the Congressman's "government guarding us from the government" scenario hardly solves the problem, Carla Dean demands, "Well, who's gonna monitor the monitors of the monitors?"

6. POLIS

The essence of urban life in its fullest and most productive sense is the sense of connectedness—of the city belonging to us and of our belonging to the city, amidst its many heterogeneous and yet intertwined and overlapping communities.[47] As I argue in this study, however, to belong to the city is not the same as to belong to all of its communities or even to any single community; rather, to ensure this fullest and most productive life in the city, one must sometimes simultaneously both belong and not belong to its communities, and this is why I also stress heterogeneity in this vision of the city. Our experience of urban life is marked by everyday encounters with unassimilable difference, and it is in these encounters that much of the pleasure and challenge of city life lies. The shorthand term that I have used throughout this study for this vision of the city defined by a simultaneous connectedness and difference within and between urban communities is the *polis*. I would now like to explain why, with this term polis, I am reaching back to the Athenian polis of the fifth century BCE for this model and how, given the many differences between that society (which had its own injustices, from a contemporary viewpoint) and ours, we might imagine a twenty-first-century, postmodern polis.[48] My understanding and use of the term polis, as urban space, society (polity), and way of life resembles that of the ancient Greeks. For them, as the historian H.D.F. Kitto argues, the polis was at once a place, a political system (the state but also the people), and "the whole communal life of the people, political, cultural, moral [and] even economic"; it was understood to be "an active, formative thing, training the minds and characters of the citizens" (75).

In the *Politics*, Aristotle defines man as the *zoon politikon*—the political animal, a creature of the polis, or, in Lewis Mumford's translation, "the animal who belongs to the polis" (*The City in History* 16–17). For its citizens (a category, it must be noted, that excluded the majority of the inhabitants of the polis, including women, slaves, and foreigners), the polis provided the ideal structure within which all his needs might be met, all his capacities developed to their fullest, and all his potential realized.[49] Requiring nearly constant engagement, the life of the Greek citizen was, in a profound sense, his public life.

This privileging of public over private life was reflected in the spatial design of the polis, in the size and arrangement (often in the familiar grid pattern) of its various spaces. Facing away from the narrow streets and built around an interior courtyard that afforded light, air and a degree of domestic privacy, private houses were generally small and sparsely furnished. The public spaces, however—the agora (which was both marketplace and public forum), Pnyx (where the Assembly met), theater, temples, gymnasium, and stadium—were spacious and well appointed, indications of their importance in the life of the polis. Then as now, the social order was inscribed in the very form of the city.

For its citizens, life in the polis was distinguished by several key characteristics: engagement, visibility, coherence, and justice. Citizens were called upon to play a role in every important institution of the polis: to defend the city in the event of war, to serve in courts of law and the Assembly, to compete in the great athletic contests, to appear in the great religious processions, and to act in and judge the comedies and tragedies performed during public festivals. The citizens' extensive engagement with the life of the polis was, of course, made possible (at least in part) by the unpaid labor of women and slaves. Yet it is also true that, as Mumford points out, the culture of ancient Greece was not, by contemporary standards, materialistic: "The Greek poleis in their best days had no great surplus of goods: what they had was a surplus of time, that is, leisure, free and untrammeled, not committed—as in America today—to excessive materialistic consumption, but available for conversation, sexual passion, intellectual reflection, and esthetic delight" (*The City in History* 127). A citizen's status was not determined by what he had but by what he did, and participation in and service to the polis were at once the citizen's greatest duty and highest honor. This high degree of engagement was accompanied by an almost unimaginable degree of visibility: a citizen's life was lived primarily in relation to and under the eyes of his fellow citizens. According to Mumford, "what distinguished the Greek polis in its developing phase was the fact that no part of its life was out of sight or out of mind . . . All that men did was open to inspection, alike in the market, the workshop, the law court, the council, the gymnasium" (*The City in History* 165–66). The ancient Greeks did not, by and large, share our sense of privacy (particularly our squeamishness about the body), which leads us to seek the shelter of walls on every side. Life in the polis was, therefore, a form of ongoing, engrossing spectacle that stimulated both creativity and critical thought. "That open, perpetually varied and animated world," Mumford concludes, "produced a correspondingly unfettered mind" (*The City in History* 168).

This visibility and the relatively small populations of the city-states (few rose above 5,000 citizens) made it possible for the ancient polis to have a conceptual coherence for its inhabitants that our huge, sprawling urban agglomerations generally lack. For the inhabitants of the polis, Mumford writes, "the whole network of urban activities had visible form and relationship" (*The City in History* 166). By comparison, inhabitants of contemporary cities often know little of the lives of others outside their class or profession. As our separation from one another grows in the fortress city, our experience of the city becomes increasingly limited and fragmented. We lack the sense of the city as an integrated whole that the citizens of the polis possessed. At the same time, one must remember that the polis had its "blind spots" as well. The only women who walked unaccompanied through the streets were prostitutes and slaves; sequestered in the home, "women of good character" were largely invisible (and even inside the home, they did not generally appear before male guests).

This coherence of the life of the city was, in turn, reflected in the life of its citizens. "Work and leisure, theory and practice, private life and public life were in rhythmic interplay," Mumford observes, "as art, gymnastic, music, conversation, speculation, politics, love, adventure, and even war, opened every aspect of existence and brought it within the compass of the city itself. One part of life flowed into another: no phase was segregated, monopolized, set apart. Or so at least it must have seemed to the full-fledged citizens, however doubtful the proposition might appear to their slaves or their womenfolk" (*The City in History* 169). This description, as Mumford's qualification indicates, again reflects an idealized reconstitution of the Greek polis, a reconstitution in part defined by our desire and need for a polis of our own. Though it might well have been, as Kitto suggests, "that the polis took its origin in the desire for Justice," one must keep in mind that these noble roots of the polis's origin and the noble vision of the polis they imply were at odds with the actual lives of many in the Greek city (72). There, justice was denied to many, and the very concept of justice was *defined* by the exclusion of many from justice. Nevertheless, the contrast between the ancient Greek polis and our contemporary compartmentalized city life is stark and significant. Denizens of "edge cities" and suburban commuters move from the closed domestic spaces of their individual homes to offices and factories located in isolated corporate "parks," dropping the children off at a neighborhood school and stopping perhaps along the way at the shopping mall. Driving down streets that feature the blank walls of gated residential developments and enclosed "retirement communities" on either side or along highways set apart from the surrounding spaces by walls or wastelands, the commuter's passage from one disconnected site to another is an exercise in alienation and monotony. Segregated by race, age, class, and profession (and even, for suburban housewives, gender), we can go through each day rarely encountering anyone substantially different from ourselves, our lives a reflection of the fragmented, ghettoized urban landscape.[50] Since we rarely see them, our sense of the vital roles played by the diverse members of American society grows hazy and vague or disappears entirely, along with our awareness of the misery of many who have been excluded or relegated to the margins of society. Our suburban enclaves and fortress cities and scanscapes are part of an effort to obscure our society's absence of economic and social justice and to shield ourselves from the consequences of this absence.

Thus, many of our contemporary cities and suburbs lack the engagement that characterized the polis of the ancient Greeks, along with the comprehensive visibility (or legibility) and coherence of its diverse public life. There are, again, many reasons why the fifth-century BCE polis neither can nor should serve as a model for the cities of the twenty-first century. Some aspects of its life (its direct, rather than representative, democracy, for example) are not scalable; others, such as the status held by women, slaves, and foreigners, we would not wish to reproduce.[51] Yet there is much we might, with proper adjustments, seek to emulate in the ancient Greek ideal and its fulfillment in Greek society, at least as we reconstitute it. The adjustments may not be insignificant, however, since our polis can only be a radically diverse polis. This diversity appears to be far beyond what the Greeks had to accommodate or even imagine, even though their world was, for its time, a diverse geopolitical world. This geopolitical character of the ancient Greek world was, as Deleuze and Guattari argue, responsible for the rise of Greek philosophy, and along with it, their concept of the polis (*What Is Philosophy?* 85–117). In this sense, too, it provides a partial, but, for the reasons explained earlier, only a partial model for us as well.

The very complexity and quality of contemporary urban life arises out of its heterogeneity, and without it, the city dies. It is a mistake to think, as some do, that life is best lived among people "of one's own kind." Nor is it true that people need to be constantly surrounded by people like themselves to feel safe. Under the right conditions, heterogeneity increases people's ability to tolerate difference (and the sense of "insecurity" it can produce) and can actually produce a more open society. As Louis Wirth argues:

> The social interaction among such a variety of personality types in the urban milieu tends to break down the rigidity of caste lines and to complicate the class structure . . . The heightened mobility of the individual, which brings him within the range of stimulation by a great number of diverse individuals and subjects him to fluctuating status in the differentiated social groups that compose the social structure of the city, tends toward the acceptance of instability and insecurity in the world at large as a norm. This fact helps to account, too, for the sophistication and cosmopolitanism of the urbanite. No single group has the undivided allegiance of the individual. The groups with which he is affiliated do not lend themselves readily to a simple hierarchical arrangement. (193)

Rather than a division into warring, homogeneous interest groups, the diversity of the urban population can, thus, under suitable conditions, erode boundaries between individuals and produce a more complex imbrication of interests and alliances across society as a whole. In fact, actual urban experience suggests that the solution to tensions arising from diversity is more diversity—not less. To see how this works, one might contrast the current situation in Los Angeles and New York.

In Los Angeles, a remarkably high percentage of the population lives in communities (many of them gated) segregated by class, race, and ethnicity, and public support for municipal government and public services has been plummeting in recent decades. By contrast, in New York there is less segregation (though still a considerable amount), and public support for municipal government and public services has not seen the precipitous fall experienced by cities such as Los Angeles. The diversity of New York City has resulted in a situation where "no single ethnic or racial majority controls the public purse": "There is no cleavage between an Anglo majority and some poor minority," the economist Edward Glaeser notes, because "in New York, everybody is a minority" (qtd. in Porter). As Eduardo Porter argues, "New York City's experience, in fact, underscores that diversity does not automatically lead to hostility among ethnic groups or toward government spending as a whole. From public education to intermarriage to the many institutions in civil society promoting mutual understanding, there are countervailing forces acting to overcome ethnic, religious or linguistic cleavages." For these countervailing forces to work, however, power cannot become too concentrated in the hands of any one group. While New York is by no means a pure ideal, it does suggest, in this distribution of power among diverse groups, one important feature of a contemporary polis.

The postmodern polis does not require some kind of overarching sense of "unity" or, in the communitarian sense of the term, "community." As Rosalyn Deutsche points out in "Evictions: Art and Spatial Politics," "the unitary image of urban space constructed in conservative urban discourse is itself produced through division, constituted through the creation of an exterior. The perception of a coherent space cannot be separated from a sense of what threatens that space, of what it would like to exclude" (403). Thus, for example, "when public space is represented as an organic unity . . . the homeless person is seen to disrupt from the outside, [so that] the homeless person becomes a positive embodiment of the element that prevents society from achieving closure" (Deutsche 403). The goal of a twenty-first-century polis, then, should not be unity, but rather inclusiveness.

This inclusiveness will not result in a kind of grand civic consensus. Nor perhaps should it, since, as Lyotard has argued against Habermas, perhaps the most prominent philosopher and advocate of the idea of consensus in recent years, such a consensus is highly unlikely to ever be achieved, and attempts to reach it are more likely to lead to the suppression of dissent and therefore the imposition of injustice (*The Postmodern Condition* 57). A heterogeneous political space might never be conflict-free or completely safe, although, as Jane Jacobs suggests, it might be safer than police surveillance can often ensure, thus giving us more "polis" and less "control" of the types discussed earlier.[52] But it can be civil—a space of dialogue and mutual tolerance—if everyone's rights are assured, at least to the degree possible. For this to happen, citizenship in the fullest sense of the word and the right to the city must be extended to all its inhabitants (in contrast to the practices of the ancient polis). In other words, the right to the city, which entails access, recognition, and representation, must be universal. Out of this universal urban citizenship and right would come a far greater sense of the coherence of the life of the city, of the roles played by all its inhabitants in the functioning of the city and of their importance.

These changes are not, however, solely in the realm of the political: they must also be fostered through the "reopening" of material public spaces to diverse populations and uses. This reopening would involve the recapturing of public spaces that have been lost to privatization and the assumption once more of municipal government's stewardship and responsibility for the city's public schools, parks, transportation, and other public spaces and services. A vital city requires what Lefebvre terms "places of simultaneity and encounters, places where exchange would not go through exchange value, commerce and profit" ("Right" 148). To be a consumer is not the same thing as being a citizen. As much as possible, we need to restore the dual function of the agora as both public forum and marketplace—a place of free exchange, rather than only commercial exchange.

"City life is the 'being together' of strangers," Iris Marion Young writes (437). Living side by side, we need above all to be open to exchange and otherness, without needing to assimilate or collapse it into the same. What can emerge from this is an acceptance of otherness, both external in the otherness of individuals different from ourselves, but also the internal otherness of our own complex and multifaceted identities. The ideal of the twenty-first-century polis, then, is the ideal of a new cosmopolitanism at work in both our cities and ourselves.

It follows from the overall argument of this chapter that the spaces and thus the nature of the twenty-first-century polis are inextricably bound up with cyberspace, and cyberspace, too, must be reimagined and recreated as a cyberpolis. To do this, we need to extend our conceptions of citizenship and its rights and obligations to cyberspace and, beyond that, consider how cyberspace might reciprocally foster the development of the polis and new forms of urban citizenship. The program for the creation of a new cyberpolis shares many of the principles articulated earlier. The rights of cybercitizenship need to be universal, which would entail both the elimination of censorship and the extension of Internet access to everyone, regardless of income. Such free access should, I believe, be regarded as a public utility, rather than a commercial product. The virtual agora, like its material counterpart, needs to become more than just another commercial space: it should also be a public forum in which the free exchange of information and views—free speech—is encouraged and protected.[53]

Aside from the threats of government and corporate surveillance and censorship detailed in this chapter, the greatest threat to this free exchange is private industry's attempt to create a tiered system that would prioritize some Internet search results and content delivery over others on the basis of who pays more. Companies and individuals who pay the requisite (presumably substantial) fees to Internet providers would have their websites given priority and delivered more speedily than others. Those who did not would be ranked lower and delivered more slowly, or else not appear at all. The battle to preserve "net neutrality" (which would continue to provide website access to all users on an equal basis) pits Internet users and consumer groups against the major telecommunications and cable companies, and it is unclear, in the current political climate, who will prevail.[54]

If cyberspace is to constitute a new polis, and be part of and help to shape a new urban polis, a new city/cyberspace polis, this intention must be "built into" its foundations: both its virtual architecture and material components (routers and so forth) must be engineered in ways that will ensure and protect free access and exchange. Cyberspace has enormous potential as both a tool of liberation and as a site within which new forms of connection and community might emerge. This potential will, however, go unrealized if, as David Tomas warned in the early days of the Internet, "its parameters are engineered primarily to function, following Gibson's dystopic vision, as a virtual world of contestatory economic activity" or governmental control (46).

There are many ways in which democracy and civic life on both local and global scales might be enhanced through the use of the Internet. In practice, it can be a valuable tool for grassroots political organization and broadening citizen participation in policy discussions on both local and international levels. Sites like Neighborhoods Online and Amsterdam's Digital City (created as a shared initiative by leaders of the local squatters movement and municipal officials) can act as resource centers for neighborhood organizers and sites in which public debate might be conducted. It can be used to publicize causes and organize protests, both locally and internationally. To an unprecedented degree, the Internet also makes possible transnational movements in human rights, consumer advocacy, and environmental protection, potentially offering a counterweight to transnational capital. The Internet thus makes possible a new, international and multicultural polis within which new models of community and community action will emerge. This new cyberpolis, combined with the Internet's potential for disseminating information to those who have historically had little access to it, will likely be cyberspace's greatest contributions to the future.

Ultimately, the battle for justice in our society and in our cities cannot be separated from the fate of cyberspace. As Lyotard points out, the computerization of society "could become the 'dream' instrument for controlling and regulating the market system, extended to include knowledge itself and governed exclusively by the performativity principle. In that case, it would inevitably involve the use of terror. But it could also aid groups discussing metaprescriptives by supplying them with the information they usually lack for making knowledgeable decisions. The line to follow for computerization to take the second of these two paths is, in principle, quite simple: give the public free access to the memory and data banks" (*The Postmodern Condition* 67). Finally the future of our cities and cyberspaces lies in our willingness to insist on the priority of the public or civic realm and its prerogatives over private, and particularly commercial, interests. Out of this willingness can emerge "a politics that would respect the desire for justice and the desire for the unknown," which, Lyotard is right to argue, is a properly postmodern form of politics (*The Postmodern Condition* 67).

4 City Moves
Urban Spaces and Motion

The automobile may well be, as John Urry argues, currently "the most important example of a global technology": its spatial, economic, and cultural dominance in much of the world is at least as significant as the media and computer technologies that, for many, have come to define globalization ("Inhabiting" 1). No other single twentieth-century technology has so dramatically transformed the urban landscape, dominated the industrial economy, and shaped the practices and ethos of everyday life.[1] The effects of this transformation were most powerful and prevalent in the first half of the twentieth century in the United States, but since the 1950s, they have become global. By now the growing resistance to the automobile's domination, particularly in urban areas, is global as well. This chapter will place this centrality of the automobile and our ambivalence towards it in the broader context of the problematic of movement in the space and culture of the modern and then postmodern city. While other modes of movement (such as bicycling) are also important in this context, I shall be primarily concerned here with the juxtaposition of automobile motion with forms of pedestrian motion, in particular those of the dérive and parkour. This juxtaposition, I believe, brings the question of postmodern "city moves" into particularly sharp focus.

Section 1 offers an outline of the concept of the *modern* city, as based on the ideas of Le Corbusier, arguably the single most important figure responsible for the modern urban imaginary, and the architectural and cultural practices defined by these ideas. Significantly grounded in the idea of automotive movement, these ideas and practices also established the relationships between the automobile and the city throughout the twentieth century, especially the transformations of urban landscapes produced by the automobile and its effects on the social and cultural life of the city.

Section 1 sets the stage for my discussion of the automobile and the city in Section 2, through a reading of Don DeLillo's novel *Cosmopolis*. This discussion is centered on the most recent and specifically postmodern aspects of "car culture" produced by the introduction of cyberspace and other virtual spaces into the interior of the car, and the effects of this cyber-car culture on urban spaces and our perceptions of them. Section 2 thus examines a different aspect of the growing imbrication of city and cyber spaces discussed in the previous two chapters. Early twenty-first-century car culture, I argue, has shifted from the traditional automobile and open-road ethos of speed and freedom to an ethos of stasis and enclosure: the paralysis of gridlock. At the same time, the proliferation of virtual spaces within the car—from GPS mapping screens to video screens (including DVD, night-vision, and surveillance-camera feeds) to Internet-connected computer screens—have made the car an integral part of the world's cyber-cities and all of their other information networks and flows. As a result, the material urban spaces experienced through the car windshield are reduced to one more set of images in an array of mobile data and images. It is this situation that, as I shall show, is powerfully captured by DeLillo's novel.

My discussion of the automobile, understood as a form of enclosed, semi-private movement, frames the analysis, undertaken in Section 3, of practices of "open" or public pedestrian movement in cities. I first discuss the proto-postmodern practice of the Situationist dérive (drift) and then move on to the new practice and worldwide youth movement of parkour, which might be thought of as a type of three-dimensional pedestrianism. Bypassing mass transit (as with the twentieth-century automobile, there has already been much interesting work done on the cultures of trains, subways, and buses), Section 3 instead explores forms of pedestrian movement practiced by individuals, though sometimes in groups, and the relationships with urban space they create, including how they remap, re-imagine, and reconfigure the spaces of the city. Like the automobile, each of these practices carries its own ethos and spatial logics. As physical disciplines, they can also be said to possess a "poetics," although my argument will primarily focus, along Deleuzean lines, on their "materials" and purposes. These practices remind us, as Sally Munt argues, that the body itself is "a product of space and a performance of space, a thing and a process, . . . a 'lived experience' where conceptualizations materialize, and are materialized, in historically specific ways" (5). In other words, as I argue here, space and the body reciprocally define and shape each other: there is no space apart from the bodies in it, and there are no bodies and no movement apart from the space in which they exist in their interactions with other bodies. Most importantly, however, the practices to be discussed here also create new ways of understanding and recreating the city as a space of freedom, creativity, and play.

1. URBAN MODERNISM AND AUTO-DOMINATION: CITY AND CITY MOVES AFTER LE CORBUSIER

A city made for speed is a city made for success.

—Le Corbusier

With each decade, it gets harder to distinguish the culture of the auto-mobile from the culture of the city.

—Mitchell Schwarzer, *Zoomscape: Architecture in Motion and Media*

Figure 4.1 Spectators at the General Motors "Futurama" model at the 1939 New York World's Fair. (Harry Ransom Humanities Research Center, The University of Texas at Austin. Courtesy Estate of Edith Lutyens Bel Geddes. Photo courtesy Estate of Margaret Bourke-White.)

I begin my discussion of urban modernism and movement with an anecdote from a decade ago. Late in 1997, a few days before Christmas, New York City's Mayor Rudolph Giuliani decided to initiate another battle in the ongoing war against the gridlock that frequently paralyzes the city's busiest streets and intersections. To prevent pedestrians from impeding the flow of turning cars, trucks, and buses when crossing the street at key intersections, the mayor ordered the erection of steel barricades at strategic points along several avenues. One such barricade was set up on the east side of Fifth Avenue, across from Rockefeller Center, on the corner where St. Patrick's Cathedral and Saks Fifth Avenue face one another on 50th Street. Crowds moving up or down Fifth Avenue approached the corner and discovered that it was impossible to cross. Pedestrians, both New Yorkers and a large, seasonal contingent of tourists, reacted at first with bewilderment and confusion. Many of the native New Yorkers (who tend to view jaywalking and crossing in defiance of "Don't Walk" signs as inalienable urban rights) turned, walked back and attempted to cross mid-block, where they were intercepted by uniformed traffic cops angrily directing them to return to the corner and cross north.[2] The crowd turned back and retraced their steps. To get to the other side of Fifth Avenue, it was necessary to cross 50th Street, cross the avenue, and then cross 50th again. As congestion built at the corner, a large, milling crowd of annoyed pedestrians began to gather on the steps of St. Patrick's Cathedral. Someone began to moo. Within moments, both sides of 50th Street were filled with mooing pedestrians—an impromptu protest against the "cattle chutes" intended to direct and discipline their movement.

The contest between pedestrians and vehicles for control of the city streets doubtless goes back at least as far as the first horse-drawn conveyances of the ancient world.[3] As Jane Jacobs, one of the most prominent critics of the automobile's domination of urban life and of post-Le Corbusier urban modernity, observes, the interchange and circulation that are the essence of urban life, the "trade in ideas, services, skills and personnel, and certainly in goods, demands efficient, fluid transportation and communication. But multiplicity of choice and intensive city trading depend also on the immense concentrations of people and on intricate minglings of uses and complex interweaving of paths" (340). Sometimes, inevitably, those uses conflict and paths collide.

Despite their chaotic surface appearance (and some actual chaos), the uses of city sidewalks and streets also have a complex order created by the rhythms of everyday life—those of people on their way to work and children off to school; of deliveries being made and stores opening; of shoppers and bench sitters; of people going out and coming back from lunch; of schools letting out and kids gathering for play dates and games; of teenagers meeting and hanging out around the neighborhood; of people coming home from work or heading out for the evening; of bars opening and movies and concerts beginning; of the night shift beginning and, later, restaurants and bars closing; and, a few hours later, of everyone getting ready to start all over again. When the preponderance of these activities is accomplished on foot, with mass transit being used as necessary for longer distances, in a dense and diverse (both users and uses) urban environment, sidewalks and streets are lively and the city works. This order, which Jacobs called the "urban ballet," with its countless intersecting and overlapping moves, involves considerable face-to-face interaction and exchange. One might also see this order as "chaosmic," to use Joyce's coinage, favored by Deleuze and Guattari, a complex interplay—a dance—of order and chance. This chaosmic urban order, Jacobs writes, "is all composed of movement and change, and although it is life, not art, we may fancifully call it the art form of the city and liken it to the dance—not to a simple-minded precision dance with everyone kicking up at same time, twirling in unison and bowing off en masse, but to an intricate ballet in which the individual dancers and ensembles all have distinctive parts which miraculously reinforce each other and compose an orderly whole. The ballet of the good city sidewalk never repeats itself from place to place, and any one place is always replete with new improvisations" (50).[4]

These interactions and exchanges are, as I argue throughout this study, crucial for both our sense of public space and of civic community. When most or all of these activities require the use of an automobile, it is not only urban spaces that are dispersed, but also urban community. As Urry points out, "automobility also dominates how non-car-users inhabit public spaces. Car-drivers are excused from normal etiquette and face-to-face interactions with all those others who are inhabiting the road. Car-travel interrupts the taskscapes of others (pedestrians, children going to school, postmen, garbage collectors . . .), whose daily routines are obstacles to the high-speed traffic cutting mercilessly through slower-moving pathways" ("Inhabiting" 4–5). In a drive-through car culture, he adds, "the 'coming together of private citizens in public space' is lost to a privatization of the mechanised self moving through emptied non-places" ("Inhabiting" 6).[5]

Contemporary cities thus face perennial dilemmas of how to preserve the density and diversity of uses (including residential, commercial, governmental, and recreational) that make for lively urban spaces while maximizing the flows of pedestrian and vehicular traffic—flows that are themselves, as my opening anecdote about the moo protest suggests, frequently in conflict. The question these conflicts raise, however, is not really one of either cars or pedestrians, though "on the ground," in particular sites, it may sometimes come down to that. Even dense "walking cities" like New York and Paris require some vehicular traffic to function: some mass transit (buses) must use the streets, taxis go where mass transit does not (and sometimes more quickly), and deliveries must be made and trash picked up. Rather, the question is one of *priority*, even though this question poses further questions and brings in new considerations concerning better balances between various forms of movement and transit in the city. While automobiles need not necessarily be "inherent destroyers of cities" (Los Angeles, for instance, is defined by the automobile and would not exist in its present form without it), it is also true that, as Jacobs remarks, "the interval of the automobile's development as everyday transportation has corresponded precisely with the interval during which the ideal of the suburbanized anti-city was developed architecturally, sociologically, legislatively and financially" (343).

The suburbanized anti-city to which Jacobs refers is typified by Le Corbusier, Oscar Niemeyer, and the Congrès internationaux d'architecture moderne (CIAM)'s visions of modern, "functional" cities composed of highrises neatly lined up, assembly-line style, amid vast, empty lawns overlaid with automotive highway grids.[6] As Lewis Mumford wrote in 1968: "Most architects, during the last thirty years, and certainly most architectural and planning schools, have been dominated by the powerful propaganda and experimental achievement of this singular man of genius, Le Corbusier. If anyone put forward what seemed a fresh and original conception of the City of Tomorrow, it was this redoubtable leader. . . . And though no one city, except Chandigarh, shows the full range of his influence, his thought has run so closely along the grain of our age that fragments of it are scattered everywhere" ("Yesterday's City" 118).

Nearly all of the urban renewal and low-income housing projects of the late 1940s, 1950s, 1960s, and early 1970s, in the U.S. and elsewhere, were based upon Le Corbusier and CIAM's conception of the "modern" city, as were quite a few postwar urban outer-ring developments, such as the "Villes Nouvelles" constructed on the outskirts of Paris.[7] It was an automobile-based urban conception and model that, whatever its initial conceptual appeal, proved, at least in its practical implementations and applications, enormously (and by and large disastrously) influential on the post-WWII generation of urban planners, including New York's "master builder," Robert Moses (Jacobs's particular bête noire).[8]

This vision of the city had several more or less obvious sources of appeal. Aesthetically, it had a marvelous futuristic aura: the "city of tomorrow" (as it was frequently known in the U.S.) was modern, clean, high-tech. Financially, it meant immense profits for developers, builders, and, not incidentally, the automobile industry (hence the French automobile manufacturer Voisin's sponsorship of Le Corbusier's "Plan Voisin" as the centerpiece of the Pavillon de l'Esprit Nouveau at the 1925 Exposition des Arts Décoratifs et Industriels Modernes in Paris, and General Motors' sponsorship of Norman Bel Geddes's "Futurama" exhibit at the 1939 New York World's Fair).[9] Arguably most importantly, it was seen by Le Corbusier and many others as the solution to the ills of congestion and crowding in rapidly growing twentieth-century cities, and, indeed, of modern life itself. "Every day the anxiety and depression of modern life spring up afresh: the city is swelling, the city is filling up," Le Corbusier lamented in *The Radiant City* (91). The street, which he regarded as "the basic organ of the city," had become "appalling, noisy, dusty, dangerous; automobiles can scarcely do more than crawl along it; the pedestrians, herded together on the sidewalks, get in each other's way, bump into each other, zigzag from side to side; the whole scene is like a glimpse of purgatory" (91).

The causes and culprits of this urban nightmare, Le Corbusier believed, were a lack of intelligent planning, greed ("A skyscraper makes a good advertisement: *the biggest in the world*," he sardonically observed), and, remarkably, the skyscraper itself (*The Radiant City* 127; his emphasis). Setting his vision of the modern "rational" city of the Plan Voisin in juxtaposition to the "romantic irrationality" of American cities, he declared Manhattan to be the result of an American "esthetic of chaos (romanticism again), an ethic that prizes confusion, a license to unleash disorder. Chaos, violence, primitive strength, the glamour of a besieging army, signs of power . . . skyscraper-propaganda" (*The Radiant City* 127). His supremely rational and functional plan, by contrast, would provide the fortunate inhabitants of this future city with *"silence, fresh air, daylight, vast horizons (wide views 'breadth of vision')"* and *"bring decent living conditions and a light-filled atmosphere to places where everything at the moment is rottenness, filth, milling crowds, din, disorder, delay, fatigue, wear and tear, and demoralization"* (*The Radiant City* 128; his emphasis). It was intended *"To create the nobility, the grandeur, the serene dignity made possible by suitable proportions. To provide a sublime expression (the mature fruit of machine-age evolution) of this century's strength. To bring back the sky. To restore a clear vision of things. Air, light, joy"* (*The Radiant City* 128–9; his emphasis).

The last phrase was no doubt also intended as a description of Le Corbusier's own vision in his manifesto. It was a powerful architectural vision that was bound to have a major influence at the time, and for a long time to come. Mumford grasped the essence of this vision and influence when he noted that "the chief reason for Le Corbusier's immediate impact lies in the fact that he brought together two architectural conceptions that separately have dominated the modern movement in architecture and city planning: the machine-made environment, standardized, bureaucratized, 'processed,' technically perfected to the last degree; and to offset this, the natural environment, treated as so much visual open space, providing sunlight, pure air, green foliage, and views" ("Yesterday's City" 118). Careful not to neglect the more earthly goods, however, Le Corbusier himself hastened to highlight the key feature of the "'great East-West throughway of Paris' which embodies the future of Paris and offers the City Council the chance to launch a gigantic financial enterprise, a 'money-making' enterprise + a source of wealth" (*The Radiant City* 207).

There are reasons to suspect that Le Corbusier's city (whose 60-story towers were to be perched on pilotis rising five to seven meters above the ground) was not so much a city to be inhabited as a city to be *viewed*: "In place of a porcupine and a vision of Dante's Inferno, we propose an

Figure 4.2 Le Corbusier, "The Plan Voisin vs. Manhattan," 1925. (© FLC/ARS, 2008.)

organized, serene, forceful, airy, ordered entity. From below, it could be sublime. From the air (we are all now learning how to look at cities from above), it will be *a symbol of the spirit*" (*The Radiant City* 134; his emphasis). The scopic regime here is that of de Certeau's (and, as discussed in Chapter 2, Descartes's) "solar Eye, looking down like a god," which offers the "pleasure of 'seeing the whole,' . . . totalizing the most immoderate of human texts [that of the city itself]" (de Certeau 92).[10] From this vantage point, one is "lifted out of the city's grasp. One's body is no longer clasped by the streets . . . His elevation transfigures him into a voyeur. It puts him at a distance. It transforms the bewitching world by which one was 'possessed' into a text that lies before one's eyes" (de Certeau 92). The panorama-city thus produced, de Certeau argues, "is the analogue of the facsimile produced, through a projection that is a way of keeping aloof, by the space planner urbanist, city planner or cartographer. . . . [It] is a 'theoretical' (that is, visual) simulacrum, in short a picture, whose condition of possibility is an oblivion and a misunderstanding of practices. The voyeur-god created by this fiction, who, like Schreber's God knows only cadavers, must disentangle himself from the murky intertwining daily behaviors and make himself alien to them" (92–93).

De Certeau contrasts this alienated image and experience of the city with that of "the ordinary practitioners of the city [who] live 'down below,' below the thresholds at which visibility begins. They walk—an elementary form of this experience of the city; they are walkers, *Wandersmän-ner*, whose bodies follow the thicks and thins of an urban text they write without being able to read it" (92–93). While de Certeau regarded this illegibility (on which point I differ with his analysis, as will be seen shortly) as an unavoidable and indeed benign characteristic of the city "written from below," as it were, Le Corbusier viewed it, within the context of the skyscraper cities of America, with horror and disgust. He was careful to draw a sharp distinction between the "tumult [and] bristling chaos" of American skyscrapers and the harmonious order of his, as he termed them, "horizontal skyscrapers" (*The Radiant City* 134); his skyscrapers—despite his use of the term 'horizontal'—were not intended to be shorter or smaller than those already crowding the cities.[11] In America, however, "skyscrapers mean anarchy," he asserted; "The skyscraper has *petrified* the cities. In an age of speed, the skyscraper has congested the city. . . . The pedestrian crawls at the feet of those skyscrapers like a beetle at the foot of a steeple . . . everyone is trampling on everyone else, because at ground-level there is no room at all; *the skyscraper has been built above yesterday's streets*" (*The Radiant City* 127–28; his emphasis).

Oddly enough, the Plan Voisin's accommodations for pedestrians, in addition to the "network of diagonal and orthogonal 'landscaped' paths" running across the great lawns in between its massive horizontal skyscrapers, included the spaces *beneath* them. As Le Corbusier explained: "Between the [pilotis] thus left to form a veritable forest in certain areas of the city's surface area, it will be possible to move about quite freely. Apart from five entrance halls for pedestrians, the space underneath the skyscraper is left vacant. Here again, as in the residential neighborhoods, the pedestrian has *the entire ground surface at his disposal*" (*The Radiant City* 132; his emphasis). Pedestrians might also make use of the underground passages that were to run underneath the streetcar lines and highways.[12] Instead of "crawling *at the feet of* those [New York] skyscrapers like a beetle," Le Corbusier apparently intended the inhabitants of his modern city to crawl *beneath* them.

Distinguished by their austere, modernist minimalism of both architectural design and landscaping, and the priority given to the sweeping superhighways that were to provide the primary means of transportation, Le Corbusier's cities present one, finally, with an image of "urban" spaces devoid of any pedestrians at all. (Indeed, the term "urban" here seems only applicable in terms of population density.) As Mumford observed in his critique of Le Corbusier's designs, "the extravagant heights of Le Corbusier's skyscrapers had no reason for existence apart from the fact that they had become technological possibilities; the open spaces in his central areas had no reason for existence either, since on the scale he imagined there was no motive during the business day for pedestrian circulation in the office quarter. By mating the utilitarian and financial image of the skyscraper city to the romantic image of the organic environment, Le Corbusier had, in fact, produced a sterile hybrid" ("Yesterday's City" 121).

Despite Le Corbusier's claims of the pedestrian having *"the entire ground surface at his disposal,"* these cities were not intended for walking; there was no place to walk *to* and no "street life" at all. His cities had a place for everything (housing, offices, shops) *except* the social and civic connections and interchanges that are the city's essential, and finally primary, raison d'être. Guy Debord clearly grasped the political implications of these designs: "The new prefabricated cities clearly exemplify the totalitarian tendency of modern capitalism's organization of life: the isolated inhabitants . . . see their lives reduced to the pure triviality of the repetitive combined with the obligatory absorption of an equally repetitive spectacle" ("Perspectives" 71).

Planners like Le Corbusier, Oscar Niemeyer, Robert Moses, and their less talented imitators tended to take a "tabula rasa" approach to city planning—with a strong emphasis on the "rasa." Their solution was not to repair the existing urban fabric: it was to first erase and then replace it. The Plan Voisin, intended for the Right Bank of the Seine but never built, would have razed two square miles of central Paris, including the historic neighborhoods (with their markedly irregular streets) of Le Marais, Temple, and Archives, and erected in their place Le Corbusier's signature cruciform skyscrapers, arranged in ranks and files amid lawns and highways. While it is clear why one would want to wander the streets of Le Marais, with its lively cafés, shops, cabarets, galleries, nightclubs, and historic landmarks (including the Place des Vosges), it is difficult to imagine why one would want to traverse the voids between Le Corbusier's identical towers—to go where, for what? His pedestrian paths are not streets. Indeed, Le Corbusier declared that city "streets no longer work. Streets are an obsolete notion. . . . we have to create something that will replace them" (121). The city of tomorrow is, above all, the city of the automobile, so that "something" that was to replace "yesterday's streets," turns out to be the superhighway and the lawn. Or perhaps only the superhighway: given the "superdensity" of his horizontal skyscrapers, it appears that Le Corbusier underestimated both the numbers of cars their inhabitants would require and the parking those cars would involve: "His vision of skyscrapers in the park," Jacobs accurately predicted, "degenerates in real life into sky scrapers in parking lots" (343).

Robert Moses, whose influence on American cities in the twentieth century was arguably greater than that of any other single individual, shared many of Le Corbusier's views and priorities. As Paul Goldberger observed, "the Moses vision of New York was less one of neighborhoods and brownstones than one of soaring towers, open parks, highways and beaches—not the sidewalks of New York but the American dream of the open road" ("Robert Moses"). "We live in a motorized civilization," Robert Moses insisted, and throughout the 1920s, 1930s, 1940s, 1950s, and into the late 1960s, he transformed the urban landscape of New York

Figure 4.3 The twenty-first-century car city: downtown Houston. (Photo by Alex S. MacLean/Landslides.)

and, through his influence on a generation of city planners and builders, of cities around the globe.[13] "His guiding hand made New York, known as the city of mass transit, also the nation's first city for the automobile age," Goldberger wrote in Moses's obituary: "Under Mr. Moses, the metropolitan area came to have more highway miles than Los Angeles does; Moses's projects anticipated such later automobile-oriented efforts as the Los Angeles freeway system" ("Robert Moses").

Several of Moses's massive highway projects, including most notoriously the Cross-Bronx Expressway, eviscerated (to use Jacobs's word) broad swaths of the densely inhabited urban fabric. His plans for the Lower Manhattan and Mid-Manhattan Expressways, which were never built, would have sundered Lower Manhattan into three parts and leveled large areas of Soho, Little Italy, and the Lower East Side.[14] To achieve the rapid and unimpeded flow of traffic, even the city itself could be sacrificed. This version of urban planning, in which traffic circulation was paramount, became, in effect, suburban planning. (As Goldberger noted, Moses's urban highways "were conceived more for the convenience of suburban automobile owners than inner-city residents" ["Robert Moses"].) The city would be, for many, simply one more scenic vista, a spectacle glimpsed through car windows as one drove swiftly by.

Though the problems created for cities by our ever-growing reliance on automobiles are considerable, it seems unrealistic to imagine that we can (or even should) do without them entirely. The viability of most older cities (those that, unlike Los Angeles, were not originally designed for automobile traffic) would, however, clearly be improved by giving more priority to the interests of pedestrians and mass transit and less to those of private automobiles.[15] This shift in priorities and resources, which may already be underway in many cities, could reverse the "erosion of cities by automobiles," and generate, at least to the extent possible, "attrition of automobiles by cities" (Jacobs 349). Widespread concerns about city viability and environmental sustainability, and a host of recent unofficial "take back the streets" movements, may be reversing or at least slowing the past half-century's dominion of the automobile in many of the world's cities.[16] Gridlock (with its attendant economic and environmental costs to cities) is, unsurprisingly, also driving this trend.

Jean-Luc Godard's 1967 film *Le Week-end*, in which a couple leave Paris in their convertible for a weekend in the country and become trapped in a seemingly endless traffic jam (punctuated by flaming wrecks and bodies strewn across the highway), is contemporaneous with and marks a decisive moment in the Western cultural relationship to the automobile.[17] The romanticized freedom associated with the automobile here becomes an apocalyptic nightmare that devolves into barbarism as the motorists indulge in theft, arson, rape, murder, and, ultimately, cannibalism. As the twentieth century drew to a close, the dominant tropes of speed and

Figure 4.4 "198-Car Pile-Up on the Long Beach Freeway," 2002. (Photo by Irfan Khan. ©2002, *Los Angeles Times*. Reprinted with permission.)

freedom in mid-century "on-the-road" narratives were being replaced by those of enormous traffic jams, horrific car crashes, and massive pile-ups.[18] Accompanying this shift in perspectives on the automobile was, I will argue here, a transformation in the perspectives on and perceptions of urban space produced *by* the automobile. I shall now examine this transformation as culminating, at least for now, in our urban world, whose more nightmarish aspects are portrayed by Don DeLillo in his *Cosmopolis*, which administers a nearly lethal dose of postmodern "reality" to the Radiant City of Le Corbusier's vision of urban modernity.

2. INSTANT TRANSFER IN SLOW MOTION: CITY, CYBERSPACE, AND CAPITAL IN DON DELILLO'S *COSMOPOLIS*

> We are before a veritable "seventh art," that of the dashboard.
>
> —Paul Virilio, "Dromoscopy"

As discussed in the preceding section, the highly automobile-dependent urbanism of Le Corbusier and CIAM, which promoted standardized housing and the compartmentalization of work, domestic, and recreational functions, was not universally applauded, even as a philosophical or aesthetic vision, let alone when put into practice, especially by lesser architects and planners. As the twentieth century progressed toward postmodernity, the forces of the philosophical, aesthetic, and practical resistance to this vision of the city and its life increased. In particular, this modern urbanism became the subject of a prescient, wide-ranging critique by the Situationists, a mid-century French avant-garde movement.[19] The urbanism produced by the capitalist car culture, the Situationists Attila Kotányi and Raoul Vaneigem argued in the 1960s, is "pure spectacular ideology" (65). For the Situationists, the position of automobile drivers (rather like that of film or television viewers transfixed before the screen), inert behind the wheel, staring through the windshield as they fulfill their dreary daily round from home to work and back again, was symbolic of the passivity, stasis, and alienation engendered by "the society of the spectacle," in which "all of life presents itself as an immense accumulation of spectacles. Everything that was directly lived . . . moved away into a representation" (Debord, *Society of the Spectacle* 1). All these screens (film, television, windshield) function not just as sites for the display of consumer capitalism's spectacles: they also serve, as the multiple meanings of "screen" suggest, to obscure, conceal, and separate us from reality.[20] Ultimately, "modern capitalism, which organizes the reduction of all social life to a spectacle, is incapable of presenting any spectacle other than that of our own alienation," Kotányi and Vaneigem argued (65).

Though the Situationists could not have anticipated the coming of the computer and Internet revolution, they clearly perceived the dangers of the society of the spectacle, of which cyberspace has become an integral part and to which it has added, quite literally, new dimensions. Their critique also pertains, with remarkably few qualifications, to the late postmodernism of our contemporary culture as it much as did to the scene of the late 1960s, when a generational backlash against consumerism emerged, however ephemerally. The Situationists saw, too, the ways in which the automobile, a powerful element and symbol of consumer culture, reconfigured everyday life, reshaped the urban landscape, and contributed to the spectacularization of the postmodern cities of signs and (a few decades later) brands, discussed in Chapter 1.

In the early 1970s, a few years after the onset of postmodernity, Robert Venturi, Denise Scott Brown, and Steven Izenour analyzed the new spatial order of the postmodern urban signscape as one "relating the automobile and highway communication in an architecture which abandons pure form in favor of mixed media" (75). Looking at (and learning from) cities like Las Vegas and Los Angeles, they argued: "It is the highway signs, through their sculptural forms or pictorial silhouettes, their particular positions in space, their inflected shapes, and their graphic meanings, that identify and unify the megatexture [of the postmodern commercial landscape]. They make verbal and symbolic connections through space, communicating a complexity of meanings through hundreds of associations in [a] few seconds from far away. Symbol dominates space. Architecture is not enough" (13). This postmodern urban space was, and still remains, a geographic and cultural landscape intended to be apprehended through a car windshield at 70 miles an hour or on the television screen in 30-second bursts.

The history of modern America, Andrew Cross suggests in "Driving the American Landscape," might be understood through the succession of frames or screens through which the country has been seen: train windows, movie screens, airplane windows, television screens, and, finally, automobile windshields. He writes: "Today there is no landscape if it is not seen through the windscreen, only a series of places, postcard snapshots separated by time and space. It is only within the frame of the windscreen that places coexist, that they become animated along the continuous narrative of the landscape through which you drive" (255). Now, of course, the computer screen would need to be added to this list.

The parallels between the views of the urban landscape seen through the car windshield and film screens are particularly striking, and they have not escaped filmmakers over the past century.[21] As Mitchell Schwarzer argues in *Zoomscape: Architecture in Motion and Media*:

> The vehicular landscape encourages an understanding of architecture that is almost cinematic—architecture in motion, buildings assembled through shots, cities understood as scenes. Sitting in a cushioned

seat, perhaps alone, the radio tuned to a favorite station, the driver watches as individual buildings or streets become like a moving picture, the frames of an architecture of indeterminate length, direction, and content. Buildings reassemble according to the driver's desires, her arrivals and departures, stops and accelerations. Like the cinema, the automobile facilitates passage into new worlds. And like kinematic cinematography, road vision, with its speed and sight, can be boldly liberating. (78)

Embedded in Schwarzer's description are many of the characteristic elements of the twentieth-century aesthetics of the windshield: speed and motion, fragmentation and selection, solitude and autonomy (accompanied perhaps by a certain narcissism and alienation), exploration and freedom. Speed—the image of movement—is the dominant, however, and it transforms the experience of the city.[22] "Speed turns the city seen through the windshield into a surface of motion, a stream of form that somehow eludes the consciousness of form" (Schwarzer 71). The urban landscape becomes flow, an experience that, as will be seen, is recaptured in a somewhat different and more active mode by dérive and parkour.

As the twentieth century recedes into the past, however, the characteristic elements of the twenty-first-century ethos and aesthetics of the windshield and of car culture itself have taken on additional and sometimes quite different aspects. If the modern American car city (roughly through the mid-1960s) was distinguished by speed (at least in the ideal) and flow, the postmodern global car city is more distinguished by gridlock, prophetically portrayed by Godard's *Le Week-end*. Once the traffic comes to a halt, as it now does with increasing frequency and duration, the enclosure of the car suddenly becomes oppressive. Stasis replaces speed, frustration erases pleasure, and the windows through which we gazed out now become apertures of exposure through which others, trapped alongside us, may peer in—a reversal of the gaze forestalled by the ostentatious tinting of windows in towncars and limousines. In this rigid, static envelope, speed appears only *inside* the automobile, in the swift flows of data and images across video, Internet, surveillance, and GPS screens.

This new culture of the cybercar and its effects on the experience of the postmodern urban landscape are brilliantly depicted in Don DeLillo's 2003 novel *Cosmopolis*. In the novel, the archetype of the automobile in the postmodern city of global capital is the anonymous white limousine, ferrying "the investment banker, the land developer, the venture capitalist . . . the software entrepreneur, the global overlord of satellite and cable, the discount broker, the beaked media chief . . . the exiled head of state of some smashed landscape of famine and war" (10). *Cosmopolis* is a "day-in-the-life" narrative of a billionaire global currency trader, Eric Packer. Leaving his 48-room apartment on First Avenue in Manhattan, he gets into his custom white limousine, which is equipped with an immense array of flat-screen visual display units across which stream the signs of global capital, "medleys of data . . . and alpine charts, the polychrome numbers pulsing" (13).

Eric is intent upon getting a haircut at a barbershop across town. His chief of security warns him that the president is in town and that traffic will, accordingly, be at a standstill in much of the city. Undeterred, Eric will spend most of the day inside the limousine, as it slowly (extremely slowly—it takes all day) makes its way, avenue by avenue, across mid-town Manhattan to the far West Side. The flow of traffic is continually obstructed by the usual midtown congestion (in which wailing emergency vehicles, streams of jaywalking pedestrians, and stalled tour buses figure prominently), which is aggravated not only by the presence of the president and his extensive entourage, but also by a water-main break, a massive street protest, a funeral cortège, a film shoot, and a bombing outside an investment bank—all but the last fairly common occurrences in the city. In *Zoomscape*, Schwarzer argues that "the aesthetics of the automobile are shaped by the brief encounter, a quick and potent mix of vision with form that almost instantaneously evaporates" (72). In the postmodern New York City of *Cosmopolis*, however, these brief encounters arise less out of the movement of the car than out of the circulation of city life *around* it as it sits frozen in gridlock. DeLillo's narration carefully tracks the limousine's progress (or lack thereof), obstacle by obstacle, avenue by avenue. The underlying structure of the narrative, thus, is defined by the limousine's halting itinerary of brief moments of movement interrupted by long interludes of paralysis.

Several times in the course of the day, by some strange synchronicity, Eric encounters his new wife, Elise. She appears, apparently by chance, in a taxi next to his limousine, in a bookstore where he has stopped to purchase a book, in a crowd on the street. Each time they meet, they have a meal: breakfast, lunch, dinner. Whether these synchronicities are meaningful coincidences or merely manifestations of random frequency remains an open question. It is possible, however, to read them as a manifestation, an effect of the reductive topology of the couple's social space, the same as that of all the wealthy New Yorkers. In this space, the inside and the outside of Eric's limousine are one and the same, forming a kind of Möbius strip, except that here everything is inside, inside the limousine, a small claustrophobic space of instant global transfer—of money and of everything else. But then, here money *is* everything; there is no "else," just as there appears to be no "outside" to the limousine. And yet, as will be seen presently, this topology is not all-inclusive, since the outside world(s), local and global, finally do invade Eric's space, and in fact have always already inhabited and inhibited it from within as well.

The limousine also pauses at multiple points in its trajectory across the city to pick up and, after brief meetings in the back seat, drop off Eric's corporate chief of technology, chief of finance, chief of theory, currency analyst, and doctor—all of whom *come to* the car.[23] Like many other pre-postmodern structures and artifacts, the office is, Eric thinks to himself, "outdated" (15). In between all these meetings, as the limousine continues its halting progress across the city, Eric also makes brief forays out of the car to have sex with a former mistress (and, later, a female bodyguard), to visit an underground dance club, to shoot a few baskets, and to get a haircut. In the course of the day, he loses his entire fortune (he is recklessly overleveraged on the yen), and then, deliberately, all of his wife's. He murders his bodyguard and, after abandoning the wreck of his limousine in the car barrens of Eleventh Avenue is, apparently, murdered in turn by an assassin who has been stalking him all day. The novel, thus, brings Eric's slow-motion urban Odyssey and itself to an end.

Cosmopolis is at once a meditation on the urban and virtual landscapes of global capital, and on the automobile in general and the postmodern limousine in particular, whose flickering screens reveal the mutual interpenetration of these two landscapes. The social hierarchy of the global city of New York extends along an automotive continuum (or, perhaps more accurately, a dis-continuum) that has the private stretch limousine at one end and the taxi at the other. The limousines of the "captains of global capital," who replaced earlier generations of "captains of industry," command the streets (until usurped by gridlock); the taxis driven by Third World refugees, "squeezed in alongside" (13). Pedestrians, sprinting for the curb as lumbering buses bear down on them, are "live prey" (41).

For Eric, the limousine is both an object of desire (and of the illusion of a fulfilled desire) and an assertion of power, "a tremendous mutant thing that stood astride every argument against it" (10). At the same time, the limousine's "presence" is curiously limited, since stretch limousines are so ubiquitous on the city streets that no one really notices them anymore. The interior of the car is an incongruous mixture of antique luxe and information-streaming high tech. The Proustian cork lining of the limousine is a sign of the automobile's literal (and anachronistic) insularity, like the Carrera marble floor, the red cedar paneling, the leather upholstery, and the ceiling mural displaying the position of the planets at Eric's birth. These anachronisms exist in intimate juxtaposition to the advanced information and imaging technologies in the limousine: up front are computer screens and a night-vision display for the infrared camera mounted on the car's exterior, and in back, along with the assemblage of visual display units on which arrays of data and video images play, the feed from the car's spycam. The limousine's contradictions are also those of Eric himself (and, to an ever greater extent, ours): the cerebral thrill of the frictionless cyber-spatial flow of data (and capital) circling the globe in nanoseconds versus the physical and emotional undertow of the material—the desire to hold, a longing for the tactile and the palpable (marble, cedar, leather), countering the conviction that everything is dematerializing, melting into air: "handheld space . . . was finished now" (13). Controlled by voice or a wave of the hand, the array of screens renders "the context . . . nearly touchless" (13).

Tropes of enclosure, insulation, and detachment proliferate around Eric. The limousine and the databanks of Packer Capital (both essentially extensions or projections of his ego) are said to be, like Eric's Cartesian fantasy of his own subjectivity, secure, impenetrable, invulnerable. (In the end, with the inevitable intervention of the reality principle, or the eruption of the real in the Lacanian sense, they turn out to be all too vulnerable.) These tropes are, as Eric's "touchless context" suggests, closely affiliated with the virtual flows of data and capital in the global markets, and with the exercises in analytical thought (cf. the Cartesian *cogito*) through which he probes their obscure patterns and discerns their "beauty and precision" (76).

Eric believes that the flows of data take him beyond the realm of human hopes and fears, that they capture something far deeper: "the zero-oneness of the world" (24). Yet Eric (and nearly everyone with whom he converses during the day) senses that something may escape even the most comprehensive and nuanced of data sets. Clearly Eric and those like him have power in the world—effects upon it—but meaning might be another matter entirely. The novel is, at least in part, a meditation on those aspects of existence that elude our technology's capture, that exceed its capacities, that cannot be digitized and downloaded. These are, it turns out, the true objects of Eric's (perhaps nostalgic) desire that motivate his seemingly quixotic day-long quest for the haircut. The significance of the haircut is intimated in Eric's reply to his chief of technology Shiner's inquiry of why, given the traffic, Eric doesn't have the barber meet him at the office or come to the car. A haircut, Eric explains, has "associations. Calendar on the wall. Mirrors everywhere. There's no barber chair here. Nothing swivels but the spycam" (15). On one, more immediate level, the haircut's meaning *is* meaning. Its more specific, personal meanings for Eric remain obscure until close to the end of the narrative. To Eric's final amazement and dismay, that meaning, for him, turns out to arise out of and be inextricably bound up with materiality (and temporality). His death is experienced as an inventory of all those elements of his life that cannot be contained or recaptured as "data."

Moving through the city, however, Eric sees signs all around him that suggest the material world (along with many of its technologies), even space, is obsolete. In the city of global capital, it is possible to feel, as Eric's currency analyst Michael Chin comments, "located totally nowhere" (23). The prototypical structures of this city are the looming towers of banks, "covert structures for all their size . . . so common and monotonic . . . [Eric] had to concentrate to see them" (36). Strangely mirage-like and distinguished by their "emptiness," the financial towers are essentially null spaces, virtual voids functioning as pure signifiers of global capital.[24] "They were in the future, a time beyond geography and touchable money and the people who stack and count it" (36). The towers seem to collapse both space and time, like the cyberspatial realms of global capital flow that are replacing them. Kinski argues that "it's cyber-capital that creates the future. . . . Because time is a corporate asset now. It belongs to the free market system. The present is harder to find. It is being sucked out of the world to make way for the future of uncontrolled markets and huge investment potential" (79).

This present–future urban geography, a space of signs and simulacra, coexists with the urban space that Eric, borrowing a term from cyberpunk, calls "meat space," a remnant of the past, a space of materiality—and nostalgia—outside (but, as nostalgia, also inside) the limousine. "There were days," he reflects, "when he wanted to eat all the time, talk to people's faces, live in meat space" (63–64). "Meat space" is also, thus, the space of corporeality, face-to-face interaction, and urban community. For Eric, the archetype of this urban space is the Diamond District, where capital still assumes its original material forms.

The materiality of the commerce and exchange that take place in the Diamond District is, Eric believes, the sign of its archaic, obsolete nature. This form of exchange produces or reproduces, in turn, archaic forms of subjectivity, community, and discourse: "Cash for gold and diamonds. Rings, coins, pearls, wholesale jewelry, antique jewelry. This was the souk, the shtetl. Here were the hagglers and talebearers, the scrapmongers, the dealers in straight talk. The street was an offense to the truth of the future" (64–65). As in the wider landscapes of global capitalism, past, present, and future modes of development coexist, however uneasily, in the global city, and Eric is amazed by "how things persist, the habits of gravity and time, in this new and fluid reality" (83). In this new "touchless" reality, nonetheless, the materiality of the city street still has unquestionable power, which he feels intensely, literally in his brain receptors (65).

Eric's own ambivalent relation to the contradictions of the materiality and virtuality of the postmodern city and era are apparent, too, in the ways he understands his own identity through the built space of the city, particularly (in ways not unlike Stan and Jimmy in Dos Passos's *Manhattan Transfer*) the high-rise residential tower he inhabits: "He felt contiguous with it. It was eighty-nine stories, a prime number . . . the tallest residential tower in the world" (8). The reference to prime numbers (divisible only by themselves and 1) and the pun on "prime" (prime real estate) is worth noting, and I shall further comment on numbers presently. While the banality of this bronze glass tower resembles that of the bank towers, it is its materiality that is significant for him in this case, as opposed to the immateriality of the bank towers, the near identity of the two images themselves notwithstanding or indeed because of it. Even leaving aside (if this is possible) the obvious phallic aspects of Eric's identification, it is clear that the materiality of the tower functions as a form of reassurance of his own substantiality: it "gave him strength and depth" (9). The tower also functions as a mirror, and in his narcissistic relation to it, one can perceive a reenactment of the Lacanian mirror stage that establishes the closed (and Cartesian), alienated, Ideal-*I*. This Ideal-*I* is indeed strictly *ideal*, an idea, since it hides a weakness and even impotence, and shallowness, which Eric's feelings of strength and depth can only superficially mask and from which they can only offer an illusion of protection. Studying the surface of the tower, Eric notes the way it reflects and refracts the light and the world around it, including his own image, reducing everything to just "a surface [that] separates inside from out and belongs no less to one than the other" (9).

While Eric is pondering the tower, however, he is also noting the obsolescence of the signifier "skyscraper" and of the old signifieds attached to it: "it belonged to the olden soul of awe, to the arrowed towers that were a narrative long before he was born" (9). This is the first of Eric's many meditations on the obsolescence of spaces (the office, the Diamond District, and so on), technologies, and their signifiers. As the rates of knowledge production and technological innovation accelerate, partly as functions of global capital and its mechanisms of "creative destruction," they increasingly render their own terms and tools obsolete. Particularly vulnerable are communication and information-processing technologies: among the words that Eric believes should be "retired" are "phone," "walkie-talkie," and "computer." Integrated into "smart" buildings, appliances (including devices such as camera phones), and clothing, computers are ceasing to exist as distinct objects. Devices (and workers) that handle cash, too, are antiquated in the world of electronic currency and transfers, and Eric wonders why cash registers are not relegated to museum displays. The dematerialization of money and capital has had a concomitant effect upon wealth and property and their signs. This effect is a variation on the latest stage of capitalism, the final *reductio ad absurdum* of the trajectory from the capitalism of things to the capitalism of signs to the capitalism of brands discussed in Chapter 1. In all of these previous forms of capitalism, though, there was still some link, however tenuous and remote, between the signifiers of wealth and some material thing (even if that thing was simply currency itself).

In the present-future of *Cosmopolis*, however, as Eric's chief of theory (also postmodern theory perhaps) Kinski observes, "all wealth has become wealth for its own sake" and "money has lost its narrative quality" (77). Like a kind of postmodern mathematics, defined only by its own reality, wealth and, as Kinski notes, property have become pure abstraction: "Money is talking to itself" (77)—about itself and only about itself. For those at the top of the capitalist food chain, property, capital in its many material incarnations, appears to be leaving behind previous paradigms of consumption—the conspicuous consumption of things, the consumption of signs promoted by the vignette-oriented advertising of the mid-twentieth century, and even the contemporary consumption of brands—and the forms of subjectivity and cities they helped to produce.[25] The concept of property has been transformed. The spectacular sums spent for land, buildings, automobiles, yachts, and private planes no longer serve the purpose of "traditional self assurances," Kinski explains. Property "is no longer about power, personality and command," nor is it a question of conspicuous consumption—"vulgar display or tasteful display" (78). What matters now is simply price—and, as Kinski argues, "the number justifies itself" (79).

Consumption at this level has become, perhaps for the first time in history, the attainment of a pure abstraction—"number itself." As Leopold Kronecker, a great nineteenth-century German mathematician and investment banker, famously said (speaking with both of his voices): "Natural numbers were the only thing created by God. Everything else was added by man." It seems possible that DeLillo might have had Kronecker's well-known pronouncement in mind here, given the novel's many references to numbers and Eric's preoccupation with them, a kind of discrete grid through which everything is seen and which reshapes everything. We recall that the number of stories in the tower where Eric lives is a prime, a piece of prime real estate signified by a (non-obvious) prime number (89). While the theory of primes is a major subject in modern number theory, of which Kronecker was one of the founders, primes have also been believed to have mystical significance throughout history. The number 89 itself has other interesting mathematical properties; for example, it is also a Fibonacci number, part of the sequence where each number is the sum of the two preceding numbers (1, 2, 3, 5, 8, 13, 21, 34, 55, 89, . . .). Fibonacci sequences (also thought, like primes, to have great mystical significance) appear in a remarkable array of natural phenomena, from the spirals of seashells and curling of waves to the branching of trees and leaves to the petals and arrangements on the seed heads of flowers. Fibonacci numbers are also related to the Golden Ratio Φ used so extensively throughout the history of architecture. DeLillo is likely to have had these easily available facts in mind, especially given his interest in mathematics and science in general, and to have used them in his portrayal of the conversion of the world into the world of numbers and/as capital in Eric's thinking, in the world in which there is nothing outside or other than numbers and capital.

The concrete manifestations of global capital are, nonetheless, still thunderingly apparent in the city. Across the urban landscape of DeLillo's cosmopolis, legions of bank towers are going up, and global capital's signifiers in the form of the names of financial institutions inscribed on buildings, too, are insistently ubiquitous. All this, however, is being superseded even as it is being produced. "The glow of cyber-capital. So radiant and seductive" illuminates the plasma screens inside Eric's limousine (78). Outside the windshield, the glow (and flow) of cybercapital can be found in the stock tickers streaming across the screens mounted on the exteriors of office towers. Distinguished by their multiplicity, abstraction, and, above all, speed, such displays are qualitatively different from the news flashes on the old Times Tower "zipper" that presented news as narrative—stories intended to be followed and understood. Now, there is only "the hellbent sprint of numbers and symbols, the fractions, decimals, stylized dollar signs, the streaming release of words . . . all too fleet to be absorbed" (80). Eric and Kinski's analysis of this scene might just as easily have been written by Debord or any of the other Situationists: what they are seeing is not "the flow of information so much as pure spectacle, or information made sacred, ritually unreadable . . . [producing] a kind of idolatry here, where crowds might gather in astonishment" (80).

Shortly thereafter crowds do gather, but not in astonishment. The anti-globalization protest, of which Eric has been seeing portents all day, begins in earnest near Times Square, where he hears plate glass shattering outside the NASDAQ Center. The protest takes two primary forms: symbolic actions (the release of swarms of rats in restaurants and hotels, a 20-foot-tall Styrofoam rat roaming the streets, people standing on corners dangling dead rats) and attacks on the sign systems of capital itself, the "video wall and logo ticker" (87).

The rats (symbols of filth, contagion, sewers, and slums) are riffs on a line from a poem: "a rat became the unit of currency."[26] The image is part of a metonymic constellation of meanings that encompasses, first, the Freudian symbolic economy (and equivalence) of money and excrement, and then, abjection and the "low Other." The protest also features the burning and trashing of cars, including Eric's limousine, which is pounded, spray painted, and pissed on. All these aspects of the protest might, in fact, be seen as an updated variation on the world-turned-upside-down of carnivalesque tradition (which it resembles in so many ways)—the "high," ruling class of globalization and its ethereal cybercapital associated with the "low," abject and excremental materiality of the rat.[27]

The protesters' attacks on the sign systems (both material and figural) of global capitalism include skateboarders graffiti-ing the ads on buses and men suspended from a rooftop, attempting to shatter the windows of a "tower [that] carried the name of a major investment bank . . . beneath a sprawling map of the world" (93). This aspect of the protest climaxes in the replacement of the electronic tickers on the face of the tower with a new message: "A SPECTER IS HAUNTING THE WORLD—THE SPECTER OF CAPITALISM" (96). The line is remarkable not just for its play on the first sentence of *The Communist Manifesto* (in which it is the specter of communism that's doing the haunting), but also for its oblique references to the spectacular (in Debord's sense) nature of global capital and to its specular virtuality. Yet, for Eric and Kinski, even the protest is ultimately reduced to merely a spectacle, even as the limousine they occupy is assaulted and trashed by the protesters.[28] "It made more sense on TV," Eric observes, as they watch the monitors in front of them (90). Kinski believes (and she might not be entirely wrong) that the protesters are only "a fantasy generated by the market. They don't exist outside the market . . . There is no outside" (90).

And yet, as Eric discovers, there are things the market and its data banks cannot completely assimilate and forces it cannot totally recuperate, including desire, chance, and death, itself ultimately a random event. Even when desire is directed, as in Eric's case on this particular day, toward currency itself and its numbers, it proves ultimately unlimited and uncontrollable, approaching the numerical infinity of Kant's mathematical sublime. "He wanted all the yen there was" (97), he thinks at one point, desire and its object here united by the double meaning of "yen." He believes what he can possess he can control, but an unfathomable (and incalculable) element of randomness enters into the yen's movements. Despite his conviction that "something" must explain the fluctuations of the yen and hence predict its behavior, the currency moves, impossibly and inexplicably, counter to his expectations.

Finally, it is death itself that proves the fallacy of capital's (and its technologies') omnipotence. Looking on as one of the protesters immolates himself, Eric is taken aback. The market, it appears, "could not claim this man or assimilate his act" (100). In death, the mind, inextricably entwined with the body, also ultimately exceeds the market's grasp. Wounded, watching the last seconds of his life tick away, Eric considers the ultimate fantasy of transcendence, now through technologies of information—the possibility of downloading his consciousness (which is, after all, a form of data) onto a computer chip, thus directly transforming human experience into yet another commodity. Yet, as he dies, he inventories all the things that define him and that cannot be turned into data, including his experiences and memories.

This final realization has, besides the immolation of the protestor, one other important precursor: the funeral cortège of a famous breakdancer that Eric comes upon late in the afternoon. What he is glimpsing, perhaps, is an intimation of a different mode of urban life, embodied in the material practices of the cortège's breakdancers and whirling dervishes. The cortège halts the flow of automobile traffic and replaces, at least for a moment, the spectacles of capital in the global city.[29] "How will we know when the global era officially ends?" Kinski asks. "When stretch limousines begin to disappear from the streets of Manhattan" (91). The limousine, too, will have, one day, to be replaced or at least displaced by other desiring-machines and by other forms of flow supported by the energy resources of the city. But which ones?

3. ACCELERATION FLOWS: FROM DÉRIVE TO PARKOUR

> The architecture of tomorrow will be a means of modifying present conceptions of time and space. It will be a *means of knowledge* and a *means of action*.
> —Ivan Chtcheglov, "Formulary for a New Urbanism"

> Find your black holes and white walls, know them. . . . it is the only way you will be able to dismantle them and draw your lines of flight.
> —Deleuze and Guattari, *A Thousand Plateaus*

"Situationism was founded upon the belief that general revolution would originate in the appropriation and alteration of the material environment and its space," Simon Sadler writes in *The Situationist City* (13). As he explains, "if one peeled away this official representation of modernity and urbanism—this 'spectacle,' as situationists termed the collapse of reality into the streams of images, products, and activities sanctioned by business and bureaucracy—one discovered the authentic life of the city teeming underneath" (15).[30]

The Situationists took the city, in particular the modernist city, as their primary object of critique, a critique carried out through what they conceived as "psychogeographical research." The latter was defined by Guy Debord as "the study of the exact laws and specific effects of the action of the geographical environment, consciously organized or not, on the emotions and behavior of individuals" ("Report" 23). Psychogeography can be seen partly as a response to the modernist architectural emphasis on the practical function of buildings and objects (exemplified, for instance, in Louis Sullivan's famous dictum that "Form follows function"), which generally failed to take into account the psychological effects they produced.[31] This research, however, was both present- and future-oriented; it involved both "active observation of present-day urban agglomerations and development of hypotheses on the structure of a [future] situationist city" ("Report" 23). In the Situationist city, a new, revolutionary mode of everyday life was to emerge as part of a program of "unitary urbanism," which aimed "to form a unitary human milieu in which separations such as work/leisure or public/private will finally be dissolved" ("Report" 23).

Beyond conceptual and ideological arguments, the Situationists' psychogeography involved a number of experimental practices or games, chief among which was the dérive, in which an individual or a small group wander (or drift) through the city streets, paying close attention to the ambiances of the places through which they pass, and to the specific emotions these ambiances evoke. The détourned collage maps Debord created (like "The Naked City" in Figure 4.5) to chart a dérive depict a Paris in fragments, linked by arrows of attraction or repulsion. Closer to Deleuze and Guattari's horizontal (rhizomic), as against vertical (arborescent) vision of life, the dérive produced a horizontal cartography of immersion (in contrast to the detached bird's-eye view of the city adopted by traditional cartographers and city planners), which intimately mapped the psychological atmospherics of the city.

In various ways, psychogeography and the dérive functioned as antidotes to what the Situationists saw as the pernicious effects of contemporary urban planning in the service of capital. In their view, modern urbanism was the spectacular ideology of modern capitalism made concrete, an exercise in organized mass alienation. "Urbanism is comparable to the advertising propagated around Coca-Cola—pure spectacular ideology. Modern capitalism, which organizes the reduction of all social life to a spectacle, is incapable of presenting any spectacle other than that of our own alienation," Attila Kotányi and Raoul Vaneigem wrote (65). This spectacularity and alienation were countered by the experiential knowledge produced by the dérive, which was at once subjective (or self-reflexive) in its emphasis on

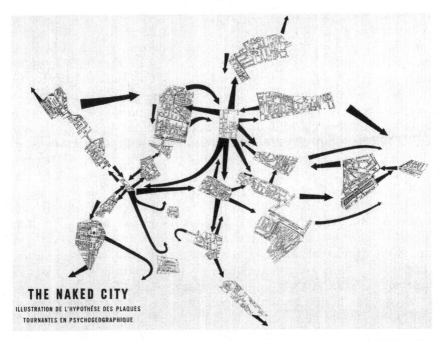

THE NAKED CITY

ILLUSTRATION DE L'HYPOTHÉSE DES PLAQUES
TOURNANTES EN PSYCHOGEOGRAPHIQUE

Figure 4.5   Guy Debord, "The Naked City," 1957. (Courtesy of RKD, The
Hague.)

the individual's interaction with the city, and objective, when undertaken
as a spontaneous group activity and in the subsequent collective critique
of the social ecology of the city. As revolutionary practice, the dérive and
other psychogeographical endeavors were also, as Sadler observes, "play-
ful, cheap, and populist . . . artistic activit[ies] carried out in the everyday
space of the street" (69).

The aleatory and transgressive nature of the "great game" of the dérive—
which Debord extended to include such activities as "slipping by night into
houses undergoing demolition, hitchhiking nonstop and without destination
through Paris during a transportation strike in the name of adding to the confusion, wandering in subterranean catacombs forbidden to the public, etc."—
undermined the Cartesian logic of Haussmannization and the rationalist grid
favored by Le Corbusier and other modernist architects and urban planners
("Theory" 53). Debord and other critics of this kind of modernism explicitly
linked this logic to the coercive power of the state, specifically, the creation
of open spaces and boulevards designed to facilitate the swift movements of
troops deployed against civil rebellions in the streets. "From any other stand-
point other than that of police control," Debord wrote, paraphrasing *Mac-
beth*, "Haussmann's Paris is a city built by an idiot, full of sound and fury,
signifying nothing" ("Introduction" 5). As discussed earlier, in the latter half
of the twentieth century, this urban strategy was amplified by forces such as

the hegemony of the automobile that led to further fragmenting and razing of historic quarters of the city. It also led to the proliferation on the outskirts of Paris of the sterile, prefab "Villes Nouvelles," whose motto, Debord claimed, could be: "On this spot nothing will ever happen, and *nothing ever has*" (*Society of the Spectacle* 177; his emphasis). Navigating the urban terrain, the dérive explored the fragments of what remained, mapped them, and wove them together into a kind of narrative, a "synchronic history." Through the practice of the dérive, unitary urbanism sought, in Henri Lefebvre's words, to "unify what has a certain unity, but a lost unity, a disappearing unity" ("Henri Lefebvre"). Lyotard would be likely to see this seeking of "a lost unity" (which could never have existed in the first place) as a form of *modernist* nostalgia, "the nostalgia for the unattainable," even if, on the positive side, it was a form of resistance to totalitarian, policing ideologies and practices of modernism, of a different modernism ("Answering" 81). For it is clear that the dérive and other Situationist practices, such as détournement and the creation of "situations," were far-reaching political gestures defining and redefining the memory of the city, including its future memory. In this respect they played an important role in the history of the movement toward postmodern spatiality, specifically more horizontal and smoother spaces in Deleuze and Guattari's sense.

In the Situationist movement, one finds not only the countering of one ideology by another, or, if one extends the Cartesian logic in question to certain modernist avant-garde movements, one avant-garde by a counter-avant-garde, or, again, one modernism by a counter-modernism, but also and more significantly, a countering of both the dominant ideology and the (destructive) urban practices defined by them through new forms of material practice. These practices directly involve citydwellers in creating new city spaces and new subjectivities through reciprocal processes that are interactively cultural, political, and aesthetic. On the deepest level, the Situationists sought to combat the modernist creation (as in the Villes Nouvelles) or imposition upon the city (as in the razing of much of Beaubourg and the Les Halles market) of a kind of Newtonian or Cartesian ambient "absolute" space (or time), into which subjects are placed, subjects that are pre-defined or determinately, rather than reciprocally, defined, including by the space. "All space is already occupied by the enemy, which has even reshaped its elementary laws, its geometry, to its own purposes," Kotányi and Vaneigem argued (67).

The result of this occupation has been and, according to the Situationists, could only ever be a universal, ever-increasing isolation and alienation of the subject in this determinate coordinate space. Through the dérive and other participatory practices, the Situationists attempted to counter the utilitarian logic (signaled by such watchwords as "the functional" and "the practical") of modern architecture and urban planning and the alienation they produced. In the "Elementary Program of the Bureau of Unitary Urbanism," Kotányi and Vaneigem propose an alternative to modernist architecture's definition or conception of "the functional": "The functional is what is practical. The only thing that is practical is the resolution of our fundamental problem: our self-realization (our escape from the system of isolation). This and nothing else is useful and utilitarian" (67). The resolution of "the fundamental problem" was to be found in the reciprocal creation of urban spaces and urban subjects, a process for which the Situationists created a material model by such practices as the dérive. Debord saw the dérive as "a rough experimentation toward a new mode of behavior . . . which is the practice of a passional journey out of the ordinary" ("Report" 24). Such experimentation was integral to the creation of a new way of life, one that would transform daily reality into creative play.

Even if one were to question certain aspects of the Situationist philosophical vision, as I suggested one could, one would still have to acknowledge in the play of the dérive itself the potential emergence of a new type of city space and a new form of subjectivity. The dérive produced a multiple and continuously varied space of possibility, "the terrain of a game in which one [indeed] participates," and a revolutionary subject, *homo ludens* ("Unitary" 144).[32] Both would emerge and develop in their continuous and reciprocal reshaping of one another.

An analogous and related, but more radical, transformation is at stake in parkour, the other form of urban movement and play that I want to discuss in this chapter as part of my exploration of postmodern urban flows and their interplay. Defined by originator David Belle as "an art to help you pass any obstacle," the practice of "parkour" or "free running" constitutes both a mode of movement and a new way of interacting with the urban environment. Parkour was created by Belle (partly in collaboration with his childhood friend Sébastien Foucan) in France in the late 1980s. Parkour practitioners (known as "traceurs") leap, spring, and vault from objects in the urban milieu that are intended to limit movement (curbs, railings, fences) or that unintentionally hamper passage (walls, lampposts, street signs, benches) through the space.

"Rush Hour," a short video trailer for BBC One featuring David Belle, was among the first media representations of parkour, and it played a major role in introducing and popularizing the practice in Britain.[33] Parkour has subsequently been widely disseminated via news reports, Nike and Toyota ads, the documentaries *Jump London* (2003) and *Jump Britain* (2005), and feature films, including Luc Besson's *Yamakasi—Les Samouraïs des temps modernes* (2001) and *Banlieue 13* (2004; released in the U.S. as *District B13*), starring David Belle and Cyril Raffaelli. Sébastien Foucan appeared in the James Bond film *Casino Royale* (2006) as Mollaka, a terrorist who is chased (parkour-style) and then killed by Bond. Madonna's 2006 "Confessions Tour" featured an extended parkour sequence (accompanying the song "Jump"), albeit one limited to the confines of a scaffold erected over the stage. Perhaps most important in the rapid development of parkour into a worldwide youth movement, however, has been the proliferation of park-our websites featuring amateur videos, photos, tutorials, and blogs.

The word *parkour* is derived from the French *parcours* (as the sport is known in France): a line, course, circuit, road, way or route; and from the verb *parcourir*: to travel through, to run over or through, to traverse. As a physical discipline, parkour might be said to have a "poetics"—first, in general, in the Aristotelian sense of constructing through its various techniques (*technē*) the drama of each parkour event. Secondly, one can approach parkour, following Aristotle's model of four-cause analysis, by considering its specific *materials* (the body and the city), *form* or vocabulary of movements (drawn primarily from gymnastics, the martial arts, and modern dance), *genre* (as against, say, gymnastics), and *purpose*, including its effects upon its audience and the traceurs themselves. The existing literature on parkour (at this point, mostly news reports or websites) tends to emphasize the elements of form or movement, such as parkour's various climbs, leaps, vaults, and drops, and the question of genre, particularly the ongoing, heated disputes among traceurs regarding what is or is not true parkour (as opposed, say, to freerunning). By contrast, I would like to focus on the materials and purpose of parkour: on the nature of the city and the body as they relate to parkour, and on the ways in which it can be seen to remap urban space and demonstrate a resistance to its disciplinary functions, particularly as manifest in the urban street grid.

As discussed in detail earlier, the institution of the street grid (or variations upon it such as Haussmann's Parisian star-configuration) facilitates

Figure 4.6 David Belle in Luc Besson's film, *Banlieue 13*.

both the intelligibility—in terms of both navigation and surveillance—and control of space in the city. It situates people in urban spaces in determinate ways and institutes a channeling of pedestrian and vehicular traffic. The grid thus carries a number of normalizing and disciplinary functions, creating in effect a "striation" of urban space in Deleuze and Guattari's sense, as considered in Chapter 2. This striation constitutes "a process of capture of flows of all kinds, populations, commodities or commerce, money or capital, etc." within a field of determinate spatial coordinates, and it establishes "fixed paths in well-defined directions, which restrict speed, regulate circulation, relativize movement, and measure in detail the relative movements of subjects and objects" (Deleuze and Guattari, *A Thousand Plateaus* 386). Many of these aspects of striation can be seen in the ways urban space is depicted in the "Rush Hour" video: in the gridlocked traffic, the flashing lights, the "STOP" light and "WAIT" sign, the sign indicating the proper directional flow of traffic, and the grim, bundled-up pedestrians trudging home en masse along the congested streets.

Against these images of conformity, regulation, and confinement, the video presents the parkour ethos of originality, "reach," escape, and freedom. Belle's (shirtless) aerial traversal of the urban space between his office and his flat—a swift, improvisational flow across the open rooftops (and the voids between them), off walls, and finally down the sloping roof into his apartment window—cuts across the striated space of the streets below and positions him, for that time, beyond the constrictions of the social realm and its "concrete" manifestations. Though parkour necessarily involves obstacles that must be overcome, the goal of parkour is to do this as smoothly and efficiently as possible, or, in the language of its practitioners, for the movement to be "fluid like water" (Law). The experience of parkour might, then, be said to transform the urban landscape into "smooth space," in Deleuze and Guattari's sense of "a field without conduits or channels" (*A Thousand Plateaus* 371), and thus into a space of uninhibited movement, at least in certain ideal moments. Parkour seems to trace a path of desire (even if the desire is simply to avoid the crowds and get home in time to watch BBC One) that moves along what Deleuze and Guattari refer to as a "line of flight," a potential avenue of escape from the forces of striation and repression. The body is propelled over or through (most parkour movement actually takes place at ground level) the strata of urban space, perhaps with the hope that, as Deleuze and Guattari suggest, "one will bolster oneself directly on a line of flight enabling one to blow apart strata, cut roots, and make new connections" (*A Thousand Plateaus* 15). In the process, parkour becomes "an art of displacement," appropriating urban space in ways that temporarily disrupt their controlling logics and even imply the possibility of a smooth space of desire.

One might equally see parkour as an overcoming of social space (and its various constrictions and inhibitions of desire, its "WAIT" and "STOP" signs) through the interplay of body and material barriers. The body becomes an instrument of freedom. This, again, is graphically conveyed in "Rush Hour" through the opening scene in which Belle strips off his business suit and through the subsequent repeated contrasts of his limber, revealed body with the rigid, swathed figures of the pedestrians below.

Through the practice of parkour, the relation between body and space is made dynamic, two reality principles in concert, interacting amid a suspension of the social strata. One might even say that the urban space is re-embodied—its rigid strata effectively liquified. In *Jump London*, the traceur Jerome Ben Aoues speaks of a Zen-like "harmony between you and the obstacle," an idealization of what is sometimes described as a state of flow, a seemingly effortless immersion in an activity with an attendant loss of self-consciousness. It suggests a different way of knowing the city, a knowledge of experience as opposed to abstract knowledge: parkour is, Jaclyn Law argues, "about curiosity and seeing possibilities—looking at a lamppost or bus shelter as an extension of the sidewalk." "You just have to look," Sébastien Foucan insists in *Jump London*, "you just have to think like children."

Most crucial for my analysis here, however, is that parkour remaps and even recreates urban space, creating a city parallel to the one defined by rigid striations and grids: a *ludic city*, a city of movement and free play within and against the city of obstacles and inhibitions. By so doing, parkour reminds us, as does the dérive but still more radically and dramatically, that, as Lefebvre put it, "the space of play has coexisted and still coexists with spaces of exchange and circulation, political space and cultural space" ("Perspective" 172). In other words, at least one smooth urban space has always coexisted and still coexists with urban striated spaces. Parkour tells us that in order to enter or re-enter this smooth space of play, we only need to make the leap.

Parkour, thus, confirms and affirms Deleuze and Guattari's assessment that it is possible to "live smooth even in the [overly striated] cities" (*A Thousand Plateaus* 482). Still, in parkour, too, "voyaging smoothly is a becoming, and a difficult, uncertain becoming at that. . . . The confrontation between the smooth and the striated, the passages, alternations, and superpositions, are underway today, running in the most varied directions" (*A Thousand Plateaus* 482). This is virtually a literal anticipatory description of parkour (anticipating it, in 1980, only by a few years and reflecting the same world of the smooth and the striated), while parkour is reciprocally an allegory of this postmodern becoming, especially the urban one. This becoming also reveals the irreducible complexity—both smooth and striated, heterogeneous and interactive, local and global, modern and postmodern—of our urban spaces and movements or moves, past, present, and future. Of course, it is the future that is especially at stake in our rethinking and reshaping of our cities and the global, geopolitical world in which they exist and which they, in turn, define.

5   Global Cities and Citizens

> To a wise man, the whole earth is open; for the native land of a good
> soul is the whole earth.
>
> —Democritus of Abdera

In 1967, at the beginning of the postmodern era, Marshall McLuhan hailed
the "brand-new world of allatonceness. 'Time' has ceased, 'space' has
vanished. We now live in a global village . . . a simultaneous happening"
(*Medium*). Some forty years later, the global interconnectedness McLuhan
perceived has only intensified as the transnational circulation of people,
capital, goods, images, and ideas reaches historically unprecedented levels.
Never before have so many people been on the move; never before has there
been such global economic integration.[1] The effects of this global circulation and integration are complex. In some respects, they foster similarities
among cultures and, in particular, a Westernization of a significant part of
the postmodern global landscape due to the power of Western capital and
its comparatively greater ability to disseminate Western culture. While the
global circulation of Western commodities and culture thus fosters some
degree of homogeneity, it often amplifies differences as well and forces
them into close spatial and temporal proximity. One might say that in this
"brand-new world," time has not so much ceased as telescoped: medieval
mindsets collide with the modern, the modern with the postmodern, and
the world seems to have more history than it can possibly assimilate or reconcile. A very different form of cultural spacetime emerges as a result.

This global landscape (or landscapes) is far from an amicable village,
however, as we tend to think of "village," or perhaps it is a different, more
discontinuous or heterogeneous (and extremely populous) type of village.
McLuhan's famous formulation of the "global village" is often taken to
imply a considerably more optimistic view than was actually the case. The
proximities created by twentieth-century advances in transportation and
communication technologies were not necessarily comfortable ones, and
the global village, as McLuhan realized, was not likely to be a peaceful
place. "The more you create village conditions, the more discontinuity and
division and diversity," he said in a 1967 interview (Stearn 314). Foresee-
ing the paradoxical divisiveness, the rising ethnic and religious conflicts
that have accompanied the shrinking globe, McLuhan argued that "the
global village absolutely insures maximal disagreement on all points. . . .

The tribal–global village is far more divisive—full of fighting—than any nationalism was. Village is fission, not fusion, in depth" (Stearn 314–15).

This statement anticipates one of the great paradoxes of postmodernity: the proliferation of transnational or supranational economic, political, technological, and cultural flows and fusions across the globe and, simultaneously, the explosion of neotribalism in the form of ethnic and religious conflict and separatism (often deploying the discourses of nationalism, national sovereignty, and self-determination)—the fissions of identity politics writ large. As Pico Iyer notes, by now "it's familiar to hear that the stories on the 'Business' and 'Technology' pages of our newspapers—about international coproductions and virtual 'town halls'—contradict the ones on our front pages (about tribal conflict and 'Balkanization')" (36). The world at our doorstep confronts us with how much we share and, simultaneously, how much we do not.

Perhaps nothing helps us to understand this new landscape of postmodern global flows better than the global cities—those cities where the local and the global intertwine, overlap, and collide, and where the impact of transnational capitalism and consumer society are most apparent. How we might best negotiate and live together amid our increasingly intimate proximities are pressing questions. The global cities are, in effect, laboratories of the future, places where we might work out the new political imaginaries that the postmodern world requires at the global, transnational, national, regional, metropolitan, and personal levels.

In this chapter, I want to conceptualize these global and urban imaginaries through different ideas of "cosmopolitanism," from (1) the "free market" cosmopolitanism that underlies and drives the globalization that is the economic framework and foundation of the global city; to (2) the cultural cosmopolitanism that is in many ways bound up with market cosmopolitanism but also might offer ways to see beyond it; to (3) the ethical-political cosmopolitanisms that are, at least in part, responses to the forces of market cosmopolitanism; and, finally, to the complex ways in which all of these cosmopolitanisms are intertwined with one another, most especially through the ideas and practices of law, justice, and hospitality.[2] I argue that all these cosmopolitanisms are, ultimately, necessary to one another: we need them all. Finally, they must function not just collectively on local, national, and global levels, but also on the personal, conscious, and critical levels. In other words, while, given their pervasiveness in our world, our unconscious cannot avoid these cosmopolitanisms, they must be lived consciously and subjected to our critical consciousness. Apart from the fact that it would be unwise and even dangerous to repress them, we need to actively shape them by our participation in them as cosmopolitans ourselves, as citizens of the world, which, as will be seen throughout this chapter, most especially in the final section, will not be easy. Even though it may be difficult and sometimes nearly impossible, however, it is still necessary.

I shall begin the chapter by outlining some of the trajectories of the idea of cosmopolitanism. The aim of this outline is not to offer a proper historical account of the subject, which would require a chapter of its own, but instead to trace, among these trajectories and junctures, two in particular that are specifically pertinent to my main subject. The first juncture, which arguably introduced the concept, is located in ancient Greek philosophy; the second is found in the Enlightenment, especially in Kant's meditations on the subject, which are indispensable to the subsequent history of the idea of cosmopolitanism and our own understanding of it. In this respect my discussion is, in Nietzsche's terms (in *On the Genealogy of Morals*), *genealogical* rather than historical, insofar as it considers the key forms of the idea of cosmopolitanism. Then I shall discuss, via some further genealogical links, the three types of contemporary or postmodern cosmopolitanisms defined earlier: "free market" cosmopolitanism, cultural cosmopolitanism, and ethical-political cosmopolitanism, and the ways in which they are connected through ideas of law, justice, and hospitality. I shall also consider in this context, most especially in Section 4, the question of postmodern subjectivity, that of the "global citizens" of my title, and specifically postmodern urban subjectivity, that of the "global cities" of my title.

My discussion throughout this chapter will be illustrated and supported by analyses of several recent films which engage these cosmopolitan themes. It may well be, to paraphrase Lenin, that of all of the arts, the most important for us is cinema, that is, the most important for our understanding and practice of postmodern cosmopolitanism (Lenin spoke of communism). I close Section 5 and the chapter with an extended discussion, via Jacques Derrida's analysis of cosmopolitanism, of Michael Haneke's film *Code Unknown*, which appears to me to portray (in a particularly dramatic fashion) the three types of cosmopolitanism, their intertwining, and their reciprocity with our postmodern subjectivities as global citizens in global cities.

1. BRIEF GENEALOGIES, ANCIENT AND MODERN

The roots of the cosmopolitan ideal lie deep in the Western tradition. Diogenes the Cynic (in the fourth century BCE) was the first Western philosopher known to actually use the term "cosmopolitan," claiming in response to a query about his origins, "I am *kosmopolitês*" (63), literally, a citizen (*politês*) of the world or universe (*kosmos*). The *idea* of cosmopolitanism and a cosmopolitan identity can, however, can be traced back at least as far as Socrates and Plato in the fifth and early fourth century BCE. We can see it articulated, for instance, by the Sophist Hippias of Elis in Plato's *Protagoras* (written around 380 BCE). The dialogue recounts a conversation that takes place among the guests assembled at the house of Callias, including

Socrates and Protagoras, whose exchanges grow increasingly contentious as the evening wears on. Near the midpoint of the dialogue, several of the other guests intervene in an attempt to reconcile Socrates and Protagoras, so that their conversation might, as Prodicus puts it, "be a discussion, not a dispute" (337b). Hippias follows up this suggestion by declaring, "Gentlemen. . . I count you all my kinsmen and family and fellow citizens—by nature [*physis*], not by custom [*nomos*]. By nature like is kin to like, but custom, the tyrant of mankind, does much violence to nature" (337c–d; translation modified).[3] The statement, like that of Diogenes, is a provocative challenge to, and implicit refusal of, the ancient Greek understanding of "citizenship" as defined by an allegiance to the city-state (the *polis*, from which the word *politês* is derived).[4] Despite Hippias's subsequent claim that the company constitutes "the intellectual leaders of Greece . . . now assembled in Athens, the center and shrine of Greek wisdom" (337d), an assertion that acknowledges a pan-Hellenic community, the appeal to a common ("like") humanity and a natural kinship among an implied "family of men," in contrast to the tyranny of custom, is a powerful one.

Hippias's statement, in the midst of a dialogue dealing with questions of ignorance and wisdom, evil and virtue, appears to suggest both an ethical and a political conception of cosmopolitanism. It is ethical insofar as it suggests a "natural" (a term that for the ancient Greeks and especially the Cynics would have implied an inherent goodness) obligation to an "other," a "stranger," that might supersede or extend one's duty beyond the city-state, and lead to a corresponding moral code; and it is political insofar as it proposes a form of citizenship that might transcend the boundaries (both territorial and governmental/administrative) of the city-state or such pan-Hellenic orders as the Greek or Delian Leagues.[5]

Both ethical and political cosmopolitanism were more fully developed by the Greek and, later, the Roman Stoics. The Greek Stoics saw the cosmos as the true polis, a "cosmopolis" ordered by the law of divine reason. To be virtuous, they believed, one should live in accord with human nature as a citizen of the cosmos, willingly extending one's ethical concern and aid to others beyond the confines of one's own (conventional) *polis* or *patria*. (For the Roman Stoics, rationality was the basis on which citizenship is extended to everyone, and the view of humans as rational beings will also be crucial for Kant's moral cosmopolitanism.) As has been noted, however, the Stoics' models of cosmopolitanism might be seen as effectively positing two potentially competing communities (*poleis* or *patriae*).

"Strict" cosmopolitans, deciding on the basis of where they might do the most good, would not necessarily give priority to helping those closest at hand, but "moderate" cosmopolitans, acknowledging a duty to their compatriots, might (such was the case in the later Stoicism of Cicero and Seneca, for instance). It is, of course, possible that one could encounter a conflict between one's duty to the *polis* or *patria* and to the cosmopolis—a conflict that has been all too familiar to modernity and then postmodernity as well, as it was to the ancient Greeks. In the postmodern world, however, this conflict does not appear to have a general, natural or universal, resolution to which one can appeal (in the way, for example, the Stoics appeal to nature or the divine in favoring the cosmopolis) but only a particular and even singular resolution, in favor of the polis or the cosmopolis, each time it arises.

Discourses on cosmopolitanism reappear, in various forms, with the rise and the development ("progress") of modernity, especially during the Enlightenment (cosmopolitan *practices* might be argued to be more common throughout modernity, roughly from the fifteenth century to the present). In eighteenth-century Europe, the terms "cosmopolitanism" and "world citizenship" frequently referred to a kind of cultural cosmopolitanism: they were used, as Pauline Kleingeld and Eric Brown note, "not as labels for determinate philosophical theories, but rather to indicate an attitude of open-mindedness and impartiality. A cosmopolitan was someone who was not subservient to a particular religious or political authority, someone who was not biased by particular loyalties or cultural prejudices" (5). The sense of a transnational community of intellectuals, a "Republic of Letters," was a part of this period's cultural cosmopolitanism, which also, however, had a political aspect because of the religious and state censorship to which many among the more prominent of them (including David Hume, Denis Diderot, Voltaire, and, later on, John Stuart Mill) were subject.[6]

The key eighteenth-century philosophical thinker of moral and political cosmopolitanism is, of course, Kant, and his work has profoundly influenced subsequent thought, such as Goethe's, and debates concerning the subject and the practices of cosmopolitanism. Kant's conceptions of morality and ethics, out of which arise his ideas on cosmopolitanism, are grounded in his definition of humans as beings of both reason and will (attributes that establish their status as "ends-in-themselves"): humans have the capacity to rationally determine what is right (i.e., moral) and wrong, and the will to act in accordance with that determination. According to Kant, reason itself dictates an unconditional moral imperative, the categorical imperative, for which he offers three formulations in *Groundwork of the Metaphysics of Morals*:

1. "Act only in accordance with that maxim through which you can at the same time will that it become a universal law" (31). This injunction effectively removes both subjectivity (in the sense of the subjective, rather than objective, character of our assessments) and particularity from our moral calculations.
2. "Act as if the maxim of your action were to become by your will a universal law of nature" (31). The addition of "nature" to what is otherwise essentially a restatement of the first formulation arguably has the effect of precluding the possibility of contradiction in moral maxims since, by definition, laws of nature cannot be contradictory.

3. "So act that you use humanity, whether in your own person or in the person of any other, always at the same time as an end, never merely as a means" (38). This injunction to treat oneself and others solely as ends-in-themselves, rather than as means to an end, is based in Kant's view of humans as beings of unconditional worth by virtue of their rationality and will.

The assumed universality of a human capacity to rationally determine what is right and of the categorical imperative implicitly suggests a form of moral cosmopolitanism (inasmuch as we are all bound by laws of morality grounded in reason). This form of moral cosmopolitanism creates a foundation for Kant's political and legal cosmopolitanism as articulated in both "Idea for a Universal History from a Cosmopolitan Point of View" and "Perpetual Peace." Kant's underlying assumptions concerning human nature have, of course, been questioned, and this questioning also poses problems for the ideal of cosmopolitanism. I shall discuss some of these problems below. For the moment, however, I shall continue to follow Kant's own cosmopolitan vision.

Kant's teleological vision of human history, set forth in his "Idea for a Universal History," foresees a future in which human beings behave "like rational citizens of the world" (12). This cosmopolitan ideal entails *the achievement of a universal civic society which administers law among men*" (16; his emphasis) and within which man's natural capacities can be developed to their fullest potential, as Nature herself intends.[7] Bringing this universal society into being depends upon establishing a lawful relation between states, which would otherwise remain antagonistic to one another and engage in war and other hostilities. And it is the evils and costs of war, Kant believes, that will ultimately compel states to institute this universal civic society—a "great league of nations" (19). Only within such a league, "a united power acting according to decisions reached under the laws of their united will," can "even the smallest state . . . expect security and justice," Kant argues (19). And only within this *"perfectly constituted state"* will human beings find the *"condition in which the capacities of mankind can be fully developed"* (21; his emphasis).

In "Perpetual Peace," Kant articulates both "preliminary" and "definitive" "articles for perpetual peace among states"—principles that should govern international relations in a new global civic order. The "preliminary" articles appear to have the dual aim of ensuring the sovereign integrity of nations (they decree that *"No Independent States . . . Shall Come under the Dominion of Another State"* and prohibit interference with the constitution or government of one state by another, for example) and of preventing friction and ensuring amity between states by, among other things, calling for the abolition of standing armies ("Perpetual Peace" 86). The injunction that *"The Civil Constitution of Every State Should Be Republican"* (which is the first "definitive" article) is also, to a great extent, based in the desire to ensure peace, which a republican constitution facilitates by requiring the consent of citizens to declarations of war ("Perpetual Peace" 93).[8]

In the second definitive article, Kant asserts that *"The Law of Nations Shall be Founded on a Federation of Free States"* that would remain distinct, rather than being "amalgamated into one" ("Perpetual Peace" 98). This federation or league of nations does not have coercive power over the member states, since such power might endanger the individual states' sovereignty and also, conceivably, the rights and freedoms of their citizens: instead, it tends "only to the maintenance and security of the state itself and of other states in league with it, without there being any need for them to submit to civil laws, and their compulsion, as men in a state of nature must submit" ("Perpetual Peace" 100). There is some debate concerning the consistency of Kant's argument (see Kleingeld and Brown), which need not be entered here. What is important here is that Kant's "law of nations" would effectively create a "third sphere" of public law—"cosmopolitan law"—"in addition to constitutional law and international law—in which both states and individuals have rights, and where individuals have these rights as 'citizens of the earth' rather than as citizens of particular states" (Kleingeld and Brown 6).

The final article of "Perpetual Peace" states that *"The Law of World Citizenship Shall Be Limited to Conditions of Universal Hospitality"* (102). "Hospitality," Kant insists, "is not a question of philanthropy but of right," and this right to hospitality is common to all men "by virtue of their common possession of the surface of the earth" (102–3). According to Kant, this right entails "the right of a stranger not to be treated as an enemy when he arrives in the land of another," although "one might refuse to receive him when this can be done without causing his destruction" (102). It does not constitute a "right to be a permanent visitor," but "only a right of temporary sojourn" (102–3). It guarantees "a right to associate," and, further, "to establish communication" (103). These last two are important aids to both cultural cosmopolitanism and, for Kant, political cosmopolitanism. He connects them directly to the project of "peaceable relations" among distant nations and to bringing the human race "closer and closer to a constitution establishing world citizenship" (103).

Writing in 1795, Kant asserted that the time was ripe for the establishment of such a constitution: "Since the narrower or wider community of the peoples of the earth has developed so far that a violation of rights in one place is felt throughout the world, the idea of a law of world citizenship is no high-flown or exaggerated notion. It is a supplement to the unwritten code of the civil and international law, indispensable for the maintenance of the public human rights and hence also of perpetual peace" ("Perpetual Peace" 105). Kant, thus, defined the geo-political "grand narrative" (in Lyotard's sense) of progress toward perpetual peace. Although none of them can be considered to have fulfilled Kant's vision and some of them may reflect the weaknesses of this vision, twentieth-century organizations such as the League of Nations and its successor, the United Nations, the International Criminal Court, and even the European Union might be seen as its inheritors.

It is equally crucial, however, that, while present-day cosmopolitanisms owe much to Kant or the Stoics and other precursors, they have also moved beyond them in important ways, as my discussion of the contemporary, postmodern, landscape(s) of cosmopolitanism in the remainder of this chapter will show. As stated at the outset, I shall address three forms of contemporary cosmopolitanism—"free market cosmopolitanism," cultural cosmopolitanism, and ethical-political cosmopolitanism—and the complex ways in which they intertwine and interact with one another, especially through the ideas of law, justice, and hospitality, and how they shape and are reciprocally shaped by urban spaces and subjectivities.

2. FREE MARKET COSMOPOLITANISM, POST-ENLIGHTENMENT AND POSTMODERN

I begin with market cosmopolitanism, which owes more to another eighteenth-century thinker, Adam Smith, than to Kant or other figures just discussed. Markets and their cosmopolitanism, I argue, *create* a strong need for new forms of cultural, political, and moral cosmopolitanisms in the global cities and world they have done so much to shape. Market cosmopolitanism might be understood as the conceptual and philosophical, or ideological, underpinning of globalization in the economic sense of the worldwide integration of markets for goods, services, capital, and labor. Guided by classic economic theory, initiated by Smith's *Wealth of Nations*, market cosmopolitans generally advocate laissez-faire capitalism, open markets, and free trade. Believing that markets are self-regulating, market cosmopolitans seek to reduce governmental involvement (including regulatory laws and restrictions on trade, tariffs, and other protectionist measures) in the economy. They rely on nations recognizing that they will maximize economic gain through international free trade and mutual cooperation, and they tend to discount the possibility that capitalist nations might find it advantageous to go to war over natural resources such as oil. They believe that free trade among nations united in one global market will bring mutual benefit, prosperity, and peace.

Since the 1980s, globalization has proceeded apace as major national industries have been privatized and deregulated around the world, national markets have become increasingly open to foreign competition and ownership, and the volume of international trade (greatly facilitated by advances in communication and transportation technologies) has grown prodigiously. These changes, as scholars such as Saskia Sassen, Peter J. Taylor, Manuel Castells, David Harvey, and Edward Soja have shown, have "re-scaled" the international economic system. Throughout the twentieth century, the key agents or "articulators" of economic flows were nation states, but now this is less and less the case. The forces of globalization are shifting power and importance away from the nation state, both upwards to global markets (including digitalized ones) and trading blocs, and downwards to cities and regions (some of them cutting across adjacent national borders).

The globalizing forces and technologies (including communication technologies that allow for "telecommuting" and videoconferencing) that many believed heralded the imminent decline or even demise of major cities have not, it turns out, had that effect. But they have reoriented and reorganized urban economies in ways that have changed the physical, demographic, social, political, and cultural character of many cities, particularly the global cities of the First World (e.g., New York, London, and Tokyo) and the megalopolises of, to use an increasingly outdated denomination (specifically in the present context), the Third World (e.g., Shanghai, Mexico City, Cairo, Mumbai, and São Paulo). To explore the effects of the developing global economy on cities, however, it is helpful to set aside, for the moment, "the familiar issues of the power of large corporations over governments and economies, or supracorporate concentration of power through interlocking directorates or organizations, such as the IMF" (which have been much studied in recent decades), and follow Sassen's shift in focus to what she refers to "as the *practice* of global control: the work of producing and reproducing the organization and management of a global production system and a global marketplace for finance" (6).[9]

The global cities of New York, London, and Tokyo are the primary sites of production (in the form of specialized services and financing) of this "new global control capability," which involves particular forms of centralization and agglomeration. The effects of the decentralization of economic activity involved in this form of production, on the other hand, can be seen in deindustrialized cities such as Detroit and Liverpool, and in the rapidly industrializing centers of the Third World: these, too, are forms of the postmodern city. Given the specific aim and scope of this study, however, in this context, too, I focus primarily on the global, First World cities, where the distinguishing features of urban postmodernity take their most dramatic form.

What is driving the growth of the global cities and shaping their particular economic structures is, as Sassen demonstrates, a complex dynamic arising out of the nature of the production involved in organizing and managing a globalized economy. She posits that "the geographic dispersal of economic activities that marks globalization, along with the simultaneous integration of such geographically dispersed activities, is a key factor feeding the growth and importance of central corporate functions," which include "managing, coordinating, servicing, [and] financing a firm's network of operations" (xix-xx). Whenever possible, many of these complex central functions not involving direct management of corporate operations

Figure 5.1   Shanghai, 2001. (Image by Corbis.)

are outsourced to independent firms specializing in legal, financial, accounting, marketing, management consulting, and computer services.

It is worth noting that the global cities themselves are not necessarily the predominant sites of corporate headquarters (particularly in countries with strong communication and transportation infrastructures), although many, especially those of banks and other financial firms, are still to be found there. Rather, they are sites where the firms that provide the array of specialized *services* required (often simultaneously) by transnational corporations are concentrated. These services now constitute the "economic backbone" or base of global cities. In other words, "the 'things' a global city makes are highly specialized services and financial goods" (Sassen 5). Significant synergies result from this concentration of specialized firms and the highly educated professionals they employ. "Being in a city," Sassen argues, "becomes synonymous with being in an extremely intense and dense information loop that . . . has as one of its value-added features the fact of unforeseen and unplanned mixes of information, expertise and talent, which can produce a higher order of information. . . . Global cities are, in this regard, production sites for the leading information industries of our time" (xx). They are, thus, fertile ground for the development and consumption of innovations both *by* and *for* these growing service industries, for example, for Microsoft in Shanghai (Figure 5.1).

The shift in the economic base from industry to services has profoundly affected the distribution of income in cities like New York and London. Whereas the often-unionized manufacturing jobs in the post-war industrial cities of the United States and United Kingdom fostered a large middle class, service jobs in the global cities turn out to promote economic polarization. At one end of the income spectrum are the highly paid service professionals—the attorneys, accountants and financial managers, the marketing and advertising specialists, the consultants, and the computer programmers. At the opposite end are the clerical workers, taxi-drivers, waiters and busboys, deliverymen, shop clerks, cleaners, and health-care and child-care workers, many of them working at or near (below or slightly above) the minimum wage, who serve the highly paid professionals, along with a remainder of low-wage, nonunionized manufacturing piece-workers. While acknowledging that the percentage of low-income workers tends to be lower in global cities than in other cities, Sassen observes that "this outcome can still coincide with growing inequality inside global cities" (249). The middle is shrinking and, increasingly, losing ground. "New York has the worst income inequality in the U.S," Sassen points out, and the trend is toward a continuing increase in this inequality: "The evidence shows that the average family income of the top fifth rose 18% since 1980 while the average incomes of the remaining four-fifths actually fell, by 12% for the middle fifth and by 13% for the lowest fifth" (270).

These developments obviously pose major challenges for the followers of Smith's ideas, however much one tries to adjust these ideas to the economic cosmos, or chaos, of postmodernity, and of course the actual practices of capitalism have always enjoyed, at best, an uneasy co-existence with these ideas. Smith was aware of and addressed some of these complexities. His argument is subtler than most of his followers like to think, particularly concerning the ethical dimensions of his understanding of "free" markets. The subjects of the free market cosmopolitanism of Smith and his followers are conceived as individuals, who, if unimpeded by the interference of governments, would steadfastly pursue their own economic interests. Guided by the "invisible hand" of the market, this pursuit will presumably result in the mutual benefit of all. While Smith is often understood to have viewed human beings as guided solely by selfish self-interest, this self-interest as he conceived it was in fact informed by what he called "prudence"—a wider sense of our mutual interdependence and responsibility to one another and to society as a whole that should, for example, prompt one to behave honorably in one's business transactions. This prudence constitutes the "enlightened" aspect of "enlightened self-interest."

Smith's vision of ethics, however, went far beyond bringing prudence into his discussion of capitalism. *An Inquiry into the Nature and Causes of the Wealth of Nations* (1776) was preceded by *The Theory of Moral Sentiments* (1759), which opens with the observation that "How selfish soever man may be supposed, there are evidently some principles in his nature which interest him in the fortune of others and render their happiness necessary to him though he derives nothing from it except the pleasure of seeing it" (1.1.1). The work goes on to examine the importance of virtues such as compassion, sympathy (arising out of our innate capacity for empathy), self-denial and self-government, and generosity and public-spiritedness. As the economist Amartya Sen points out, Smith "outlined the *social* benefit from being public-spirited, but left it open as to how much that would actually change *individual* behaviour, especially of the wealthy and the powerful. To some extent his hope was that behavioural norms may emerge that are not conditional on calculations of self-interest in each case, but dependent rather on taking them to be 'proper' rules of behaviour, reflecting established conventions that are to be standardly followed" ("What Difference" 5; his emphasis). A right calculation of self-interest, then, should be informed by all of these virtues, and perhaps most of all by a keen recognition of how our individual interests are bound up with those of others. Further, this recognition is essential at all levels of calculation—from the family to the neighborhood, to the nation, to the world—and for *all* agents, including corporations and states.

Recognition alone is, of course, not all that is necessary for these calculations. Equally important is the weight or priority given to these interests, and ethical or moral cosmopolitanism is, arguably, especially important in establishing these priorities and making the calculations they entail. Such calculations, I would argue, require a far more holistic sense of "economics" in the broad sense, extending from the household (the etymology of "economy" derives from the ancient Greek word for household, *oikonomia*) outwards, and of costs and benefits than has historically been the rule in Western societies. (Non-Western societies have sometimes been better at viewing economics in more holistic ways.)

At the level of corporations, for example, such cost-benefit calculations would involve, first, considerably broadening the definitions of both costs and benefits. The "costs" of widget production would include not only raw materials, capital investment (in machines, factories, and so forth), and labor. They would also include the costs that corporations incur but do not pay—what economists call "negative externalities." These include the costs borne by workers and communities, not only for work-related physical or psychological injuries (e.g., alienation and stress), for example, but also for the upheaval and displacement that results when industries relocate to take advantage of cheaper labor, and workers must uproot themselves and their families from their communities to find work elsewhere. Currently these costs are off-loaded onto individuals and communities in the form of escalating social, health care and unemployment costs, faltering local economies, and decimated tax bases. (It is worth noting that corporations rarely miss an opportunity to tout—and use as leverage to obtain tax abatements and other accommodations—the employment and tax benefits that result when they locate to a particular community; they are rarely as eager to calculate the losses to individuals and communities when they depart.) Finally, the environmental costs of widget production, including pollution and depletion of natural resources should also be factored in. The benefits of production—including of the value of widgets (whether things or services), wages, and profits—then, would need to be recalculated, taking these additional, more comprehensively defined costs into account.

Consideration of a few of these unregarded costs is occasionally forced by the tactical actions of disaffected workers, including slowing production, providing substandard service, monkeywrenching, and pilfering supplies or company time by recreationally surfing the Web during working hours, for example. Sen argues that "paying attention to equity may, in many circumstances, help to *promote* . . . efficiency (rather than hindering it), because people's behaviour may be dependent on their sense of fairness and their reading as to whether others are behaving fairly" ("What Difference" 6; Sen's emphasis). Such cost considerations are also sometimes imposed from "outside," for example, by governments requiring corporations to assume financial responsibility for the clean-up of toxic production sites and waste dumps. Yet many such costs are incurred or borne beyond the purview or control of local, state, and national governments: a mining concern incorporated in the U.S. pollutes rivers in Africa, Chinese power plants burning coal pollute the air over Japan, and so forth. Even in cases of "national industries," the interests of the nation and the industries might conflict, as for example, when General Motors moves its factories to countries with cheaper labor (Mexico, Thailand, Chile, Colombia), leaving the "costs" of these corporate decisions to be borne by the legions of unemployed American workers left behind and by entire cities and regions whose economic base has been destroyed.[10]

Once, it was true that the interests of major corporations generally coincided or overlapped with those of the nations in which they were founded and headquartered, as manifest in the proverbial "What's good for General Motors is good for the country." As subsequent developments in the automobile and other major industries have demonstrated, however, this is less and less the case. The interests of transnational corporations, whose production, marketing, and distribution might involve operations in dozens of countries or more (ExxonMobil, for example, claims to have "operations in nearly 200 countries and territories," which, since there are only 192 countries in the world, makes one wonder where they *don't* have operations of some kind), clearly transcend national and regional interests.[11] As a survey of maps of the world found in corporate annual reports of such major transnationals as ExxonMobil suggests, they are likely to view national borders as increasingly inconsequential.[12] Indeed, the greatest growth in First World economies and in the global cities is in those industries (especially financial and service) that are most reliant on the global economy and thus least tied to national interests.

Given the immense economic power of major corporations and the political power that accompanies it, the disengagement of national and corporate interests and the possibilities of conflicts between them are of increasing concern. Consider that, based on a comparison of 2005 corporate sales and national gross domestic products (GDPs), 45 of the 100 largest economies in the world were corporations.[13] The 2005 sales of *each* of the five largest corporations (Citigroup, General Electric, American International Group, Bank of America, and HSBC Group) were greater than the GDPs of 137 of the world's 192 countries.[14] This power differential between corporations and nations, which grows greater every year, makes more and more nations vulnerable to the exploitation of both their natural resources and labor by corporate interests beyond or exceeding (i.e., over-powering) national control.[15]

Decisions made in the boardrooms and management offices of transnational corporations frequently have immense effects on the lives and well-being (economic and otherwise) of millions of individuals far from the control centers where they are made and well beyond the reach of even the most powerful nations' laws and regulations. History is rife with instances in which corporate owners and managers have given priority to narrowly conceived profits over broader interests, even when those broader interests are no farther away than their own children and neighbors. It is a common but nonetheless peculiar and willful myopia that, for example, would lead one to poison the very air that one's children and neighbors (not to mention one's self) must breathe or the water they must drink. At a distance, say, in the case of effects of decisions on some Third World nation on the other side of the globe, this myopia can only grow worse: as a rule, the greater the distance, whether spatial or temporal (as might be the case when the effects of decisions made now might not be manifest until some future time, beyond the conceptual range of the quarterly earnings report or even the ten-year strategic plan), the greater the attenuation of the sense of responsibility. I would, therefore, argue that "market cosmopolitanism" needs to be reimagined and reconstituted, its view expanded, as much as possible, through this broader conception of "costs," which includes *all* the effects of production decisions—both intended and unintended, near and far, now and in the future. At present, global corporations all too frequently have far too narrow and parochial a view of their own interests—and ours.[16]

One might argue that what I am proposing here is in fact prioritizing moral or ethical forms of cosmopolitanism over market cosmopolitanism, or else conflating them (as some argue that Smith himself does in adding "enlightened" to "self-interest"). Such an argument would be based in a (not uncommonly held) assumption that the two are or should be separated. Yet clearly they are inextricably intertwined: our economic cosmopolitan interdependence extends beyond particular communities and nations. Even against themselves, as Kleingeld observes, "market cosmopolitans do presuppose a thin form of moral cosmopolitanism, insofar as they consider tolerance important, take all human beings as equal trading partners, and couch their ideals in terms of 'natural human rights'" ("Six Varieties" 520). As noted earlier, however, Smith's vision of enlightened self-interest clearly went beyond this "thin" form of moral cosmopolitanism and entailed a far more exacting moral compass. How often and to what degree the proponents of laissez-faire capitalism that succeeded him have recognized or employed this compass is, of course, a different matter. Working outward from Smith, Sen makes a persuasive argument for the necessity of "seeing the interdependence between equity and efficiency, and between values and institutions":

> If, for example, social opportunities of basic education are denied through the absence of school facilities to many, or basic economic rights are withheld because of massive inequalities in ownership (reinforced by the absence of counteracting policies such as land reforms, microcredit facilities, etc.), then the results will go well beyond the presence of only that inequality. The results will tend to include other restraining effects related to the nature of economic expansion, the flourishing of political and cultural developments, and even the expectable reductions in mortality and fertility rates—all of which could suffer because of the presence of inequality in educational or economic opportunities. ("What Difference" 11)

Sen's essay encourages businesses to take a far broader view of how their decisions might affect their own long-term interests and those of the societies upon which they inevitably depend. Such considerations suggest that corporations might "do well by doing good," a frequently cited formulation of enlightened self-interest. In the affluent First World, we might look to governments to offset some of the costs of economic displacement; in the Third World, however, governments are far less able to do this. Ben Bernanke, the chairman of the Federal Reserve, has argued that "the challenge for policymakers is to ensure that the benefits of global economic integration are sufficiently widely shared—for example, by helping displaced workers get the necessary training to take advantage of new opportunities—that a consensus for welfare-enhancing change can be obtained. Building such a consensus may be far from easy, at both the national and the global levels. However, the effort is well worth making, as the potential benefits of increased global economic integration are large indeed." Where personal or corporate ethics fail and where national entities find themselves either unequal to the task or outflanked, international organizations (including NGOs) and laws have proven to be the best recourse. The new power differentials between corporations and nations have been among the motivating factors in the creation of extranational organizations, treaties, and accords (e.g., the European Union and the Kyoto Accords), alongside older attempts at restraining and adjudicating among nation states such as the United Nations. In this way, then, corporations are inadvertently contributing to the rise of new versions of political and, I will argue below, cultural cosmopolitanism.

It is, accordingly, fitting to close this section with a discussion of how markets and their cosmopolitanism enter the domains of cultural cosmopolitanism, to be addressed as such in the next section. Marx and Engels's "Communist Manifesto" provides a suitable point of departure for this discussion. Their sketch of the expansive imperatives of capital there suggests some of the ways in which market cosmopolitanism both establishes the conditions for and actively produces cultural cosmopolitanism:

> The need of a constantly expanding market for its products chases the bourgeoisie over the entire surface of the globe. It must nestle everywhere, settle everywhere, establish connections everywhere. . . . The bourgeoisie has, through its exploitation of the world market, given a cosmopolitan character to production and consumption in every country. . . . In place of the old wants, satisfied by the production of the country, we find new wants, requiring for their satisfaction the products of distant lands and climes. In place of the old local and national seclusion and self-sufficiency, we have intercourse in every direction, universal inter-dependence of nations. And as in material, so also in intellectual production. The intellectual creations of individual nations become common property. National one-sidedness and narrow-mindedness become more and more impossible. (212–13)

Restless capital gathers and produces commodities (including the previously uncommodified) all over the world and puts them into circulation. It creates global networks and circuits—both material and digital—through which flow the ceaseless production of goods (including cultural products like books, films, television shows, and music), information, images, and ideas. These flows, combined with flows of migrants of all types (from travelers to economic immigrants to refugees), disseminate cultures and produce invaluable and vibrant combinations, conjunctions, convergences, fusions, hybrids, and transformations among them.[17] "Mélange, hotch-potch," this is, Salman Rushdie observes in *Imaginary Homelands*, "how newness enters the world. It is the great possibility that mass migration gives the world" (394).

Looking across history at the effects of cultural cross-pollination on the development of human civilizations, it is clear that Rushdie is right. At the same time, these cultural migrations and flows are not without their costs and conflicts: the forces of globalization both disseminate *and* sometimes eradicate cultural diversity, as the discussion of homogenization in Chapter 1 would suggest as well. Beyond its considerable costs to individuals and families, the seemingly perpetual mobility and displacement produced by global capitalism can uproot communities and destroy traditional ways of life. The threat or experience of such losses is a source of great anxiety and unrest for many who experience globalization as only the most recent version of an economic colonization that exploits the less powerful. Along with this economic colonization also comes what's been called "Coca-Colonization," the imposition of or infiltration by a Westernized (frequently Americanized) consumer culture and ethos.[18] Even more objectionable to many, particularly in "traditional" patriarchal and religious societies, are the ideas and mores—secularism, the equality of women, and sexual freedom, among them—that are embedded in and disseminated through Western television shows, Internet websites, films, music, books, magazines and newspapers, fashion, and even consumer goods like cosmetics (Figure 5.2). Authoritarian regimes have similar fears about purportedly Western concepts of democracy and human rights. Cultural purists everywhere deplore the very mélange and hybridization that Rushdie celebrates.

These creative combinations and destructive conflicts are played out in various ways nearly everywhere, but they are ever-present features of urban life in global cities, where the in-gatherings of people from all over the world are greatest. Those who inhabit the global cities are obviously not all cosmopolitans with relationships to numerous, multinational cultures; many are locals who live their lives, as much as possible, within the confines of close-knit, essentially "closed," homogeneous communities. The senses of "local" and "community" used here, it should be emphasized, are not necessarily limited to one particular *geographic* locale, say, the Italian-American,

Figure 5.2   Dubai, United Arab Emirates, 2005. (© Steve Raymer/Corbis.)

Roman Catholic community of Bayside, Queens, though they may be. Today it is not uncommon for immigrants, especially "labor migrants," to inhabit communities that are located in two places at once: in the community of origin, for example, a neighborhood or village in Mexico or India, and in the counterpart neighborhood in a global city where members of the original community settle. The bonds between the two geographically separate parts of the community are maintained through frequent travel and communication (telephones, the Internet, and so forth), and social ties are reinforced through such practices as only marrying "someone from the neighborhood" or returning to the original community in order to find a spouse. Within such communities, much energy can go into maintaining the original language, culture, and traditions, and into attempting, when necessary, to assimilate elements of the new into those original forms in order to maintain their integrity. The degree of attachment to the two parts of the bilateral community might vary: for the first-generation immigrants, "home" might always be in the country of origin and the new country might be a "home away from home"; for the second generation, the reverse is likely to be true.

Refugees and exiles, despite their mobility from one culture to another, are not necessarily cosmopolitans either, since their shifts between cultures, unlike those of cosmopolitans, are involuntary. For them, as Ulf Hannerz observes, "at best, life in another country is home plus safety, or home plus freedom, but often it is just not home at all. He [the exile] is surrounded by the foreign culture but does not immerse himself in it . . . he may reluctantly build up a competence, but he does not enjoy it" (243). Tourists, on the other hand, may enjoy their contact with the foreign culture and even immerse themselves in it as much as possible (that is, as far as their knowledge of language and local mores might allow), but they do not participate extensively in the culture, one of the principal markers of cosmopolitanism. Yet tourism, depending upon the level of interchange with the foreign culture, might arguably help to foster a cosmopolitan sense of the world by making one aware—in a concrete rather than abstract sense—of the existence and thus the real possibility of different ways of understanding and living in the world. Similarly, one's reception (whether of welcome or hostility) in another culture and the reasons behind it can sometimes provide an illuminating glimpse of both that culture and one's own from outside— a perspective that Americans in particular frequently seem to lack.

Even in the best of circumstances, however, market and cultural cosmopolitanisms do not necessarily harmonize with each other. As I have suggested, "market cosmopolitanism" clearly creates many of the necessary conditions for, and actually plays a large role in actively producing, cultural cosmopolitanism. It is also clear, however, that, rather than a true cultural cosmopolitanism, the result of globalization might all too easily turn out to be primarily a form of "consumerpolitanism," as Edward Spence has termed it, in which the wealthy segments of the First World simply continue to consume more and more of the world's goods and resources while remaining largely oblivious to the economic, cultural, political, and ethical implications of the global system that produces them, and in which the striving inhabitants of the Third World find that the economic and cultural benefits of globalization are too often either elusive or unequal.[19] If we are to create a viable twenty-first century cultural cosmopolitanism, we will need to make use of all of the resources of globalization (including the Internet) while thinking far beyond the banal versions of cultural cosmopolitanism—from "How to Make a Deal in 100 Languages" to "buy[ing] the world a Coke"—that it offers.[20]

3. CULTURAL COSMOPOLITANISM

The cultural cosmopolitanism I will discuss here involves both a sense of community and a sense of subjectivity. At this point in history, we are all part of a vast web of relationships that span the globe, and many of these relationships, arguably the most defining ones, are cultural, and, in this context, any relationship may involve a cultural component. To conceive of how this web might evolve into a community that is productively cosmopolitan will require both a thinking through of currently existing ideas of cultural community (including what, exactly, a cultural community is and what it means to belong to one) and the creation of a new, cosmopolitan understanding of community out of which a new cosmopolitan reality might emerge. Such a conception would, I argue, inevitably be at odds with the inherently traditional and conservative understandings of community espoused by present-day communitarians and, to a lesser but still marked extent, traditional Enlightenment-based liberalism—both of which offer coherent (and sometimes overlapping) accounts of the nature of community, the individual, and the relationships between them.

The conceptions of "community" adopted by most communitarians are those of community in a broadly nationalist sense: that of, in Jeremy Waldron's words, "a particular people sharing a heritage of custom, ritual, and way of life that is in some real or imagined sense immemorial, being referred back to a shared history and shared provenance or homeland" ("Minority" 756).[21] It is this sense of national "community" that has generated both the greatest loyalty and the greatest destruction on both a local and global scale over the past two centuries. Such understandings of the nation are often overlaid with or underpinned by discourses of religion, ethnicity, race and "blood"—as in, for example, the (highly dubious) assertions that "America is a Christian nation" or that "India is a Hindu nation," and, reciprocally, it is common for racist groups like the Aryan Nation or even religious groups to deploy the discourses of "nation" or rough equivalents like the Islamic "Umma" (the worldwide community or nation of Muslims).[22] Nationalists in this sense and communitarians in general attribute to such communities (their own and those of others) a defining homogeneity and unity (even in the face of manifest diversity, one hears such inarguable claims as, "We're all Americans"). Most communitarian arguments about the nature and purpose of community clearly share these same assumptions. As will be seen later, the political and ethical consequences of these understandings of community are considerable. First, however, I would like to consider their cultural aspects and compare them to a more *cosmopolitan* (in the present sense) understanding of community. My argument against the validity of such conceptions of community and identity, and of their value for our communal life, is based on three primary critical considerations concerning them: their lack of accuracy (and, therefore, necessity); their obsolescence; and, finally, their frequent (and in some cases, inevitable) conflicts with certain human rights that might be considered essential for our productive existence and, possibly, survival in our global world. Such essential or "basic" rights include the right to life (including such security rights as the right not to be murdered, raped, tortured, or enslaved) and liberty (including the right of free movement, freedom of belief and religion, freedom of association and assembly, and freedom of thought and expression), the right to due process (including the protections of *habeas corpus*) and equality before the law, and finally, the right to political representation and participation in one's government. While it may not be altogether impossible to question the absolute, universal validity of these rights, it would be difficult to deny the fact that most of them are accepted as basic (and not only in Western societies). In fact, many communitarians accept these rights as well.

As I noted earlier, national discourses and narratives inevitably involve particular claims of a shared history, language, religion, ethnicity, and way of life.[23] Such narratives tend to be highly selective in their accounts of history, denying or underplaying the inevitable heterogeneities of every "nation" or "people." The consequences of these selective histories and of what Salman Rushdie refers to as "the absolutism of the pure" are often detrimental both for particular communal entities and for the relationships between and among them. In particular, in times of social, economic, or political tension, the rhetorical insistence (often mobilized for the local political advantage of individual politicians or parties) upon such purity and homogeneity is likely to lead to violent attempts to purify or homogenize the "nation" in fact. In such situations, the historical closeness of various groups is no guarantee of amity. In *Civilization and Its Discontents*, Freud analyzes the phenomenon he termed "the narcissism of minor differences," noting that "it is precisely communities with adjoining territories, and related to each other in other ways as well, who are engaged in constant feuds and ridiculing each other— like the Spaniards and Portuguese, for instance" (72). Such conflicts have always been among the primary means by which "nations" are established and maintained. "It is always possible to bind together a considerable number of people in love," Freud points out, "so long as there are other people left over to receive the manifestations of their aggressiveness" (72). It may also be noted that nationalism, however grounded or expressly defined (including in ethnic, religious, and racial terms), has often, all too often, expressly announced or assumed that the corresponding community is or should be valued above all others and even above life itself, that is, that one should be willing to die, and kill, for one's "country" or "people," even without a compelling necessity (e.g., defending one's country against invaders) to do so. The twentieth century alone, with its hundreds of millions dead as a consequence of this understanding of community, provides us with too many examples—from the Nazi genocide of the Jews (including those who were German citizens), to the genocide of the Muslims by the Serbs in Bosnia-Herzegovina, to the genocide of the Tutsis by the Hutus in Rwanda in the mid-1990s, to the current genocide of black African Sudanese by their Arab countrymen, and the internecine warfare in Iraq between the Sunnis and the Shiites. It should also be acknowledged that, in certain circumstances, nationalism, sometimes linked to religion, can play and has played a positive role, for example, in colonial liberation movements or in the resistance to the oppressive power of the Soviet regime in the countries of the former Soviet bloc. It is also worth noting that the former Soviet regime not only acted in the name of internationalism, but that it was in some respects internationalist in fact, although it was also nationalist in other respects and often implicitly governed (in either sense) by Russian nationalism. These complexities should of course be acknowledged and kept in mind, for otherwise one can easily slide into naïve and uncritical, and hence problematic, reversals of nationalist or communitarian thinking, rather than develop a rigorous and practicable alternative. These complexities do, as will be discussed below, pose certain, sometimes difficult, problems for postmodern cosmopolitan thinking and practices. They do not, however, help the communitarian view(s), at least of the kind considered here.

Supporters (including present-day communitarians such as Will Kymlicka, Michael J. Sandel, and Michael Walzer) and the political and religious enforcers of such versions of "community" all over the world insist upon their necessity, claiming that we derive our identities only within and through membership in a community, usually the community of our birth. In addition, as I mentioned earlier, they also generally insist upon the constitutive coherence, uniqueness, and homogeneity of such a community. It is hardly surprising that such claims, and the arguments based on them, have encountered persistent criticisms, such as those by Waldron (already cited). These claims are fundamentally problematic, for the following reasons, some of which are nearly self-evident.

First of all, individuals frequently derive some part of their identities from aspirations and identifications that have little or nothing to do with any individual community to which they might belong (beyond the community of the human race, that is). An individual, for example, might define herself as a physician, and while becoming a physician inevitably makes one a member of the community or communities of physicians, the identity (particularly in its aspirational form—"When I grow up, I want to be a doctor") probably arises more out of the profession and its activities than out of a sense of community per se. This is not to diminish the extent to which we are all "interpellated" by our communities (and I will discuss this aspect of our communal life further presently), but instead to suggest that our identities are shaped by many forces, including internal ones that might have little to do with "community."

Further, the communitarian claims in question are belied by the realities of the contemporary world, in which everyone is, one way or another, simultaneously part of numerous and frequently highly diverse "communities" of varying scale, reach, and cohesiveness. The numbers and types of community to which an individual might belong is, to some extent, determined by such factors as age, education, and what might broadly be understood as "access," which has been vastly expanded by the increasing ease and speed of travel and by communication technologies like the Internet, but which still primarily correlates with wealth. The "self-awareness" of these communities is also, it is worth pointing out, sometimes contingent: the ties that connect us to others are not always conscious or even known to us, though they may affect us in important ways.

Such networks of unknowing connections have been the subject of several powerful films, in particular, Robert Altman's *Short Cuts* (1993), which traced out the connections among inhabitants of Los Angeles, and, more recently, Michael Haneke's *Code Unknown* (2000) and Delphine Gleize's *Carnage* (2002), which explore the connections created by the economic and political forces of globalization or, more narrowly, Europeanization. *Carnage* is a parable of the intricate transnational web of relations produced by consumption, in this case, the consumption of a bull. The film opens with a bullfight in Andalusia in which both the young toreador and the bull are gored. The toreador is dispatched to the hospital and the bull to the slaughterhouse in parallel, the ambulance and the truck carrying the bull's carcass traveling side-by-side in separate lanes on the same highway. As the toreador sinks into a coma, the bull's carcass is dressed and parts of it are distributed across Europe. In parallel, rhyming mises-en-scène, we witness the effects of the bull's "consumption" on twelve Spanish, French, Belgian, and Italian individuals, among them, the little girl, Winnie, who watches the bullfight on the television, her parents, and their Great Dane, Fred, for whom they buy a bone from the bull; Winnie's kindergarten teacher and her teacher's mother, who dines on *toro en riojo* and whose liver is transplanted into the comatose toreador after her death; an old woman who buys the horns for her taxidermist son; and a scientist who examines the bull's eyes (and discovers in its semiblindness an explanation for the toreador's disastrous inability to predict its movements) and his very pregnant, distraught wife. As the narrative progresses, we see that the characters are linked by much more than the bull: the trajectories of its parts are not only those of consumption, but also of carnality (in many guises), hunger, and desire—powerful forces that underpin human behavior and link us to one another in communities that extend far beyond our limited comprehensions of them. The significance of these forces in shaping our communities makes the communitarian understanding of community (whether based in nationalism, ethnicity, or religion) simply obsolete in this technologically advanced era of global exchange and migration.

Cities have always constituted a living proof of Waldron's argument that "we need cultural meanings, but we do not need homogeneous cultural frameworks. We need to understand our choices in the contexts in which they make sense, but we do not need any single context to structure all our choices. To put it crudely, we need culture, but we do not need cultural integrity" ("Minority" 786). Urban life is, in its very essence, an embrace of difference and interchange. In all of their multiplicity and heterogeneity, cities have always offered the possibility of escaping the confines of a too-narrow community, of multiplying and extending both the scale and reach (if not cohesiveness) of senses of community, and of finding, among the immense diversity of urban inhabitants, new communities of those who share one's multiple affinities. Indeed, such possibilities have always been among the primary attractions of cities. The number, range, and diversity of "local" urban communities to which the individual city-dweller might belong are immense, including, for example, co-workers or other professional alliances; neighbors (both within apartment buildings and within geographically distinct neighborhoods); political parties and action groups; sports fans, leagues, and informal athletic groups; neighborhood restaurant and bar regulars; church members; subscribers to cultural organizations such as museums, theaters, music, film, book, and dance groups; and educational groups, including college students and, in the case of public and private primary and secondary students, their parents, too. While ostensibly "local," many of these communities might also extend far beyond the geographical boundaries of the city and nation. The diversity, complexity, and vitality of these many intertwined communities and the ways in which they bring together individuals from every national, religious, ethnic, racial, and class background are a more accurate and authentic representation of the world's nearly infinite interconnections than any fantasy of a hermetically sealed monoculture.

The respective value that individuals place on each of the communities to which they might belong will obviously vary, depending upon the perceived importance of the attachment, but it would be a rare person today who would not see him or herself as simultaneously part of several, diverse communities. A mapping of these attachments would resemble a vast, endlessly shifting global network with individuals at "nodes" or intersection points of various communities that are, further, in themselves heterogeneous in various ways. These communities might also sometimes be considered to be at cross-purposes with one another (in this, they might be seen to reflect the complexities, and sometimes contradictions, of the ongoing creation of subjectivity itself). "Coherence," "unity," and "homogeneity," then, are not terms easily applied to such assemblages of communities, even if individuals do not perceive any particular contradictions or conflicts among them. We are not only all different: we are, as Sen puts it, *"diversely different"*— different in different ways, since each of us constitutes a unique assemblage of connections among various communities (*Identity* xiv). "Indeed," he points out, "many of the conflicts and barbarities in the world are sustained through the illusion of a unique and choiceless identity. The art of constructing hatred takes the form of invoking the magical power of some allegedly predominant identity that drowns other affiliations, and in a conveniently bellicose form can also overpower any human sympathy or natural kindness that we may normally have. The result can be homespun elemental violence, or globally artful violence and terrorism" (*Identity* xv).

Communitarians and nationalists also generally assume that our rights and choices are—and should be—"framed" and determined by the community.[24] These assumptions are, it seems to me, both unnecessarily restrictive (and, once put into practice, sometimes genuinely oppressive) and in any event are, again, obsolete, particularly in the postmodern world, even though our choices are sometimes determined or limited by our communities. But they need not be and certainly, in most cases, should not be. And, again, by which among the communities to which we simultaneously belong should they be limited? For those who lack access to or knowledge of other communities, an individual's rights and choices may well be de facto determined by the one or ones into which they are born. Access and knowledge, however, are material barriers—they can be, and increasingly are, overcome, given the will and resources: representational government (including most especially the participation of women), economic development, and education would seem to be the most vital forces for diminishing these barriers. One could of course think of reasons why a society or community would wish to be protected or insulated from ideological challenges to its practices, for example, when a community or those groups within it that hold power over it benefit from such isolation. Whether such "protection" is practically possible in the contemporary world of the Internet, television, and jet travel is doubtful, of course, at least over the long run. In any event, one might argue, especially against the proponents of the communitarian views under discussion but also more generally, that most of the historical progress in human rights has come from just such ideological challenges to structures that have traditionally served primarily to benefit the powerful and the status quo.

Even more problematic are claims by communitarians that rights and choices *should be* determined and limited by a given community. A 1979 United Nations Report on Article 27 of the International Covenant on Civil and Political Rights appears to suggest just this (Capotorti 40–41, 98–99). The report rejected the view of Article 27 as principally a provision against discrimination.[25] Instead, the defense of the fundamental human rights of minority cultures, the report asserts, requires both nondiscrimination *and* "affirmative measures." Such measures might include, for example, "the recognition that minority cultures are entitled to protect themselves by placing limits on the incursions of outsiders and limits on their own members' choices about career, family, lifestyle, loyalty, and exit, limits that might be unpalatable in the wider liberal context" (Waldron, "Minority" 758). Whatever the benefits of this interpretation might be (and they seem rather limited to me, even for "subsidized" minority cultures), the problems seem immense. It would leave, for instance, signatory countries in the position of not only condoning such practices as female "circumcision," but also perhaps of aiding the community's enforcement of it, by, for example, returning to the "custody" of the community women who have fled in order to escape it or refusing such women formal rights of refuge and asylum.

From the perspective of cosmopolitanism as understood here (and with qualifications given earlier), when there is a contest between basic human rights and the rights of community, the basic human rights should prevail. That is, even when some members of the community might willingly accede to the community's mandates, as in the case of women who adopt the veil, the nation or international community should not be in the position of enforcing such mandates or restrictions and should, in some cases, endeavor to bring about their change through nonviolent means.[26] Further, they should do everything to ensure the availability of other options and the right of exit. It is not enough to assume that because some accede to them, certain forms of control are truly voluntary or acceptable. This view is also suggested by Lyotard's argument for the postmodern practice of justice, which I invoked earlier and to which I shall return in the next section. As, however, already in 1762 Rousseau argued in *The Social Contract*, "Nothing can be more certain than that every man born *in* slavery is born *for* slavery. Slaves lose everything in their chains, *even the desire of escaping from them*: they love their servitude . . . If then there are slaves by nature, it is because there have been slaves against nature. Force made the first slaves" (2:14; my emphasis). Certain rights might be, and from the present cosmopolitan perspective would be, inalienable, irrespective of what an individual, community, or country might desire at a particular moment in history, and denials of certain fundamental human rights cannot be justified, even by claims of "tradition" or "cultural integrity."[27]

4. POSTMODERN COSMOPOLITANISM: COMMUNITIES AND SUBJECTIVITIES, POLITICS AND ETHICS

> This race—this race between the destroying planes and the struggling Parliament of Man—it sticks in all our heads. The city at last perfectly illustrates both the universal dilemma and the general solution, this riddle in steel and stone is at once the perfect target and the perfect demonstration of nonviolence, of racial brotherhood, this lofty target

scraping the skies and meeting the destroying planes halfway, home of all people and all nations, capital of everything, housing the deliberations by which the planes are to be stayed and their errand forestalled.

—E.B. White, "Here is New York"

In "Multiculturalism and Mélange," Waldron asks a series of hypothetical questions: "What if there has been nothing but mélange all the way down? What if cultures have always been implicated with one another, through trade, war, curiosity, and other forms of intercommunal relation? What if the mingling of cultures is as immemorial as cultural roots themselves? What if purity and homogeneity have always been myths?" (107). In spite of all of the current overwrought and simplistic rhetoric about "the clash of civilizations," a careful examination of world history would confirm that Waldron's hypotheticals constitute a more accurate précis of the history of human culture than idealized visions of monolithic civilizations arising and flourishing in splendid isolation. Throughout human history, cities have been the loci of "civilizations," in large part by virtue of their invaluable role as centers of cross-cultural encounter and exchange. The diversity of urban populations is both a cause and a reflection of the many cultural influences that merge to form "civilization."

The creation of a self-consciously cosmopolitan community might begin with the abandonment of myths of civilizations' homogeneity and cultural purity, and the acknowledgment of the extent to which every civilization and culture is the product of centuries and even millennia of cultural exchanges of goods, technologies, ideas, customs, narratives, and images. This acknowledgment does not entail a denial of the distinctiveness of different cultures, but it does highlight the multitudes of connections and commonalities that link them to one another, and it suggests the advantages of multicultural hybridization over monocultural ghettoization (voluntary or not). This understanding of human cultural development would also help to sever the imaginary linkage of culture with heredity (whether conceived in terms of race, ethnicity, or "blood")—the essentialism that is the foundation of racist and other sectarian ideologies.

A cosmopolitan community would seem to require a considerable degree of open-mindedness on the part of its members, an acceptance of cultural diversity, hybridity, and heterogeneity, and a concomitant refusal of parochialism in all its guises. It would, in other words, be more meaningfully multicultural, with an emphasis on the importance of interaction and exchange. It is important to differentiate this version of multiculturalism from the assemblage of "plural monocultures," in which groups sequester themselves (or are sequestered) in ethnic, racial, or religious enclaves that strive to keep interaction with other communities to an absolute minimum.[28] If it were to envision a "world culture," it would be, as Hannerz suggests, one "marked by an organization of diversity rather than by a replication of uniformity" (237).

This cosmopolitanism would eschew the search for (or insistence upon) a single, dominant cultural or cognitive paradigm. It would involve not a forsaking of the search for truth, but rather the realization that no one truth can be everyone's ("universal") Truth, that what we will have instead are many truths, for which there might be different standards of validity and value for different people in different contexts. As Nietzsche observes in *Thus Spoke Zarathustra*, "Never yet has truth hung on the arm of the unconditional" [Niemals noch hängte sich die Wahrheit an den Arm eines Unbedingten] (52). In other words, "truth" is always irreducibly conditional, and thus contingent and, as Nietzsche often notes, perspectival, never universal or absolute. This cosmopolitanism would also involve the recognition that cultural meanings are inherently contextual, contingent, eternally in process, and prone to proliferate beyond any individual or group's control.

The engagement with the Other entailed by cultural cosmopolitanism might take many forms, but the willingness to engage in conversation would likely be chief among them. The ability (and willingness) to engage in the conversations I have in mind here would arise out of the rights to establish communication and to associate envisioned by Kant's right to hospitality. Though it is linked to Kant's project of establishing "peaceable relations" among distant nations, I do not conceive this conversation as having the creation of a Habermasian consensus as its goal. I do not think that if we just begin or keep talking to one another, we will all ultimately agree. But a willingness to engage with the ideas and experiences of others will help us to find our commonalities as well as our differences. "Conversation," as Kwame Anthony Appiah argues, "doesn't have to lead to consensus about anything, especially not values; it's enough that it helps people get used to one another" (*Cosmopolitanism* 85). It would, in my view, be better to say "a consensus about everything" rather than "anything." Appiah does, however, have a point in stressing the value of conversation or dialogue as such; cosmopolitanism crucially depends on keeping it and its very possibility open. The "rules" of such dialogues (language games) are, of course, an important question and would sometimes need to be negotiated. And there are, admittedly, situations in which silence might well be the best choice (and a necessary right).

The benefits of these conversations are likely to go far beyond simply becoming accustomed to one another. At any given point in history, many people are seeking solutions to many of the same problems—from theoretical and practical questions of justice, rights, and equality to pragmatic questions of how to raise children and organize the family, how to structure education and work, and how to care for the ill and the elderly—and there is much we can learn from one another's perspectives and experiences. There are also global problems that cannot be solved by individuals or nations working alone: they will require global solutions, involving multiple interactions and dialogues between individuals, communities, cultures, and nations. A good set of examples is provided by what Bruno Latour calls "hybrid" phenomena and problems. Global warming, deforestation, and the erosion of the ozone layer, for instance, are not simply scientific or environmental problems: they are also political, economic, and technological problems, and their solutions or formulations, to begin, will, therefore, require complex interactions between different fields of knowledge and different small- and large-scale communities, national and international.[29]

One can also consider this situation through the workings of what Lyotard (building upon Wittgenstein's concept) defines as heterogeneous "language games"—different discourses (e.g., political, economic, scientific, philosophical) that deploy different vocabularies (or "technical jargons") and types of statements (denotative, prescriptive, and so forth), and, accordingly, different rules for what can be said and how the validity of those pronouncements is determined.[30] Even language games assumed to be common throughout much of the world (e.g., the scientific), however, might take on somewhat different forms in different cultures (rather like the different versions of poker). We move, deliberately or not, among various language games and networks of games in different contexts. As Lyotard points out, "the social bond is linguistic, but is not woven with a single thread. It is a fabric formed by the intersection of at least two (and in reality an indeterminate number of) language games, obeying different rules" (*The Postmodern Condition* 40). At the same time, the language games and their rules are "heteromorphous," so they can neither be reduced to one another nor subsumed beneath some universal metalanguage. From this and the present perspective, the main problem postmodernity faces is not the development of consensus, communal or other, but that of the coexistence and, when possible, negotiations between heterogeneous language games (in this broad sense) in the absence or indeed given the impossibility of a unifying consensus. This is a complex and difficult problem, as Lyotard is well aware and as he explains, especially in *The Differend: Phrases in Dispute*. But, unlike that of consensus (which appears hopeless), it may actually be a soluble problem.

To navigate the postmodern world and its heterogeneous language games, people must be taught the vocabularies and rules of as many fields as possible and, as Lyotard suggests, the procedures that will make it possible to connect the fields that have been separated by the traditional (i.e., Aristotelian) organization of knowledge. These procedures and the flexibility they entail might, in turn, help us to negotiate different cultures and, perhaps, to sometimes bridge the divides among their perspectives. Although such an education in "postmodern knowledge" would have its pragmatic uses, it is not, as Lyotard argues, "simply a tool of the authorities; it refines our sensitivity to differences and reinforces our ability to tolerate the incommensurable. Its principle is not the expert's homology, but the inventor's paralogy" (*The Postmodern Condition* xxv). We will need, in this context, both new "moves" and new "rules."

It is difficult to predict how successful our attempts at conversation will be. But success is not, again, to be measured by whether or not it will be possible to achieve consensus (it seems, in many cases, highly unlikely). We might instead come to some agreements, and we might also "agree to disagree" in some instances. Some matters will need to be adjudicated through an appeal to or imposition of justice, but it would need to be a somewhat different version of justice than we have inherited. We should, as Lyotard suggests, attempt to "arrive at an idea and practice of justice that is not linked to that of a consensus," since all too often, previous "consensuses" required the suppression of minority dissent (*The Postmodern Condition* 66). In order for this to come about, we would need, first, to acknowledge the inherently heteromorphous nature of language games. This acknowledgment, Lyotard argues "obviously implies a renunciation of terror, which assumes that they [language games] are isomorphic and tries to make them so" (*The Postmodern Condition* 66). Further, the determination of "the rules defining a game and the 'moves' playable within it must be local, in other words, agreed on by its present players and subject to eventual cancellation" (*The Postmodern Condition* 66).

This "postmodern" approach to the heterogeneity of our discourses (or language games) would seem, at least in principle, to offer a new and better ground for the practice of justice than one that relied upon achieving consensus. With its heterogeneous interests and worldviews, postmodernity allows previously marginalized or oppressed groups to make claims upon justice, even in the absence of a majority consensus regarding those claims. We need, thus, to approach the problem of justice in new ways. We will doubtless face practical problems to which there is currently no solution, but thinking about them differently might give us a place to start.

In Stephen Frears's 1987 film *Sammy and Rosie Get Laid*, the two main characters, Sammy and Rosie, live together in a tumultuous, multiethnic, low-income London neighborhood during the Thatcher era. Sammy's father Rafi arrives from Pakistan, a politician on the run from investigations and retribution for his collaboration with the military dictatorship. The product of an English upbringing and Oxbridge education, Rafi is nostalgic for the British Empire and appalled by Sammy and Rosie's "disorderly" multicultural neighborhood. Sammy and Rosie, however, owe their allegiance to something else. "We don't live in England, we live in London," they explain, but it is a very different London from the one Rafi remembers and romanticizes. Rather than recoiling from their encounters with the diverse othernesses in this multicultural London, Sammy and Rosie embrace them. Refusing to define themselves through their ancestry, language, or citizenship, they are, as Waldron suggests cosmopolitans must be, "creature[s] of modernity, conscious of living in a mixed-up world and having a mixed-up self" ("Minority" 754). More accurately, they are creatures of postmodernity.

Present-day cosmopolitan subjectivities might be best understood through postmodern conceptions of subjectivity as inherently fragmented and contingent, less a "self" in the Cartesian sense than a series of fluctuating subject "positions" at the intersection of multiple discourses, cultures, and social structures. We are all subject to the interpellations of multiple social forces, but at the same time, like Sammy and Rosie, we have some degree of freedom and choice in our allegiances and affinities, which is different from how a wholly autonomous individuality is envisioned by traditional liberalism. The cosmopolitan will cultivate the ability to move as gracefully as possible among many cultures. This ability requires mastering language games beyond one's native or even previously acquired repertoire. It demands the capacity to manage a multiplicity of allegiances and, thus, a certain tolerance for ambiguity and, inevitably, contradiction. It involves, as Hannerz argues, both the ability to "surrender" oneself to the "alien" culture and also to disengage, including from one's original culture(s).

Most importantly, however, the cosmopolitan must be defined by an essential willingness to engage with and, beyond that, to extend hospitality to the Other. In some ways, this turns out to be a complex matter since, as Derrida points out in "Politics and Friendship," "the Other is not simply the Other as coming from the outside. . . . the Other is already inside, and has to be sheltered and welcomed in a certain way." There are always at least two "Others" at any given moment—the Other without and within— and they are inseparable. One might also see this situation through the psychological connections between repression and projection. The Other within, as Freud observed, is the bearer of those parts of ourselves (desires, feelings, tendencies, and qualities) that we reject or refuse to recognize, and so repress, relegating them to the realm of the unconscious. Expelled from the conscious self in order to defend it, these repressed othernesses tend, nonetheless, to reappear in the form of externalized projections. Refusing to see them in ourselves, we instead see them in (or as) Others. The external Other's perceived alterity is, then, largely a reflection, a return, of our own unperceived, internal otherness—of all those things we refuse either to *recognize* in ourselves or to *be* in ourselves.

The roots of our fear and hatred of Others lie not just in the fear of the unknown stranger who might harm us, but also in this dialectic of our own repression and projection. Our internal repressions are, accordingly, linked to the oppression of various racial, ethnic, or religious Others who are the objects of our projections. Toni Morrison's *Beloved* contains a meditation, rendered in appropriately primal terms, on the damage this dialectic produces in ourselves and in others:

Whitepeople believed that whatever the manners, under every dark skin was a jungle. Swift unnavigable waters, swinging screaming baboons, sleeping snakes, red gums ready for their sweet white blood. In a way, he thought, they were right. The more coloredpeople spent their strength trying to convince them how gentle they were, how clever and loving, how human, the more they used themselves up to persuade whites of something Negroes believed could not be questioned, the deeper and more tangled the jungle grew inside. But it wasn't the jungle blacks brought with them to this place from the other (livable) place. It was the jungle whitefolks planted in them. And it grew. It spread. In, through and after life, it spread, until it invaded the whites who had made it. Touched them every one. Changed and altered them. Made them bloody, silly, worse than even they wanted to be, so scared were they of the jungle they had made. The screaming baboon lived under their own white skin; the red gums were their own. (198–99)

Those who cannot reconcile with or at least tolerate the Other within will project both that otherness and their fear and aggression toward it outward, onto the exterior Other. As Derrida argues, in order to be hospitable to the Other, it is first necessary "to negotiate this hospitality within ourselves," to welcome what is "already a society" within oneself, "a multiplicity of heterogeneous singularities" ("Politics").

In 1996, Derrida addressed the International Parliament of Writers in Strasbourg on the issue of "cosmopolitan rights" for refugees, asylum seekers, and immigrants. In that address, later published as "On Cosmopolitanism," he raised the possibility of a new instantiation of the historical "cities of refuge," an "open city" emerging out of and requiring a new *cosmopolitics* that encompasses both the duty of and the right to hospitality. Within the present context of global cities and globalization, such a cosmopolitics would require us to think about hospitality, democracy, and justice beyond the borders of the nation state—it would, in effect, require the creation of a new political imaginary. As a way of thinking through this cosmopolitics— what it might involve, the difficulties we would have to overcome in order to bring it about, and how we might begin—I want to discuss the question of hospitality in Michael Haneke's film, *Code Unknown: Incomplete Tales of Several Journeys.*

Composed of a series of fragmented, interlocking storylines, *Code Unknown* opens with a brief, silent scene sandwiched amid the opening credits. In the scene, a young girl slowly shrinks against a wall and crouches for a moment. Then, she stands up. The camera cuts from her to the face of another child who, in sign language, asks, "Alone?" The girl shakes her head. Another child signs, "Hiding place?" And she shakes her head again. We are, we realize, watching a game of charades played by children who are deaf. None of the guesses—"Gangster? Bad conscience? Sad? Imprisoned?"—elicits a nod. The screen reverts to the opening titles.

As we discover, this strange prologue telegraphs some of the key questions posed by the film. There is, first and most obviously, the eponymous unknown code, often linked to an indecipherable message, which is central to many of the situations depicted in the film. For example, in one of the many echoes or reversals in the film, the little girl's gestures will be repeated at several points by the character Marie, an illegal immigrant from Romania. The questions the children pose—alone, hiding place, gangster, bad conscience, sad, and imprisoned—will resonate throughout the film's depictions of isolation, of desperate refugees and immigrants, of pervasive violence, of guilt and misery. *Code Unknown* is set in Paris, depicted as a global, heterogeneous city, where the many languages of its inhabitants (the film includes dialogue in French, German, English, Malinka, Romanian, and Arabic, in addition to the children's sign language) routinely appear as unknown codes for one another, as do their customs, values, and intentions. The theme is developed from a different ethnic angle in Haneke's more recent film, *Caché*. Both films, however, to varying degrees (in *Caché*, it is the central underlying conflict), feature violent returns of the colonial repressed. In *Code Unknown*, it is the confrontation between the "petit Arabe" and Anne. The characters of *Code Unknown* face one another across a series of cultural divides that separate them from one another and fragment the city—divisions that are formally emphasized by the brief cuts to black that separate one scene from another throughout the film. Placing us within this divided city, the film repeatedly suggests the question, what do we owe to others? To our relatives and friends and neighbors? To passersby and foreigners in our midst? To our former colonial subjects? To those who seek refuge among us?

The first scene, after the opening credits, is of a chance encounter at a busy Paris intersection that brings together Marie, the illegal immigrant from Romania, mentioned earlier; Jean, a French young man from the provinces; Amadou, a young teacher of African descent; and Anne, a Parisian actress. Entitled "One Paper Bag," the scene begins with Anne coming out of the door of her apartment building onto a busy street. Jean, the younger brother of Anne's boyfriend Georges, is waiting for her outside. He has run away from his father and the farm, he explains, and he needs a place to stay. He would have come upstairs, but the code to the electronic lock on the door has been changed, and he did not know the new one—yet another "unknown code" in the film. He tried to call, but Anne was in the bath and didn't hear the phone, so he got the answering machine. His brother Georges is away photographing the war in Kosovo, Anne tells him, and she is on her way to a meeting. She and Jean have a quick conversation as they walk, and, after buying him a pastry and reminding him that "there isn't room for three" in her apartment, she gives him the code and the keys.

On his way back, Jean passes Marie, who is sitting against a wall just inside an alley, begging. He tosses the empty, crumpled up pastry bag into her lap and keeps walking. But Amadou, the son of Senegalese immigrants, sees this and decides to intervene. He confronts Jean, asking him, "Was that a good thing to do? Do you feel that was right?" and demands that he apologize to the woman. They scuffle, Anne returns and demands to know why Amadou is beating up on Jean, and the police arrive. They ask for everyone's papers, they arrest Amadou, and the next time we see Marie, she is being escorted, in handcuffs, onto a flight back to Romania.

On multiple levels, this scene might be seen as a series of failures of hospitality: Jean's failure to offer hospitality to Marie (which is then made "official" by the police), but also Anne's failure to offer hospitality to Jean (which might be part of what triggers Jean's subsequent mistreatment of Marie), and, finally, the failure of Amadou's attempt to correct the situation with Marie by forcing Jean to apologize and acknowledge her right to be treated with dignity, and thus to reinstate hospitality. We may understand these failures and the nature of hospitality itself with the help of Derrida's analysis of the subject, which I would like to enter by way of Sigmund Freud's comment on altruism.

In *Civilization and Its Discontents*, Freud argues that no ideal runs so counter to our original natures as altruism—the command that we love one another as ourselves—and that we are therefore not naturally inclined to offer much hospitality, let alone love, to our neighbors, much less strangers. *Homo homini lupus.* (Man is wolf to man.) Although not in disagreement with Freud's argument, Derrida, following (in a qualified way) Kant and Levinas, nevertheless believes in the possibility of hospitality, a certain form of hospitality, at least in principle or at least *as* a principle, even toward a complete stranger. According to Derrida, hospitality is "an unconditional injunction—I have to welcome the Other whoever he or she is unconditionally, without asking for a document, a name, a context, or a passport. That is the very first opening of my relation to the Other: to open my space, my home—my house, my language, my culture, my nation, my state, and myself" ("Politics"). As he points out, however, an enactment of the hospitality of this (unconditional) type in practice is not possible without conditions. First, in order to offer hospitality, one must be the "master" of the house or nation—one must in some sense control it, have sovereignty over it—in order to be able to "host" at all. But the control does not stop there, for the host must have some degree of control over his guests, as well. If they take over the house, he is no longer the host. Extending hospitality might, given a bad guest, result in the displacement, undermining, or destruction of everything—and everyone—in the house, in the space of hospitality. The host, therefore, has the duty, Derrida argues, "of choosing, electing, filtering, selecting [his] invitees, visitors, or guests, those to whom [he] decide[s] to grant asylum, the right of visiting, or hospitality" (*Of Hospitality* 55).

Embedded in hospitality, then, there are several impasses or, in Derrida's terms, "aporias" defined by the conflicts between the (unconditional) principles of hospitality and the conditions, ultimately irreducible (as against what the principles in question would require), under which these principles must be implemented. Thus, while the moral injunction to hospitality might be "unconditional" in principle, in practice it does involve conditions, and these conditions are not without their troubling implications. There is,

Derrida says, "no hospitality, in the classic[al] sense, without sovereignty of oneself over one's home, but since there is also no hospitality without finitude, sovereignty can only be exercised by filtering, choosing, and thus by excluding and doing violence. Injustice, a certain injustice . . . begins right away, from the very threshold of the right to hospitality" (*Of Hospitality* 55). Accordingly, the ethical imperative to offer unconditional hospitality is inevitably bound up with political considerations of property, sovereignty, and control. Thus, as against Levinas's more strictly ethical view and closer to that of Kant (without, however, fully endorsing the latter either), Derrida's vision of hospitality necessarily encompasses both the ethical and the political domains, which we must always negotiate. Derrida argues that "we will always be threatened by this dilemma between, on the one hand, unconditional [ethical] hospitality that dispenses with law, duty, or even politics, and, on the other, [political] hospitality circumscribed by law and duty. One of them can always corrupt the other, and this capacity for perversion remains irreducible" (*Of Hospitality* 135).

Even leaving aside certain psychological or psychoanalytic complexities (on which I shall comment below), Derrida's analysis directs us towards the apparently irreducible ethical-political complexity, almost impossibility, of hospitality, while still insisting on the necessity, the imperative, of practicing it. For Derrida, and on this point he departs from both Kant and Levinas, hospitality is both necessary *and* impossible. There is no formula, no decidable or decipherable algorithm for hospitality, which would establish or guarantee it once and for all. This does not mean, however, that we shouldn't institute or practice certain general ethical, political, or legal laws of hospitality. Quite the contrary: such laws are *necessary*, including and in particular those that guarantee our rights, such as the right to political asylum, which is also one of Derrida's points. Laws, however, are *never sufficient*, for each situation is ultimately singular, unique, and what worked in one case might fail in another, seemingly similar situation.

Thus, in *Code Unknown*, we might see Amadou as caught within some of the impasses, the conflicting demands, of hospitality, including those of a psychological nature, between which we all must navigate, and with a much greater chance to fail than to succeed. First, though, it is necessary to acknowledge that Amadou's own aims are divided and therefore problematic. He sees that an injury (itself arguably a gesture of inhospitality or at least a failure of hospitality) has been done to Marie. In what might be construed as a gesture of hospitality, he seeks to remedy it, to affirm her dignity as a person. But he also wants to teach Jean a lesson: he wants him to apologize, to admit that he was wrong. He wants Jean to acknowledge Marie's humanity, in a sense, to make the gesture of hospitality *for him*. But Amadou cannot offer her someone else's hospitality; he cannot host what he does not control. He could, of course, have simply directed his attention, his hospitality to Marie from the very beginning. He might have asked her, for example, what she needed, and then helped her as much as he could.

But while Amadou is seizing the moral high ground, feeling righteous (and most of us are probably cheering for him), he has also brought Marie to the attention of the police, who will ensure her deportation. The involvement of the police reminds him (and us) that issues of law—not just ethical but also juridical law—are implicated in hospitality, and that hospitality has its unhappy exclusionary aspects, its inevitable violence. The police's handling of the situation raises other questions as well. Since they do not arrest Jean or even take him in for questioning, they have apparently decided, despite the conflicting accounts, that Amadou, who is polite, reasonable, articulate, but, nonetheless, black, must be at fault. (We later learn that he's beaten by the police, who also ransack his family's apartment.)

The scene is also an object lesson in the perils of unintended consequences: we can never be absolutely certain, when we try to help, whether we might instead be doing harm. Yet the film is hardly an apology for noninvolvement. In several scenes, Haneke shows us the consequences of not intervening, of standing back, of thinking some failures of hospitality are none of our business. In the film, the most grievous, large-scale failure of hospitality is that of the recent Balkan wars, invoked by Georges's photographs. The mutilated and murdered Muslim inhabitants of Kosovo might be seen as victims of the Serbs' brutal failure of hospitality to, as Derrida puts it, "Others as our own," as fellow citizens of Yugoslavia, whatever their religion or heritage, or just as fellow human beings. Georges's photographs of the slaughter also offer compelling witness to the international community's failure to intervene in a timely manner, and to the costs of this political and ethical neglect.

The category of the "stranger," the Other, is of course not limited to those from other countries or ethnicities or races or religions whom we might encounter in foreign lands or in those places we consider ours: our countries, cities, and towns, however much we might consider them to be "our homes." The stranger seeking welcome might come to us as a neighbor, one whom we believe we "know."

Even among neighbors, however, where close proximity would seem to lend a particular urgency, we do not always intervene. One night Anne's ironing is interrupted by the screams of a child down the hall. She stops, mutes the television, listens, but then, after a moment, she starts to iron again. A note asking for help appears under her door, but she cannot "decode" it, she cannot decide whether it is really a plea for help or a joke. Nor is she certain of the identity of its sender. The woman across the hall refuses to look at it, but assures Anne that she did not write it. Anne doubts that a ten-year-old girl would sign herself "a defenseless child." She is reluctant to act without being sure. And not long after, she is standing mute over the child's grave. The incident raises the question of what we owe those whose identity and intentions are unknown or uncertain. As Hannerz observes, "Trust tends to be a matter of shared perspectives, of 'I know, and I know that you know, and I know that you know that I know'. And this formula for the social organization of meaning does not necessarily apply to the relationship between local and cosmopolitan" (248). Welcoming Others into our midst, what have we the right to expect from them? That they tell us truly who they are? That they make known their peaceful intentions? And what of those who conceal their identities, loyalties, and intentions, and who mean us harm? Clearly we do not have to welcome the latter, but it is related to a more difficult question: to what extent are we obligated to tolerate the intolerant? The film does not answer, at least not definitively, these questions, but it makes us pose and re-pose them, and pursue possible and necessary answers, both in our thought and, hopefully, eventually in our lives.

There are, the film demonstrates, many barriers, psychological as well as practical, that cause our hospitality to fail, or us to fail in our hospitality. We see this, for example, in the story that Marie relates to a friend, after she returns to Paris. "One day, in Certeze," she begins, "I gave some money to a gypsy beggar. She was so dirty, I ran to wash my hands to avoid catching a disease. She simply disgusted me." She pauses for a moment and then continues. "Last winter, on Boulevard St. Germain, a well-dressed man was about to give me twenty francs. . . . But when he saw my outstretched hand, he threw the bill into my lap as if I nauseated him. I rushed back here and hid myself in the attic. I cried my eyes out all day. It was so embarrassing. Do you see?"

This scene might be understood as an inverted allegory of an encounter with one's own, internal otherness. Marie is first in the position of rejecting the abject Other, whose "dirt" threatens to be contagious and must be washed off. Marie's disgust, however understandable, might be a sign of something deeper: that in some sense the gypsy beggar was also experienced (perhaps unconsciously) as a reflection of herself, specifically of her own repressed feelings or desires. The second incident she describes is a mirror of the first: now the debased, abject Other is revealed to be herself. She has, then, occupied both positions (of the ambivalent charity-giver and of the abject Other) in what is essentially the same, twice-told narrative. While the reversal in these two instances of failed or aborted hospitality is ironic, the lesson we might draw from it might have more to do with the necessity of negotiating the hospitality within ourselves in order to be able to extend it to others. And we realize, too, that these two scenes were echoed in the opening scene in which Jean tosses his empty pastry bag into Marie's lap—a gesture of inhospitality, however, that thus inverts the intent of the previous two, which at least originated in a kind of hospitality.

There is, in fact, only one scene of wholly positive intervention in the film, and it occurs on Anne's behalf, when, in a crowded metro car, she is harassed, followed, threatened, and finally spit upon by a young man who mockingly refers to himself as "un petit Arabe." An older man, identified in the credits as "the old Arab," intervenes and chastises the young man saying, "Shame on you!" When the young man challenges him physically, the old man silently hands his eyeglasses across the aisle to Anne and stands up to face him. In a city riven by ethnic boundaries, the old man crosses them and asserts the primacy of a basic decency. The scene is also a reminder of the possibility that we might all, at one time or another, find ourselves in need of help and hospitality, even in our own cities.

There is very little to alleviate the darkness of Haneke's vision of the global city in *Code Unknown*. As the film comes to a conclusion, it cycles back through a variation of the opening scenes—Marie returns to find someone else has taken up her place in the alley; she finds another place but is threatened and chased away, and, then, ominously, followed. Georges returns home and finds the code to the front door has been changed, and Anne, again, does not hear the phone ringing. A child performs an elaborate, indecipherable pantomime. Whatever spaces of hospitality might have emerged appear to be dissolved now.

Most of the failures of hospitality in the film may well be failures of ethical rather than political hospitality, but if we are to make our heterogeneous, globalized cities work, if we are to make them hospitable, we will need both, and a balance of both. The practice of ethical-political hospitality is difficult, nearly impossible, but it is also absolutely necessary. If we could speak in terms of codes here, the codes of this hospitality are unknown, which may be the ultimate meaning of Haneke's title. It appears, however, that in order to improve the inhospitable world of the new cosmopolis, we must work with unknown codes or even with codes that may never become fully known. For, as Derrida argues and Haneke's *Code Unknown* shows, hospitality is always singular, a matter of an act or event or decision without a code to underlie or guarantee it. We need to find new types of solidarity, new ways of imagining and practicing hospitality among our cities and ourselves, as we encounter one another on our journeys, of which we can only give each other incomplete tales.

Notes

NOTES TO CHAPTER 1

1. The relationships between the formal aspects of *Sister Carrie* and *Manhattan Transfer* and their respective representations of the city have been examined by numerous critics. On *Sister Carrie*, see Christophe Den Tandt, Philip Fisher, June Howard, Richard Lehan (1969, Pizer 1991), and Donald Pizer (1984). On *Manhattan Transfer*, see Bart Keunen, Todd Gibson, A.C. Goodson, and Pizer (1991). For more wide-ranging discussions of these relationships, see Robert Alter, Graham Clarke (ed.), Blanche Housman Gelfant (1954), Lehan (1998), Diane Wolfe Levy, Raymond Williams (1973), and William Sharpe and Leonard Wallock (eds.).
2. In 2006, according to the *Forbes 100* ranking, eleven of the twenty largest corporations in the world (ranked on a composite score for sales, profits, assets, and market value) were banking/investment companies.
3. There are several excellent Marxist and New Historicist studies of *Sister Carrie* that focus on capitalism, commodity fetishism, and the construction of identity. See in particular Rachel Bowlby, Amy Kaplan, Kevin R. McNamara, Walter Benn Michaels, and Robert Shulman. By contrast, my approach focuses on how desire is specifically connected to transformations of the urban environment. For the history of Chicago and the transformation of the urban environment from the Great Chicago Fire of 1871 through the mid-1890s, in which *Sister Carrie* is set, see Carl Smith's *Urban Disorder and the Shape of Belief*.
4. Cayce has (phonetically) the same name as Case, the protagonist of Gibson's *Neuromancer* (discussed in the next section), in what is likely a deliberate allusion to Pynchon's, analogously gendered, pairing of his protagonist Oedipa Maas in *The Crying of Lot 49* with Sophocles's Oedipus. This set of interactive allusions indicates that at stake in all these works is the search for knowledge and even the ultimate knowledge of, to use Lucretius's great title, "the nature of things," and the question of gendering this search. The nature of the search for knowledge in *The Crying of Lot 49* has been the subject of much discussion and debate during recent decades, including in the context of the relationships between modernism and postmodernism in contemporary literature. See, for example, Brian McHale's important discussion of the novel in this context in his *Postmodernist Fiction* (21–25).
5. In the 1900s, these electric signs (sometimes called "fire signs") were still concentrated on Broadway and around what was then known as Longacre Square (now Times Square) due to a restriction imposed by an agreement between the Broadway and Fifth Avenue owners' associations (Berman 109). On the history of Times Square, see Marshall Berman and William R. Taylor.

By 1925, the year Dos Passos's *Manhattan Transfer* was published, it is estimated that there were over 12,000 electric advertising signs in New York City (Brevda 80). For histories of street lighting and how it transformed the urban night, see David Nye, Wolfgang Schivelbusch, and David Nasaw.

6. On the other hand, these two modes of retail, the pushcart and the department store, have been at odds from the first appearance of department stores in the mid-nineteenth century to the present. One can also see this conflict—and the replacement of the wandering peddlers and small tradesmen by kiosks and department stores (with their modern merchandising displays) through what Guillaume Le Gall terms an "imposed immobility"—in Eugène Atget's early twentieth-century photographs of the Paris streets (30). On the history of this conflict in New York City, see Daniel Bluestone.

7. Though it focuses primarily on French department stores, Rosalind H. Williams's *Dream Worlds* remains one of the best explorations of the history of consumption and of the development of department stores.

8. Clare Eby offers a perceptive reading of *Sister Carrie* via Veblen's theory of pecuniary emulation and invidious comparison, and conversely of Veblen's theories via Dreiser's works. She also takes up the "psychology of desire" operative in "the shift from a production-oriented economy to a consumption-driven one" (109).

9. See Derrida, *Grammatology* 27–73; and Lacan, *Écrits* 412–44.

10. For Saussure's schema of signification, see *Course in General Linguistics*; for Lacan's, see "The Instance of the Letter in the Unconscious."

11. As Derrida persuasively argues, the privileged role of the signified meaning in the economy of signification defines the history of Western thinking concerning signification and, in many respects, the history of Western thought itself. This view also dominates most political-economical thinking, such as that of Marx, whose concept of commodity fetishism, as articulated in *Capital*, for example, is defined by this dominance.

12. The same can be said of Hurstwood's clothing and manner. In conversation with Hurstwood, Carrie "heard, instead of his words, the voices of the things which he represented. How suave was the counsel of his appearance! How feelingly did his superior state speak for itself!" (88).

13. In his analysis of *Sister Carrie* in *Hard Facts*, Philip Fisher traces Dreiser's hierarchy of labor determined by a progressively greater "selling of the self" (162).

14. For a useful discussion of gender and consumption in *Sister Carrie*, see Gelfant's "What More Can Carrie Want?" For a broader view of the subject, see Victoria De Grazia and Ellen Furlough's edited collection, *The Sex of Things*.

15. The situation becomes even subtler if one considers that Nicole was sexually abused by her father and that her husband is her psychiatrist, and that Fitzgerald's novel itself is clearly written against the background of psychoanalysis, on the one hand, and capitalism and its conspicuous consumption, on the other. The economy (in either sense) of Nicole's desire is one of the more complex and rarely explored aspects of Fitzgerald's novel.

16. See in particular *This Sex Which Is Not One*. Of course, I merely offer here a very general summary statement of Irigaray's agenda. Her analysis itself and, by the same token, inevitably the relationships between her thought and that of Freud and Lacan are vastly more complicated. For the complexities of Lacan's economy of desire, both in this set of contexts and in general, see Jean-Michel Rabaté's chapters, "*Ravishing* Duras, or the Gift of Love" and "Joyce's *Jouissance*, or a New Literary Symptom," in his *Jacques Lacan: Psychoanalysis and the Subject of Literature*.

17. See Irigaray's *Speculum of the Other Woman* and *This Sex Which Is Not One.*

18. The page number from *Mrs. Dalloway* is from the edition Deleuze and Guattari cite.

19. I use *interpellation* here in the Althusserian sense of the "hailing" or "summoning" of the subject by an agency of capital, urging her to take up a particular subject position. The concept owes as much to Lacan, including his ideas discussed in this chapter, as to Marx.

20. In his autobiographical work *Dawn*, Dreiser reports that the merchandise at the hardware company he worked for in Chicago similarly called out to him, "You need me! You need me! You need me!" (338–39).

21. Lacan discusses the first moment in which the "Ideal-*I*" is precipitated through the child's recognition and identification with his or her mirror image in "The Mirror Stage." Lacan emphasizes that this recognition and identification are actually a mis-recognition (he uses the word "méconnaisance") and mis-identification: the Ideal-*I* is precipitated through a confusion of the image in the mirror with the being standing before it. This original conflation of the self with the mirror image is the source or prototype for many of the subject's subsequent secondary identifications (with "role models" and the idealized images presented by advertising, for instance).

22. In his deconstructionist reading of *Manhattan Transfer*, Walter Brevda argues that "for Dos Passos, then, the latent meaning of 1925 Times Square was its portent as the first sign of the postmodern age of representation, self-referentiality, and skepticism. Indeed, there is much in *Manhattan Transfer* which today we might call postmodern" (89).

23. It is true that Freud also distinguishes between things (objects which sometimes function as symbols or signs) and words (signs which can also, as in some cases of schizophrenia, function as things), and considers the role of both in the overall economy of desire. For Freud, however, this economy is ultimately governed by the connection to things or, along the Saussurean lines discussed earlier, to the primary relations between the signified and the thing itself. Thus, the ultimate prototype of the fetish (phallus) is always the materiality of the penis. For Lacan, by contrast, the economy of desire is governed by the signifier and more specifically by the signifier's form, such as the lack itself of castration or the form (triangularity) of Oedipal triangulation. The signifier thus becomes detached from the ultimate material referent or even from the signified. This is the type of detachment that we find in Dos Passos's depiction of urban subjectivity. This difference between Freudian and Lacanian economies of desire is significant, even though both economies share the determination of desire in terms of lack or absence, and as such are both criticized by Deleuze and Guattari.

24. For studies of the interrelationship between early twentieth-century New York skyscrapers and corporate identity, see also Gail Fenske and Deryck Holdsworth's "Corporate Identity and the New York Office Building: 1895–1915" and Olivier Zunz's "Inside the Skyscraper" in *Making America Corporate: 1870–1920.*

25. The criteria defining "global cities" and their respective rankings within the first, second, and third tiers have been the subjects of numerous studies. See in particular Saskia Sassen's *The Global City*, John Friedmann's "The World City Hypothesis," and Mark Abrahamson's *Global Cities*. I consider the phenomenon of postmodern global cities in the final chapter of this book, "Global Cities and Citizens."

26. Reproductions of New York and other cities in video games reflect this signscape, too, no matter how tidy the streets might be. In "Tycoon City: New

York," for example, "real-life corporate logos litter billboards and mar-
quees—Lacoste, Nokia, Toys'R'Us—but the streets themselves are spotless,
the landscaping immaculate" (Morgan 4).

27. Figures from the United Nations "Human Development Report" (1998) and
Robert Coen/Universal McCann's "Insiders Report."

28. The capacity of capital to co-opt and neutralize critique is immense. A
signal example of such a situation is Mercedes-Benz's use of Janis Joplin's
satirical send-up of consumerism, "Mercedes Benz" (1971), in a 1995 television advertising campaign that appealed to Baby Boomers (now presumably affluent enough to purchase one) through a mixture of nostalgia and
knowing irony.

29. "Sampling" and "remixes" of rock and rap music have also been a particular
area of controversy, for example, *The Grey Album*, the Danger Mouse remix
of the vocals from Jay-Z's *The Black Album* and the Beatles' *White Album*,
to which EMI (which owns the rights to the *White Album* master) responded
with a cease-and-desist order. Despite Danger Mouse's compliance, bootleg
copies continue to circulate on the Web.

30. For a survey of the tactics of antibrand campaigns, see Naomi Klein's *No
Logo*, particularly the chapter entitled "The Brand Boomerang."

31. Cayce's encounters with the footage are evocative of Oedipa Maas's night
odyssey through San Francisco in Pynchon's *The Crying of Lot 49*. Oedipa's
trip through "the infected city" (86) becomes a passage through a landscape
littered with images of the muted post horn. The muted post horn is simultaneously an ominous sign of the Trystero, a vast and evil conspiracy, and
of the covert mail system known as WASTE, used by a number of resistant
undergrounds (which may or may not be connected by anything more than
the sign itself), and perhaps more generally of the ambiguity of signification
itself, which pervades Oedipa's search, as Thomas Schaub argues in *Pynchon: The Voice of Ambiguity*.

32. According to the market research firm Yankelovich, a person living in a city
30 years ago saw up to an estimated 2,000 ad messages a day, compared with
5,000 today. Roughly half of the 4,110 people surveyed said that "marketing
and advertising today was out of control" (Story).

33. Individuals' consumption patterns can be tracked via data obtained from
charge cards (including "preferred customer cards" in drugstores and super-
markets), from catalogue and on-line sales, and from consumer surveys and
covert observations of consumer behavior, among other sources. This data is
then aggregated by zip codes.

34. In *Ways of Seeing*, Berger argues that advertising "turns consumption into
a substitute for democracy. The choice of what one eats (or wears or drives)
takes the place of significant political choice. [Advertising] helps to mask and
compensate for all that is undemocratic within society. And it also masks
what is happening in the rest of the world" (149).

35. In his *Postmodernism, or, the Cultural Logic of Late Capitalism*, Fredric
Jameson takes up the issue of the legibility or mappability of space as part
of his broader discussion of postmodern culture. Arguing that "our daily
life, our psychic experience, our cultural languages, are today dominated by
categories of space" (16), Jameson uses Los Angeles's Westin Bonaventure
hotel, which constitutes "something like a mutation in built space itself"
(38), as an exemplar of the illegibility or unmappability of the postmodern
world. The design of the interior of the Bonaventure, with its symmetrical
towers, multiple balconies, and hanging streamers, obscures its form and,
Jameson argues, "makes it impossible for us to use the language of volume
or volumes any longer, since these are impossible to seize" (43). The space

generates a kind of sensory overload, "a constant busyness [that] gives the feeling that emptiness is here absolutely packed, that it is an element within which you yourself are immersed, without any of that distance that formerly enabled the perception of perspective or volume" (43). The difficulty that one experiences in mapping this space, organizing it into a coherent mental image, and locating one's own position in it is, for Jameson, an allegory of the difficulty we experience as postmodern subjects in creating a "cognitive map" of our positions within the social, economic, and political structures of global capitalism.

36. See Malcolm Gladwell's 2004 *New Yorker* history of the mall, "The Terrazo Jungle," for a fascinating portrait of Victor Gruen. Gruen, Gladwell observes, "may well have been the most influential architect of the twentieth century. He invented the mall." Gruen also designed Fort Worth, Texas's automobile-free downtown—a scheme that has effectively turned the city itself into a vast shopping mall.

37. The ad in its static billboard form is of the same genre as the Camel and Gillette ads discussed earlier.

38. I have considered the work of Jenny Holzer and Barbara Kruger in more detail in the articles devoted to them in Hans Bertens and Joseph Natoli's *Postmodernism: Key Figures*, where I also provide a bibliography of other scholarly work on their art. See reproductions of Kruger's work in Kruger, *Love for Sale*, and of Holzer's work in Diane Waldman, *Jenny Holzer*.

39. In 2003, Kruger produced façade banners, billboards, subway posters, and bus wraps for the British department store chain Selfridges (which frequently commissions seasonal displays by contemporary artists). This participation of artists in department store commerce is not new: Andy Warhol was a window dresser for Bonwit Teller, and Tiffany commissioned window displays by Jasper Johns and Robert Rauschenberg. There is, nonetheless, something disconcerting in Kruger accepting such commissions, given the critical nature of her art. While it is unclear whether Kruger intended them to be somehow still oppositional or disruptive in nature, it seems that this use of her work constitutes a commercial recuperation or détournement of it and has the unhappy effect of neutralizing its critique, as did the previously discussed appropriation of Janis Joplin's "Mercedes Benz." In the summer of 2006, Kruger's signs were featured throughout the London Selfridges, among them, "Buy me. I'll change your life."; "I shop, therefore I am."; and "See it. Want it. Buy it. Forget it."

40. For more on "culture jamming," see *Adbusters* magazine, the website of the Billboard Liberation Front, Mark Dery's "Culture Jamming: Hacking, Slashing, and Sniping the Empire of Signs," Robert Goldman and Stephen Papson's *Sign Wars: The Cluttered Landscape of Advertising*, and Klein's *No Logo*.

NOTES TO CHAPTER 2

1. "Cyberspace" is also known by various other names, most commonly the "Web" and the "Net," but also the "Metaverse," the "Matrix," "terminal space," and the "Grid."

2. Stills of depictions of cyberspace from *Tron* (1982), *Johnny Mnemonic* (1995), *Hackers* (1995) and *The Matrix* (1999) may be viewed at *An Atlas of Cyberspaces*. The *Atlas* is also an excellent source for conceptual, historic, and other maps of cyberspaces.

3. In "The Lessons of Cyberpunk," Peter Fitting offers the following etymology of the term: "*cyber* of course suggests 'cyborg' and 'cybernetics' and the

increasing presence of computers in our lives, while *punk* is an attempt to identify this new writing in terms of its edge and texture" and to relate it to "punk values in terms of both social resistance and punk's aesthetic rebellion" (296).

4. The phrase "Newton's sleep" occurs in Blake's "Letter to Thomas Butts, 22 November 1802" (693).

5. It is not possible to trace here the rich and complex history of Cartesian thinking (in the broad sense it acquired as modernity developed), but the territory has already been well explored in the scholarly literature, including that on postmodernity and its history.

6. For more detailed studies of Le Corbusier, see William J.R. Curtis's *Le Corbusier: Ideas and Forms*; Kenneth Frampton's *Le Corbusier: Architect of the Twentieth Century*; Peter Blake's *The Master Builders: Le Corbusier, Mies Van Der Rohe, and Frank Lloyd Wright*; and Stephen V. Ward's *Planning the Twentieth-Century City: The Advanced Capitalist World*.

7. The authoritative and authoritarian tenor of Le Corbusier's rhetoric and thought are neither accidental nor incidental. At the top of the title page of *The Radiant City*, above both Le Corbusier's name and the book's title, is the inscription: "This work is dedicated to AUTHORITY."

8. "The philosophers have only interpreted the world, in various ways; the point is to change it" ("Theses on Feuerbach" 23).

9. See Peter Marcuse's "The Grid as City Plan: New York City and Laissez-Faire Planning in the Nineteenth Century," including for some of the critiques of the 1811 Plan, among them that of Frederick Law Olmsted (who subsequently designed a competing, more suburban plan for the 1870 extension that was rejected), and for accounts of the competing interests involved in both plans.

10. See Elizabeth A.T. Smith's "Re-Examining Architecture and Its History at the End of the Century" (Ferguson 22–99) and Zeynep Çelik's "Cultural Intersections: Re-Visioning Architecture and the City in the Twentieth Century" (Ferguson 190–228) for more on this and other features of modernist colonial city design.

11. Heisenberg's uncertainty principle states that we can measure or precisely predict either the position or the momentum of a quantum object, such as an electron, but never both simultaneously, as we can in classical physics, which, by the same token, allows us to ascribe both reality and causality to classical physical objects. The uncertainty relations make such an assignment impossible in quantum physics.

12. For a detailed analysis of these connections, see Arkady Plotnitsky's *The Knowable and the Unknowable: Modern Science, Nonclassical Thought, and the "Two Cultures."*

13. Gödel's incompleteness theorems prevent us from ever rigorously, mathematically guaranteeing the truth or falsity of all mathematical propositions and the noncontradictory nature of mathematics itself, provided that the mathematical field considered is sufficiently rich to include arithmetic.

14. The Villa Savoye is also perhaps the greatest realization of Le Corbusier's concept of the "machine à habiter" [the machine for living (in)].

15. Rosalind Krauss's *The Originality of the Avant-Garde and Other Modernist Myths* similarly misreads Mondrian, in my view.

16. "Bedwin" is a re-spelling of "Bedouine," the feminine form of Bedouin.

17. See the interview with Gibson and Timothy Leary, "High Tech High Life."

18. Fitting's reference to "cognitive mapping" here implicitly references Jameson's well-known essay, "Cognitive Mapping."

19. Stephenson's visions of both cyberspace and the near-future geography of Southern California are probably due to more than imagination: he majored in geography as an undergraduate at Boston University.

20. Tomas made this observation in reference to Tim McFadden's "The Structure of Cyberspace and the Ballistic Actors Model—an Extended Abstract," presented at the conference and later published in Benedikt's *Cyberspace: First Steps* under a slightly different title.
21. Benedikt does note that "this fully developed kind of cyberspace does not yet exist outside of science fiction and the imagination of a few thousand people" (123). He cites (in the note to this assertion) the works of Gibson, Brunner, and Vinge.
22. For more on Google Earth's capabilities and origins, see John Hanke's speech at the 2005 O'Reilly Media *Where 2.0 Conference.*
23. The complete Metaverse Roadmap Summit Report is available on-line (Acceleration Studies Foundation). For a summary of the draft report, see Terdiman.

NOTES TO CHAPTER 3

1. Among the more important of these urban imaginaries must be our cyber-simulations of cities, such as those created by the interrelated programs ArcMap and ArcGlobe, used by urban planners. For further analysis of the underlying assumptions built into SimCity, see Kenneth Kolson's "The Politics of SimCity" and Mark Schone's "Building Rome in a Day."
2. Many such maps, tracking the flow of Internet traffic via the NFSNET/ANSNET backbone, for example, already exist. See Terry Harpold's article, "Dark Continents: Critique of Internet Metageographies," and also the *Atlas of Cyberspaces.*
3. In the U.S., there are also two primary metropolitan high-tech research centers or what Saskia Sassen refers to as "regional" global cities: the San Francisco–San Jose axis, which encompasses Silicon Valley, and the Boston–Route 128 area. Silicon Valley (centered around San Jose) is an area of particularly rapid growth. In 2008, San Jose's population surpassed that of Detroit.
4. For a detailed analysis of these relations, see Stephen Graham and Simon Marvin's *Telecommunications and the City: Electronic Spaces, Urban Places.* Graham's edited collection, *The Cybercities Reader,* also contains useful essays on these issues.
5. See also Soja's more recent work on postmodern cities and on their relations to cyberspace in *Thirdspace* and *Postmetropolis.*
6. The phenomenon of suburbanization itself was, however, hardly new. The ancient Romans had a term for the outskirts of Rome where the estates of the wealthy were located: *suburbium.*
7. See Lawrence Mishel, Jared Bernstein, and Sylvia Allegretto's *The State of Working America.*
8. See Teresa Tritch, "The Rise of the Super-Rich."
9. See Boddy's analysis in "Underground and Overhead: Building the Analogous City."
10. See especially the chapter "Fortress L.A." in *City of Quartz.*
11. For an analysis of how structural features of plazas and other public spaces affect their uses, see William H. Whyte's landmark study, *The Social Life of Small Urban Spaces.*
12. See Peter Marcuse's "Not Chaos, But Walls" and "The Partitioned City in History"; Peter Marcuse and Ronald Van Kempen, eds., *Of States and Cities*; and Steven Flusty's *Building Paranoia.*
13. There have been several important recent studies of gated communities. See in particular Susan Bickford's excellent "Constructing Inequality: City

Spaces and the Architecture of Citizenship"; Edward J. Blakely's study for the Brookings Institution, *Fortress America: Gated Communities in the United States*; Margaret Kohn's *Brave New Neighborhoods: the Privatization of Public Space*; Setha Low's *Behind the Gates: Life, Security, and the Pursuit of Happiness in Fortress America* and also her essay "How Private Interests Take Over Public Space: Zoning, Taxes, and Incorporation of Gated Communities"; Steve Macek's "Gated Communities"; and Evan McKenzie's *Privatopia: Homeowner Associations and the Rise of Residential Private Government.*

14. Cited in Clemence.

15. Many studies have found that racial and ethnic diversity "tends to undermine support for government spending on 'public goods' of all types, whether health care, roads or welfare programs for the disadvantaged" (Porter 4).

16. In most enclosed neighborhoods crime has indeed decreased. It seems likely, however, that this particular strategy of crime prevention might not so much prevent it as just shift it (along with the traffic) to other, less protected environments. Much depends on the safety of the neighborhood to begin with. Enclosure has "backfired" in some neighborhoods in Southern California, for example, by making them "more conducive to gang activity" (Owens). As a former police officer explained, "If a neighborhood is already controlled by a gang, creating cul-de-sacs only gives them more control over the territory" (Owens).

17. See Virilio, *Speed & Politics.*

18. Brand made this (often misattributed) pronouncement in a slightly different form at the first Hackers' Conference in 1984, and it later appeared in his 1987 book, *The Media Lab: Inventing the Future at MIT,* in the following form: "Information wants to be free. Information also wants to be expensive. Information wants to be free because it has become so cheap to distribute, copy, and recombine—too cheap to meter. It wants to be expensive because it can be immeasurably valuable to the recipient. That tension will not go away" (202). It is noteworthy that only the first part of his statement has been endlessly circulated; he was perhaps more accurate in his second assertion.

19. William J. Mitchell's *City of Bits* was one of the very first explorations of the profound effects that cyberspace might have on urban space and our conceptions of it, particularly the ways in which "the worldwide computer network— the electronic agora—subverts, displaces, and radically redefines our notions of gathering place, community, and urban life" (8). Mitchell predicted that cyberspace would "play as crucial a role in twenty-first-century urbanity as the centrally located, spatially bounded, architecturally celebrated agora did . . . in the life of the Greek polis" (8). While Mitchell might have overemphasized the extent to which cyberspace would come to *replace* urban space, he was right about many of the ways in which cyberspace has come to resemble urban space. At the same time, as mentioned earlier, for the first time in history the majority of the world's population now lives in cities.

20. For the most comprehensive study of how global capital represents itself, technology, and globalization in its advertising, see Robert Goldman, Stephen Papson, and Noah Kersey's multimedia, Web-based book, *Landscapes of Global Capital.* The website features downloads of the ads that are analyzed in the study.

21. For the history of the struggles over Internet governance and control of the Internet root, from which much of the following account is drawn, see Goldsmith and Wu, and also Milton L. Mueller's *Ruling the Root.*

22. Domain names (popularly known as URLs) are the easy-to-remember names for Internet computers and websites, for example, www.amazon.com. These

are connected to Internet Protocol (IP) addresses that serve as routing directions to particular computers. The domain name system (DNS) translates Internet names into the IP numbers needed for the transmission of messages across the Internet.

23. See Internet World Stats, "Top Ten Languages Used on the Web."
24. Internet Growth for Language (2000–2007): English (139%), Chinese (392%) (Internet World Stats, "Top Ten Languages").
25. In 2005, Yahoo took their participation in Chinese political repression a step further by helping Chinese state security agents track down (via his e-mail address) the sender of a post to a pro-democracy website, the journalist Shi Tao, who was subsequently sentenced to ten years in prison.
26. It has not, however, thus far been able to prevent the well-publicized problem of unintentional "overblocking," in which, for example, filters set up to screen sexual content end up also blocking websites dealing with breast cancer. Overblocking can, as the OpenNet Initiative website explains, constitute "a significant challenge to the access of information on the Internet for it can put control over access in the hands of private corporations and unaccountable governmental institutions."
27. For a detailed "mapping" of the vast holdings of media conglomerates Sony, Newscorp (Rupert Murdoch), Viacom, Walt Disney, AOL Time Warner, Bertelsmann, and Vivendi Universal, see the web page for the PBS Frontline documentary, "The Merchants of Cool: Media Giants."
28. See, for example, C. Edwin Baker, *Media, Markets and Democracy*; William M. Kunz, *Culture Conglomerates: Consolidation in the Motion Picture and Television Industries*; and Peter Wilkin, *The Political Economy of Global Communication: An Introduction*.
29. The world's largest photo archives, for example, are now in the hands of two corporations, Getty Images and Corbis (owned by Bill Gates), which has recently acquired the historic photo archives of UPI, Sygma, and the Bettmann Archive.
30. The copyright period previously extended for the life of an individual author plus 50 years, or, for "corporate authors" (such as Disney) for 75 years. Now, they extend for 70 years and 95 years, respectively. It is worth remembering that few works are copyrighted by individuals any longer: publishers generally require authors to sign away their copyrights to the works they publish.
31. See the "Estimated Quarterly U.S. Retail Sales (Adjusted): Total and E-commerce," Table 3 of the U.S. Department of Commerce, U.S. Census Bureau's survey of "Quarterly Retail e-Commerce Sales" for the first quarter of 2006 (United States).
32. In "The Game is Virtual. The Profit Is Real," Mark Wallace writes that "for many people, what are known as massively multiplayer online games have become significant sources of income. Web sites have sprung up that allow players to use real currency to buy items—like weapons or real estate—that they may want or need for games" (7). In "How Much for a Jetpack?" Brad Stone reports: "Second Life has become . . . the Net's fastest-growing virtual world, with a robust marketplace whose dynamics mimic the vicissitudes of a real national economy."
33. On the new forms of community emerging in cyberspace, see in particular Steven G. Jones's two edited collections, *CyberSociety: Computer-Mediated Communication and Community* and *CyberSociety 2.0: Revisiting Computer-Mediated Communication and Community*; Howard Rheingold's *The Virtual Community: Homesteading on the Virtual Frontier*; and Donna Haraway's "A Cyborg Manifesto: Science, Technology and Socialist-Feminism in the Late Twentieth Century."

34. In *Flame Wars*, Mark Dery argues that "the upside of incorporeal interaction" on the Internet is a "technologically enabled, post-multicultural
vision of identity disengaged from gender, ethnicity, and other problematic
constructions. On line, users can float free of biological and sociological
cultural determinants" (2–3). As David J. Gunkel and Ann Hetzel Gunkel
point out, "according to this logic, cyberspace would surpass the dissonance
of multiculturalism, liberating identity from the problematic constructions
embodied in biological and sociocultural difference" (130). They argue
that "it is precisely in the attempt to transcend the meat of the body that
western thought has instituted and accomplished a violent erasure of other
bodies and the body of the other. Therefore, the cyberspatial researchers
who forecast and celebrate a utopian community that is 'raceless, gender-
less, and classless,' do so at the expense of those others who are always
already excluded from participating in this magnificent technology precisely
because of their gender, race, and class. Far from resolving the crises of the
multicultural society, cyberspace would perpetuate and reinforce current
systems of domination" (131). They are, of course, correct. Yet it is also
true that many users subscribe to the logic of transcendence and experience
their presence on the Internet in this way. There are many excellent studies
of virtual subjectivity: see especially Scott Bukatman's *Terminal Identity:
The Virtual Subject in Postmodern Science Fiction* (which also discusses
"terminal spaces," including cybercities); Katie Hafner and John Markoff's
Cyberpunk: Outlaws and Hackers on the Computer Frontier; N. Kath-
erine Hayles's *How We Became Posthuman: Virtual Bodies in Cybernet-
ics, Literature, and Informatics*; Tsugio Makimoto and David Manners's
Digital Nomad; Andrew Ross's "Hacking Away at the Counterculture";
Vivian Sobchak's "The Scene of the Screen: Towards a Phenomenology of
Cinematic and Electronic Presence"; Allucquere Rosanne Stone's "Will the
Real Body Please Stand Up?: Boundary Stories about Virtual Cultures"; and
Sherry Turkle's *Life on the Screen*.

35. The physical and conceptual resemblances of mall space and cyberspace have
been noted by several critics. In a critique of the generic blandness of early
cyberspace environments, "Virtual Downtown," Trip Gabriel argued that
"Subscribers who dial up America Online find themselves in the most familiar of settings, navigating with a computer interface that is meant to look like
a mall. But to some, that sense of Anytown, U.S.A., a faceless environment
that reflects mass tastes, is exactly what is wrong with cyberspace."

36. See Dolores Hayden's examinations of how the expansion of suburbia (aided
by both federal policies and tax subsidies) diminishes public space in *Building
Suburbia* and "Building the American Way: Public Subsidy, Private Space."

37. The recent proliferation of similar security strategies (CCTV surveillance
and security guards posted inside and outside building lobbies) in many
American cities can also be seen to be part of an attempt to recapture retail
customers who have been deserting the commercial districts of cities for suburban malls since the 1960s.

38. This is not to say that the profile created through the assembling and analysis of all of our personal data is an accurate one. See Jeffrey Rosen's "The
Eroded Self" for a detailed consideration of the problems inherent in these
constructions of our identities.

39. Beyond the narrative and thematic intertextualities between the two films,
there are several visual ones, such as the reuse of a photo of Hackman as
Harry Caul in *Conversation* for the NSA dossier on Edward "Brill" Lyle in
Enemy, and the similar abandoned warehouses used by both characters as
their worksites.

40. As Nunn points out, "these technologies are being diffused among cities, aided by organizations like the Defense Advanced Research Projects Agency, NASA, the US military, national research laboratories, the Office of Law Enforcement Technology Commercialization of the National Institute of Justice, and others" (1).

41. Barron, "Civil Liberties Group Worries as City's Electronic Eyes Multiply." For the complete survey report, see the New York Civil Liberties Union's "Surveillance Camera Project." A 2006 survey by Privacy International reported that there were an estimated 4.2 million cameras surveilling Britain (Reuters, "Britain's Ranking on Surveillance Worries Privacy Advocate").

42. The widespread availability of satellite images via Google Earth and other commercial services has turned out to be of some concern to governments around the world. See Katie Hafner and Saritha Rai, "Governments Tremble at Google's Bird's-Eye View."

43. See Christopher Caldwell's "A Pass on Privacy?" on the implications of the widespread use of E-Z Pass technologies that "give you the option of trading a bit of privacy for a load of convenience" (13).

44. See Nunn for an extensive survey and "taxonomy" of the sophisticated defense technologies now being commonly deployed by urban police departments, including biometrics, monitoring, imaging, communications, decision support, record-keeping, and weaponry.

45. See Bryan Appleyard, "No Hiding Place: The Surveillance Trap / Your Whole Life Laid Bare."

46. I say "particularly prevalent" because Russia, China, and other repressive regimes are not conducting popular polls on the matter.

47. For an extended discussion of urban communities, see Sharon Zukin.

48. On Athenian concepts of democracy and citizenship, see G.E.M. de Ste. Croix's *Athenian Democratic Origins: And Other Essays.*

49. While the citizen class of ancient Greece included women (the daughters of citizens, who were eligible to marry within this class), they were not, in any political or economic sense, "citizens," since they lived under the rule of male guardians and could not own property, vote, or enter into legal contracts. "Respectable" women lived almost entirely within the confines of the household.

50. The isolation of the suburban housewife has been the subject of much critique since the early 1960s, when Betty Friedan published *The Feminine Mystique.* Dolores Hayden, who has written on the design of a "non-sexist city," points out that "the private suburban house was the stage set for the effective sexual division of labor. It was the commodity par excellence, a spur for male paid labor and a container for female unpaid labor. It made gender appear a more important self-definition than class, and consumption more involving than production" ("What Would a Non-Sexist City" 169).

51. In "Evictions," Rosalyn Deutsche cautions against the vision of democratic civic life as an "organic unity" that is found, for instance, in some nostalgic invocations of the ancient Greek polis.

52. See "The Uses of Sidewalks: Safety" in Jacobs's *The Death and Life of Great American Cities* (31–32).

53. It is worth remembering that capital, too, requires the access and interchange of the polis (or some particular version of it) for its proper functioning. The censorship and restriction of access to the Internet can only, in the long run, suppress the creativity and innovation that drives not just a vital society but also commerce itself.

54. See Stephen Labaton's "Congress to Take Up Net's Future" and "Protecting Internet Democracy" (*New York Times* editorials), and Adam Cohen's "Why the Democratic Ethic of the World Wide Web May Be about to End."

NOTES TO CHAPTER 4

1. The role of the automobile in twentieth-century economic and cultural life (particularly in cities) has been examined in depth in the works of authors such as Peter E.S. Freund and George Martin, Jane Holtz Kay, J. Abbott Miller, Lewis Mumford (especially in *The Highway and the City*), Wolfgang Sachs, Mitchell Schwarzer, Richard Sennett, John Urry, Martin Wachs and Margaret Crawford, and Peter Wollen and Joe Kerr.

2. Most of the pedestrians interviewed by *New York Times* reporter Alan Finder were vociferous in their disapproval of the mayor's scheme. "The idea that automobiles should get priority in the city is insane," insisted Graham Wyatt, a native New Yorker. His wife Joy commented, "It's almost a joke to New Yorkers, the notion that someone can tell them not to cross the street." Another New Yorker, Sunny O'Neill, wondered "if we're developing a police state, rules and all." Drivers, however, were predictably enthusiastic.

3. Motor vehicles actually constituted a considerable improvement over horses, not only because they are faster and can carry more weight, but because they generate less noise (the clatter of iron-shod hooves and wooden or metal wheels on cobblestones has been notorious throughout history) and less pollution (a horse produces 35 to 50 lbs. of wet manure daily, for an annual accumulation of more than 9 tons of manure *per horse*) (Westendorf and Krogmann).

4. In some ways, Jacobs's city ballet and the sense of the city (essentially a vision of the city as polis) might be seen to be related to the ancient Greek activity of *agorazein*, which Jacob Burckhardt describes in *The Greeks and Greek Civilization*: "Here, in full view of the ships, surrounded by as many temples, civic buildings, monuments, shops and moneychangers' stalls as there was room for, the Greeks could occupy themselves with *agorazein*, that activity no northerner can render in a single word. Dictionaries give: 'go about in the marketplace, shopping, chatting, consulting', but can never convey the delightful leisurely mixture of doing business, conversing, standing and strolling about together. It is enough to know that the morning hours were generally described by it: the time when everybody is in the agora" (52). One should, again, keep in mind the idealized nature of Burckhardt's reconstitution of ancient Greek culture and the unavoidably hypothetical nature of many features of any such reconstitution. The main point here, however, is the concepts, such as *agorazein*, that have shaped our ideas and culture ever since, even if through such reconstitutions.

5. Urry's appeal to "non-places" as defining the physical and cultural urban topology dominated by the automobile here is an implicit reference to Marc Augé's *Non-Places: Introduction to an Anthropology of Supermodernity*, which argues that the "non-places" of transportation routes, vehicles, airports and rail stations, and their adjunct facilities such as hotel chains "are the real measure of our time" (79).

6. Le Corbusier's plans for the "Ville Contemporaine" (1922), the "Plan Voisin" (1925), the "Ville Cartésienne" (1930s), and the "Ville Radieuse" (1930–36) are all variations on this theme, as are the cities envisioned in CIAM's famous "Athens Charter" of 1933 (published in 1943 and edited by Le Corbusier). As numerous critics, including Mumford, Jacobs, and the Situationists, have pointed out, most of these high-rise versions of suburban sprawl were essentially anti-urban. They constituted, in effect, a suburbanization of the city itself.

7. The examples of the few successes (New York's Stuyvesant Town, for instance) and many failures (most of the low-income housing projects built during this era) of this urban model can be found in cities around the world today.

8. Jacobs's highly influential critiques of urban renewal, Le Corbusier's "Radiant City," and Robert Moses's highway projects (including the Cross-Bronx, Lower Manhattan, and Mid-Manhattan Expressways) in *The Death and Life of Great American Cities*, while correct on most counts, are not without their weaknesses. See, for example, Mumford's response in his mixed (and sometimes scathing) review, entitled "Mother Jacobs' Home Remedies for Urban Cancer," in the *New Yorker*. For a more positive (and, I think, more balanced) view of Jacobs's legacy, see Paul Goldberger's "Uncommon Sense: Remembering Jane Jacobs, the 20th Century's Most Influential City Critic."

9. Le Corbusier had first approached both André Citroën and Louis Renault, chief executives of the two largest French automobile manufacturers, before persuading Gabriel Voisin to act as sponsor. In gratitude, Le Corbusier christened this variation on his earlier "Ville Contemporaine" the "Plan Voisin" (Shaw 44). For more on the "Futurama," which is frequently credited with first introducing the idea of the superhighway into America, see Norman Bel Geddes's *Magic Motorways* and Paul Mason Fotsch's "The Building of a Superhighway Future at the New York World's Fair."

10. De Certeau has set the scene here from the vantage point of the "Top of the World" observation area on the 110th floor of the World Trade Center (South Tower) in Manhattan.

11. Le Corbusier believed the solution to the congestion of existing cities lay, paradoxically, in *increasing* the population density. "Here is the solution," he wrote, "provided by such calculation to the problem of the business center of a great city: superdensity: 3,200 occupants to the hectare" (*The Radiant City* 131). The "superdensity" of his skyscrapers would, he thought, make it possible to devote more space at ground level to lawns and other amenities for pedestrians.

12. One might contrast this scheme with Pynchon's depiction, discussed in Chapter 3, of the spaces under the California freeways (where the clandestine mail drops of WASTE can be found) as sites of resistance. Here, the spaces beneath the highways of Le Corbusier's Plan Voisin are sites of legitimate and *orderly* circulation.

13. Robert Moses left behind an enormous legacy, including the construction, in New York State alone, of a vast network (some 416 miles) of urban highways and parkways; numerous public housing projects in Harlem and on Manhattan's Lower East Side, in Morrissania (the Bronx), and Brownsville (Brooklyn); Jones Beach, Orchard Beach, and Jacob Riis Parks; Lincoln Center for the Performing Arts; 658 playgrounds; and the New York 1964–5 World's Fair. He was also instrumental in the building of the United Nations, Shea Stadium, Co-op City, and the 35-building Stuyvesant Town complex on Manhattan's East Side (he used his political influence to arrange both tax breaks and slum-clearance authority for its developers, Metropolitan Life). His models of superhighways, slum clearance, and superblock housing projects were widely imitated both in the U.S. and abroad. For the history and analysis of his complex legacy, see Hilary Ballon and Kenneth T. Jackson's edited collection *Robert Moses and the Modern City: The Transformation of New York*; Robert Caro's *The Power Broker: Robert Moses and the Fall of New York*; and Joel Schwartz's *The New York Approach: Robert Moses, Urban Liberals, and Redevelopment of the Inner City*.

14. Jacobs played a key role in organizing the successful popular opposition to the Lower Manhattan Expressway.

15. Rather than culture, politics, education, income, or even climate, the two critical factors determining automobile dependency in cities turn out to be bad urban design coupled with a lack of population and employment density (which automobiles, in turn, diminish). See Peter W.G. Newman and Jeffrey R. Kenworthy 1989, 1999, and especially their 2006 study, "Urban Design to Reduce Automobile Dependency."

16. Many such movements have sprung up around the world. In the mid-1990s, Reclaim the Streets, a British group that refers to itself as a "disorganization," staged a series of impromptu street parties on major highways and streets in Camden, Manchester, Brighton, Cambridge, Leeds, and London. See Jay Griffiths, "Life in the Fast Lane on the M41" for a detailed account. In Bogotá, Colombia, there is a long-running institution called the "ciclovia" (bike path), in which 70 miles of city streets are "closed to cars every Sunday but open for jogging, biking, dancing, playing ball, walking pets, strolling with babies—anything but driving" (Wood). The enormously popular ciclovia (an estimated 1.5 million people participate in it each week) has served as a model for other cities in Latin America, which have turned parks and even entire city districts into car-free zones. By 2007, more than twenty cities in the U.S., including San Francisco, New York, Atlanta, Philadelphia, Cleveland, Chicago, and El Paso, had also begun closing parks to cars on certain days (Wood).

17. The film's closing titles, reading respectively, "Fin du Film" and "Fin du Cinéma" ("End of Film" and "End of Cinema"), might as well have included "Fin de l'Automobile," thus bringing to a close the aesthetic and culture of speed and of space and time that emerged in the end of the nineteenth century and defined much of modernism, as considered earlier. For the emergence of this culture of space and time, and of speed, in the late-nineteenth and early twentieth centuries, see Stephen Kern's *The Culture of Time and Space: 1880–1918*, which, historically, brings us to the time of Le Corbusier, where this chapter began.

18. See, for example, the very different David Cronenberg 1996 film *Crash* (based on the J.G. Ballard novel) and Paul Haggis's 2005 *Crash* (which won the 2006 Academy Award for Best Film), Brian DePalma's 1990 *Bonfire of the Vanities* (based on the Tom Wolfe novel), and Joel Schumacher's 1993 *Falling Down*. Commercials for cars, which still portray travel by automobile as a form of liberation, are (unsurprisingly) among the few exceptions to this shift.

19. The Situationist International (SI) emerged out of Guy Debord's Lettrist International (LI), and Asger Jorn and Constant Nieuwenhuys' International Movement for an Imaginist Bauhaus (IMIB), a successor to CoBrA. In its early period (1957–1962), the Situationist International was essentially a continuation of the LI and the IMIB, and it reflected their focus on art and issues of urbanism, architecture, and design. For a detailed analysis of the Situationists' urban theories and practices, see Simon Sadler's *The Situationist City*, the definitive text on the subject.

20. Among the hidden aspects of "reality," according to the Situationists, would be our actual (as opposed to imaginary) relationship to the real conditions of our existence. It is worth mentioning, in the context of the link between spectacularity and ideology, that Althusser defines ideology as "the imaginary relationship of individuals to their real conditions of existence" (162). While these ideologies or "'world outlooks' are largely imaginary, i.e. do not 'correspond to reality,'" and thus "constitute an illusion," he notes that they also "make allusion to reality, and that they need only be 'interpreted' to discover

the reality of the world behind their imaginary representation of that world (ideology=illusion/allusion)" (162).

21. From its earliest days, cinema was bound up with the fascination of mechanical movement (one of Edison's first kinetoscopes was shot from the front of a moving subway train).

22. For a philosophical (and sometimes poetic) analysis of the epistemology of the automobile windscreen, see Paul Virilio's "Dromoscopy, or The Ecstasy of Enormities." For a more scientific and technical analysis, see Stephen Carr and Dale Schissler's "The City as a Trip" and Donald Appleyard, Kevin Lynch, and John R. Myer's *The View from the Road.*

23. Moses apparently shared this practice, as Goldberger reported in his obituary: "He maintained several offices, one of which was in his limousine; so eager was he to use every minute that he often held meetings in his car, taking his guest along in whatever direction Mr. Moses happened to be going. When Mr. Moses had finished talking with his guest, the second limousine, which had been following, would pick up the guest and take him back to his office as Mr. Moses continued on to his destination in the first car. . . . He was the nation's first great builder of highways, but ironically he never learned to drive a car himself, and he maintained a staff of chauffeurs on 24-hour call" ("Robert Moses").

24. Or, one might say, "nul," the computer's hexadecimal (base 16) 00 character used to indicate a missing printed or displayed character. "Nul" is also the ASCII term for a zero-value character.

25. As I note in Chapter 1, these transformations of urban spaces, like the transformations in the economic base that bring them about, are complex and uneven. Even today, there is a complicated balance of things, signs, brands, and this new "pure" signifier of capital. Thus, Eric sees tourists standing in line for cut-rate theater tickets in Times Square as "stunted humans in the shadow of the underwear gods that adorned the soaring billboards" (83). Except for the underwear, the description could equally fit the subjects of ancient Assyria, Egypt, Greece, or Rome, dwarfed before the monolithic sculptures of their gods and kings.

26. The line, which also serves as the novel's epigraph, is from "Report from the Besieged City," by the Polish poet Zbigniew Herbert. The poem (not cited beyond that one partial line) works well as a commentary on DeLillo's project and on the novel's principal themes.

27. On these tropes and phenomena, see Freud's "Character and Anal Eroticism," and Peter Stallybrass and Allon White's *The Politics and Poetics of Transgression,* especially Chapter 3, "The City: the Sewer, the Gaze, and the Contaminating Touch."

28. Lefebvre notes the insularity of the automobile and the detachment from the life of the city it produces in *Everyday Life in the Modern World.* "Motorized traffic," he observes, "enables people and objects to congregate and mix without meeting . . . each element remaining enclosed in its own compartment, tucked away in its own shell" (qtd. in Friedman 240).

29. How much potential the automobile might have as a means of political subversion is an intriguing question. In *The City in History,* Mumford recounted one such use of it: "In the recent Caracas revolution that deposed a brutal dictatorship in Venezuela, the starting signal, I have been told by an eyewitness, was the honking of motor car horns. That honking, growing louder, coming nearer, converging from every quarter of the city upon the palace, struck terror into the hearts of the rulers. That, too, was an urban phenomenon" (513).

30. Many of the ideas examined in this chapter were first developed by Debord, Jorn, Constant, and Ivan Chtcheglov prior to their founding of the SI (which officially lasted from 1957–1972), but subsequently became integral features of the SI's early program. Here, I will follow Sadler's lead in referring to these key figures as "Situationists."

31. "Functionalists ignore the psychological function of surroundings," Asger Jorn argued in *Potlatch* 15: "The appearances of the buildings and of the objects that we use and that form our environment have a function that is separate from their practical use."

32. *Homo Ludens*, "Man the Player" or "the playing man," is an alternative or perhaps companion to *Homo Faber*, "Man the Maker" or "the working man"—conceptions of the human being with long and complex histories. *Homo Faber* is a concept most closely associated in modernity with Marx (who refers to it in *Capital*), Henri Bergson (who uses it in *L'Évolution Créatrice*), and, in the mid-twentieth century, with Max Frisch, the author of the great novel *Homo Faber: Ein Bericht*, and Hannah Arendt, particularly in *The Human Condition*. Most relevant in this context of the dérive and other urban practices of subversive movement and play, however, is the work of the Dutch historian Johan Huizinga, *Homo Ludens: A Study of the Play Element in Culture*, which was a great influence on the Situationists' theories and practice. The concept of "play" was central to Huizinga's understanding of human history, and he argued that "civilization arises and unfolds in and as play" (Foreword).

33. This video is accessible in several versions on YouTube and Google Video.

NOTES TO CHAPTER 5

1. According to the International Organization for Migration, "there are now about 192 million people living outside their place of birth, which is about three per cent of the world's population. This means that roughly one of every thirty-five persons in the world is a migrant. Between 1965 and 1990, the number of international migrants increased by 45 million—an annual growth rate of about 2.1 per cent. The current annual growth rate is about 2.9 per cent" ("About Migration"). A major indication of the degree of global economic integration is the fact that global merchandise exports, as a percentage of world gross domestic product, are increasing faster than at any previous time in human history. In 1913, it was approximately 8%. By 1990, it had risen to a little under 15%. Since 2000, global merchandise exports have accounted for more than 20% of the world's GDP (cited in Bernanke).

2. It should be noted that "ethical" and "political" are generally different denominations and may, accordingly, and often do function differently in our discourse, theoretical or practical. In particular, one can distinguish them, as I shall more or less do here, along Levinasian lines by seeing "ethical" as referring to the relationships between individual beings and "political" as referring to the relationships between groups. Both denominations, however, have been inextricably intertwined, both conceptually and practically, throughout the history of their use as terms, a difficulty further exacerbated by other denominations, such as and in particular, "moral," used in the same set of contexts, and the differences all of these usages have in different languages. This intertwining is of course not surprising, given the connections between such concepts in many practical situations, and most major thinkers of both problematics, such as Levinas (or Kant, Hegel, Heidegger, and others

before Levinas), explored the relationships between both denominations, as, say, they are used along the Levinasian lines just defined. Since my discussion here will deal primarily with these and related interconnections in the context of cosmopolitanism, I will speak, as in this elaboration, in terms of the "ethical-political."

3. The passage and, in particular, the terms *physis* [nature] and *nomos* [custom] pose certain difficulties of interpretation and, hence, translation, which cannot be properly addressed here, although they cannot be altogether avoided either. It may be argued, however, that *physis* carries here the meaning of our essential nature, whereby we are all kinsmen as human beings by virtue of this shared essential nature. This "nature" could also be potentially related to the essential or ideal forms of goodness, virtue, and so forth, which would also be a *natural* assumption within the overall framework of the dialogue, while "local" customs or "laws" (another meaning of *nomos*) split us into groups—communities, cities, states, eventually nations, and so forth, which cannot be essential or ideal. This argumentation is, to some degree, questioned in the chapter. For, "postmodern" cosmopolitanism implies the "peaceful coexistence" of differences, defined by local *nomos* (local "normative universes," a concept sometimes designated by the term 'nomos' in recent literature), rather than grounds itself only in shared commonalities, cultural or "natural" (a problematic concept from the postmodern perspective).

4. By contrast, our Latinate "city" derives from *civitas*, a body of citizens.

5. There are considerable complexities when it comes to the actual practice of cosmopolitanism in ancient Greece, and indeed to the set of, sometimes ambiguous, attitudes that transpire in Plato's dialogues, in which the "strangers" sometimes appear in a negative light, as in *Sophist*. I shall, however, bypass these complexities, since they do not affect my main point, which concerns the idea and ideal of cosmopolitanism, here in part those of the Cynics and the Stoics.

6. Advocacy organizations such as International PEN and the International Institute of Letters, are, in many ways, contemporary, more politicized heirs to the Republic of Letters.

7. Kant's teleology invokes a Nature that has purposefully endowed human beings with both reason and freedom of will in order that they might, in time, realize its "*secret plan to bring forth a perfectly constituted state*" (21; emphasis in original).

8. This insistence upon a republican constitution is, of course, much in keeping with the revolutionary spirit of the times, and the rhetoric of both the American and French revolutions had its cosmopolitan aspects, particularly in their assertions of God- or Nature-given indefeasible and inalienable rights in the American Declaration of Independence and in the French 1789 Declaration of Human Rights, which became the preamble to the first constitution of the French Revolution in 1791.

9. Sassen's economic model of the global city is built upon a series of hypotheses which have, since she published the first edition of *The Global City* in 1991, been largely confirmed. See the section entitled "The Global City Model: Organizing Hypotheses" in the "Preface to the Second Edition," xix-xxii.

10. The benefits, of course, are part of this calculation, including the benefits of employment for workers in Mexico, Thailand, and so forth. Such benefits might well also include considerations of equity, as in the right of Third World workers to have the same access to good jobs and development that workers in the First World often enjoy.

11. See ExxonMobil, "Why ExxonMobil?"

12. See Crystal Bartolovich's analysis in "Boundary Disputes: Textuality and the Flows of Transnational Capital" and "Mapping the New World Order."
13. Based upon the International Monetary Fund's 2005 ranking of countries of the world by nominal Gross Domestic Product and the 2005 "Forbes Global 2000" rankings of public corporations (worldwide) based on sales.
14. The 2005 "Forbes 2000" ranking of public corporations used here is based upon "a composite ranking from four metrics: sales, profits, assets and market value," rather than just from sales (as above). The ranking of countries by nominal GDP is again from IMF statistics.
15. This situation was, in fact, one of the earliest effects of capitalism, beginning at least with the East India Company, which was established in 1600. The Company's history provides many a cautionary tale about the depredations of unbridled corporate *and* national (imperialistic) power on a global scale. Unbridled state power in the form of excessive control over national economies is also of concern, though with the collapse of the former Soviet Union and Eastern bloc, this seems to have waned considerably, while corporate power has burgeoned. It is also possible for the two to go together, as in the kleptocratic dictatorships of Ferdinand Marcos in the Philippines, Mobutu Sese Seko in Zaire, and Jean-Claude Duvalier in Haiti, for example.
16. In a 2006 speech on the history of global economic integration, Ben Bernanke acknowledged that much of the opposition to global economic integration "arises because changes in the patterns of production are likely to threaten the livelihoods of some workers and the profits of some firms, even when these changes lead to greater productivity and output overall." Bernanke seemed to suggest that the responsibility for addressing such negative effects of globalization belonged to governments, however, rather than to the corporations.
17. The word "culture" is, as Raymond Williams observes in *Keywords*, "one of the two or three most complicated words in the English language," and its meaning and usage vary among different academic disciplines and popular vernaculars. It has, according to Williams, three principal contemporary uses: (1) an "independent and abstract noun which describes a general process of intellectual, spiritual and aesthetic development"; (2) an "independent noun . . . which indicates a particular way of life, whether of a people, a period, a group, or humanity in general"; and (3) a noun which describes the works and practices of intellectual and especially artistic culture" (90). My discussion uses it in all three senses, sometimes separately, depending upon the context of the argument, and sometimes interactively. The concept of course requires further critical analysis, which cannot be pursued within my limits here.
18. For a compelling argument on globalization "from below," see Steven Flusty's *De-Coca-Colonization: Making the Globe from the Inside Out.*
19. Whether consumption can be a part of the creation of "resistant identities" is, I think, still an open question that should be explored. It is true that individuals, as Urry says, "can imagine ourselves as members (or supporters) of resistant organisations through purchases, wearing the T-shirt, hearing the CD, surfing to the page on the Web, buying the video of iconic figures and so on," but the impact of such "support" is debatable ("Global Media" 6). At the same time, there is no doubt that corporations are increasingly attempting to fashion themselves as good citizens of the world (cf. Starbucks "fair trade" coffee, Walmart's "organic" products, and so forth), a welcome sign, at least. Certainly, it cannot hurt to "think globally and act locally" when we act as consumers.
20. This reference is to one of the most popular advertising campaigns in history, the famous 1971 "hilltop" Coke ad in which a chorus of dozens of adoles-

cents from all over the world sang, "I'd like to teach the world to sing, in perfect harmony. I'd like to buy the world a Coke, and keep it company."

21. Even more problematic is the currently widespread tendency to define community in even greater, monolithic terms as clashing cultural "civilizations," as Samuel P. Huntington does in *The Clash of Civilizations*, in which he divides the contemporary world into Sinic, Japanese, Hindu, Islamic, Orthodox, Western, Latin American, and African "possibly" (45–47).

22. Language, too, is a lesser, but nonetheless highly symbolic, marker of community identity, as can be seen, for example, in political attempts to establish—and enforce—a "national language."

23. "If nation-states are widely conceded to be 'new' and 'historical,' the nations to which they give political expression always loom out of an immemorial past, and, still more important, glide into a limitless future," Benedikt Anderson writes in *Imagined Communities*. "It is the magic of nationalism to turn chance into destiny" (11–12).

24. For detailed critiques of such views, see both Waldron's "Minority Cultures and the Cosmopolitan Alternative" and Amartya Sen's *Identity and Violence: The Illusion of Destiny*, both of which inform my treatment of the subject here.

25. Article 27 of the "International Covenant on Civil and Political Rights" (1966) states: "In those States in which ethnic, religious or linguistic minorities exist, persons belonging to such minorities shall not be denied the right, in community with other members of their group, to enjoy their own culture, to profess and practise their own religion, or to use their own language."

26. In cases in which such mandates are imposed upon those who have no power to consent (as in the case of female circumcision, which is practiced upon children) or no power to choose, those mandates can be regarded as essentially illegitimate.

27. Such claims tend, as Appiah, Sen, and other critics have pointed out, to be based in highly selective and dubious versions of such communities' "tradition." Indeed, this is likely true of all hegemonic senses of tradition, which, as Raymond Williams argues, constitute "a deliberately selective and connecting process which offers a historical and cultural ratification of a contemporary order" (*Marxism and Literature* 115).

28. Cf. also Appiah's critique of "counter-cosmopolitanism" in his *Cosmopolitanism: Ethics in a World of Strangers* and *The Ethics of Identity*.

29. For a detailed analysis of hybrid phenomena and the challenges they present, see Latour's *We Have Never Been Modern*.

30. In *The Postmodern Condition*, Lyotard differentiates, for example, among the "denotative" game (whose statements have "cognitive value" and emphasize the truth or falsity of empirical fact [36, 40, 46]), the "technical" game (which emphasizes efficiency or inefficiency, a distinction that combines fact and, usually, values [44]), and the "prescriptive" game (which emphasizes moral/ethical considerations of the just and unjust, right and wrong, good and evil [36, 40]). Different communities use different versions and combinations of these to constitute their own "games"; so, for instance, scientists might work mostly within the provinces of the denotative (ascertained via "the scientific method"), politicians within the technical and prescriptive, and so on.

Bibliography

Abrahamson, Mark. *Global Cities*. New York: Oxford UP, 2004.

Acceleration Studies Foundation. "Metaverse Roadmap Summit Report." Accessed on 11 July 2007. <http://metaverseroadmap.org>.

Alphaville. Dir. Jean-Luc Goddard. Athos Films et al., 1965.

Alter, Robert. *Imagined Cities: Urban Experience and the Language of the Novel*. New Haven: Yale UP, 2005.

Althusser, Louis. "Ideology and Ideological State Apparatuses (Notes towards an Investigation)." *Lenin and Philosophy and Other Essays*. Trans. Ben Brewster. New York: Monthly Review P, 1971. 127–86.

Anders, Peter. *Envisioning Cyberspace: Designing 3D Electronic Spaces*. New York: McGraw, 1999.

Anderson, Benedikt. *Imagined Communities: Reflections on the Origin and Spread of Nationalism*. Rev. ed. New York: Verso, 1991.

Appiah, Kwame Anthony. *Cosmopolitanism: Ethics in a World of Strangers*. Issues of Our Times. New York: Norton, 2006.

———. *The Ethics of Identity*. Princeton: Princeton UP, 2005.

Appleyard, Bryan. "No Hiding Place: The Surveillance Trap / Your Whole Life Laid Bare." *Sunday (London) Times Magazine* 15 April 2001. Accessed on 6 November 2008. <http://cryptome.info/no-hiding.htm>.

Appleyard, Donald, Kevin Lynch, and John R. Myers. *The View from the Road*. Cambridge: MIT P, 1964.

Arendt, Hannah. *The Human Condition*. 2nd ed. Chicago: U of Chicago P, 1998.

Aristotle. "Politics." *The Collected Works of Aristotle*. Vol. 2. Bollingen Ser. LXXI.2. Ed. Jonathan Barnes. Princeton: Princeton UP, 1984. 1986–2129.

Atlas of Cyberspaces. Ed. Martin Dodge. Accessed on 8 November 2008. <http://personalpages.manchester.ac.uk/staff/m.dodge/cybergeography/atlas/wireless.html>.

Augé, Marc. *Non-Places: Introduction to an Anthropology of Supermodernity*. Trans. John Howe. London and New York: Verso, 1995.

Aurigi, Alessandro, and Stephen Graham. "Cyberspace and the City: The 'Virtual City' in Europe." *A Companion to the City*. Ed. Gary Bridge and Sophie Watson. Blackwell Companions to Geography. Oxford: Blackwell, 2000. 489–502.

Bacharach, Burt, and Hal David. "Do You Know the Way to San Jose?" Perf. Dionne Warwick. Scepter Records, 1968.

Baker, C. Edwin. *Media, Markets and Democracy*. New York: Cambridge UP, 2002.

Ballon, Hilary, and Kenneth T. Jackson, eds. *Robert Moses and the Modern City: The Transformation of New York*. New York: Norton, 2007.

Banham, Reyner. *Los Angeles: The Architecture of Four Ecologies*. New York: Harper, 1971.

Banlieue 13 (U.S. rel. *District B13*). Dir. Pierre Morel. Europa Corp. et al., 2004.

Barron, James. "Civil Liberties Group Worries as City's Electronic Eyes Multiply." *New York Times* 14 December 2006. Accessed on 1 August 2007. <http://select.nytimes.com/search/restricted/article?res=F40E14F63E550C778DDDAB0994DE404482>.

Bartolovich, Crystal. "Boundary Disputes: Textuality and the Flows of Transnational Capital." *Mediations* 17.1 (December 1992): 21–33.

———. "Mapping the New World Order." Invited lecture, Humanities Institute, SUNY Stony Brook. March 1995.

Baudrillard, Jean. *For a Critique of the Political Economy of the Sign.* Trans. Charles Levin. New York: Telos P, 1981.

The Beatles. *The Beatles (The White Album).* Capitol, 1968.

Bedwin Hacker. Dir. Nadia El Fani. Canal+ Horizons et al., 2003.

Benedikt, Michael, ed. *Cyberspace:First Steps.* Cambridge: MIT P, 1991.

Berger, John. *Ways of Seeing.* London: BBC and Penguin, 1972.

Berman, Marshall. *On the Town: One Hundred Years of Spectacle in Times Square.* New York: Random, 2006.

Bernanke, Ben S. "Global Economic Integration: What's New and What's Not?" Address. Federal Reserve Bank of Kansas City's Thirtieth Annual Economic Symposium, Jackson Hole, Wyoming. 25 August 2006. Accessed on 11 July 2007. <http://www.federalreserve.gov/boarddocs/speeches/2006/20060825/default.htm>.

Bertens, Hans, and Joseph Natoli, eds. *Postmodernism: Key Figures.* Oxford: Blackwell, 2002.

Bettig, Ronald V. "The Enclosure of Cyberspace." *Critical Studies in Mass Communication* 14 (1997): 138–57.

Bickford, Susan. "Constructing Inequality: City Spaces and the Architecture of Citizenship." *Political Theory* 28:3 (2000): 355–76.

Billboard Liberation Front. Accessed on 8 November 2008. <http://www.billboardliberation.com/>.

Blade Runner. Dir. Ridley Scott. Ladd Company et al., 1982.

Blake, Peter. *The Master Builders: Le Corbusier, Mies Van Der Rohe, and Frank Lloyd Wright.* New York: Norton, 1996.

Blake, William. *The Complete Poetry and Prose of William Blake.* Ed. David V. Erdman. Berkeley: U of California P, 1982.

Blakely, Edward J., and Mary Gail Snyder. *Fortress America: Gated Communities in the United States.* Washington, DC: Brookings Institution P, 1997.

Bluestone, Daniel. "The Pushcart Evil." Ward and Zunz 287–312.

Boddy, Trevor. "Underground and Overhead: Building the Analogous City." Sorkin 123–53.

The Bonfire of the Vanities. Dir. Brian De Palma. Warner Bros., 1990.

Bowlby, Rachel. *Just Looking: Consumer Culture in Dreiser, Gissing and Zola.* New York: Methuen, 1985.

Brand, Stewart. *The Media Lab: Inventing the Future at MIT.* New York: Viking Penguin, 1987.

Brevda, William. "How Do I Get to Broadway? Reading Dos Passos's *Manhattan Transfer* Sign." *Texas Studies in Literature and Language* 38:1 (1996): 79–114.

Bridge, Gary, and Sophie Watson, eds. *The Blackwell City Reader.* Oxford: Blackwell, 2002.

"Britain's Ranking on Surveillance Worries Privacy Advocate." *New York Times* 3 November 2006. Accessed on 1 August 2007. <http://select.nytimes.com/search/restricted/article?res=FA0A11FF3B5B0C708CDDA80994DE404482>.

Bukatman, Scott. *Terminal Identity: The Virtual Subject in Postmodern Science Fiction.* Durham: Duke UP, 1993.

Burckhardt, Jacob. *The Greeks and Greek Civilization*. Ed. Oswyn Murray. Trans. Sheila Stern. New York: St. Martin's P, 1998.

Caché. Dir. Michael Haneke. Les Films du Losange et al., 2005.

Caldwell, Christopher. "A Pass on Privacy?" *New York Times Magazine* 17 July 2005: 13–14. Accessed on 1 August 2007. <http://www.nytimes.com/2005/07/17/magazine/17WWLN.html?ex=1187150400&en=97aa3e48e414aa0f&ei=5070>.

Calvino, Italo. *Invisible Cities*. Trans. William Weaver. New York: Harcourt, 1974.

Campanella, Tommaso. *City of the Sun*. Lenox: Hard P, 2006.

Campbell, Colin. *The Romantic Ethic and the Spirit of Modern Consumerism*. Oxford and New York: Blackwell, 1987.

Capotorti, Francesco. *Study on the Rights of Persons Belonging to Ethnic, Religious and Linguistic Minorities*. U.N. Doc. E/CN.4Sub.2/384/Rev. 1 (1979).

Carnage (Carnages). Dir. Delphine Gleize. Balthazar Productions et al., 2002.

Caro, Robert A. *The Power Broker: Robert Moses and the Fall of New York*. New York: Knopf, 1974.

Carr, Stephen, and Dale Schissler. "The City as a Trip: Perceptual Selection and Memory in the View from the Road." *Environment and Behavior* 1:1 (1969):7–35.

Casino Royale. Dir. Martin Campbell. MGM, 2006.

Castells, Manuel. *The Urban Question: A Marxist Approach*. London: Edward Arnold, 1977.

Çelik, Zeynep. "Cultural Intersections: Re-Visioning Architecture and the City in the Twentieth Century." Ferguson 190–228.

Certeau, Michel de. *The Practice of Everyday Life*. Trans. Steven Rendall. Berkeley: U of California P, 1984.

Chtcheglov, Ivan. "Formulary for a New Urbanism." Knabb 1–4.

Clarke, Graham, ed. *The American City: Literary and Cultural Perspectives*. New York: St. Martin's P, 1988.

Clemence, Sara. "Most Expensive Gated Communities 2005." *Forbes.com* 18 November 2005. Accessed on 1 July 2007. <http://www.forbes.com/real-estate/2005/11/17/expensive-gated-communities-cx_sc_1118home_ls.html>.

Clines, Francis X. "The City Life: Unbearable Memories of Marketing." *New York Times* 2 June 2004. Accessed on 1 August 2007. <http://select.nytimes.com/search/restricted/article?res=F20616FE3F550C718CDDAF0894DC404482>.

Code Unknown: Incomplete Tales of Several Journeys (Code inconnu: Récit incomplet de divers voyages). Dir. Michael Haneke. Bavaria Film et al., 2000.

Coen, Robert, and Universal McCann. "Insiders Report." December 2005. Accessed on 10 July 2007. <www.universalmccann.com/pdf/Insiders1205.pdf>.

Cohen, Adam. "*Why the Democratic Ethic of the World Wide Web May Be about to End*." Editorial. *New York Times* 28 May 2006. Accessed on 10 November 2008. <http://www.nytimes.com/2006/05/28/opinion/28sun3.html>.

The Conversation. Dir. Francis Ford Coppola. American Zoetrope et al., 1974.

Cortázar, Julio. *Hopscotch*. Trans. Gregory Rabassa. London: Collins, Harvill P, 1967.

Cose, Ellis. "Drawing Up Safer Cities." *Newsweek* 11 July 1994. Accessed on 10 November 2008. <http://www.newsweek.com/id/134193>.

Crash. Dir. David Cronenberg. Alliance Communications et al., 1996.

Crash. Dir. Paul Haggis. Bob Yari Productions et al., 2004.

Crawford, Margaret. "The World in a Shopping Mall." Sorkin 3–30.

Cross, Andrew. "Driving the American Landscape." Wollen and Kerr 249–58.

Curtis, William J.R. *Le Corbusier: Ideas and Forms*. New York: Rizzoli, 1986.

Danger Mouse. *The Grey Album*. (Mash-up), 2004.

Davis, Mike. *City of Quartz: Excavating the Future in Los Angeles.* New York: Vintage, 1992.

Dear, Michael, and Steven Flusty. "Postmodern Urbanism." *Annals of the Association of American Geographers* 88:1 (1998): 50–72.

Debord, Guy. "Introduction to a Critique of Urban Geography." Knabb 5–8.

———. Perspectives for Conscious Alterations in Everyday Life." Knabb 68–75.

———. "Report on the Construction of Situations and on the International Situationist Tendency's Conditions of Organization and Action." Knabb 17–25.

———. *Society of the Spectacle.* Detroit: Black & Red, 1983.

———. "Theory of the Dérive." Knabb 50–54.

De Grazia, Victoria, and Ellen Furlough, eds. *The Sex of Things: Gender and Consumption.* Berkeley: U of California P, 1996.

Deleuze, Gilles. "Postscript on the Societies of Control." Leach 309–13.

Deleuze, Gilles, and Félix Guattari. *Anti-Oedipus: Capitalism and Schizophrenia.* Trans. Robert Hurley, Mark Seem, and Helen R. Lane. Minneapolis: U of Minnesota P, 1983.

———. *Kafka: Toward a Minor Literature.* Trans. Dana Polan. Minneapolis: U of Minnesota P, 1986.

———. *A Thousand Plateaus: Capitalism and Schizophrenia.* Trans. Brian Massumi. Minneapolis: U of Minnesota P, 1987.

———. *What Is Philosophy?* Trans. Hugh Tomlinson and Graham Burckell. New York: Columbia UP, 1994.

DeLillo, Don. *Cosmopolis.* New York: Scribner's, 2003.

———. *White Noise.* New York: Penguin, 1984.

Den Tandt, Christophe. *The Urban Sublime in American Literary Naturalism.* Urbana: U of Illinois P, 1998.

Derrida, Jacques. *Of Grammatology.* Trans. Gayatri Chakravorty Spivak. Baltimore: Johns Hopkins UP, 1974.

———. "On Cosmopolitanism." Trans. Mark Dooley. *On Cosmopolitanism and Forgiveness.* Trans. Mark Dooley and Michael Hughes. London and New York: Routledge, 2001. 3–24.

———. "Politics and Friendship: A Discussion with Jacques Derrida." Centre for Modern French Thought, University of Sussex, 1 December 1997. Accessed on 10 July 2007. <http://www.hydra.umn.edu/derrida/pol+fr.html>.

Derrida, Jacques, and Anne Dufourmantelle. *Of Hospitality: Anne Dufourmantelle Invites Jacques Derrida to Respond.* Trans. Rachel Bowlby. Stanford: Stanford UP, 2000.

Dery, Mark. *Culture Jamming: Hacking, Slashing, and Sniping in the Empire of the Signs.* Np.: Open Magazine Pamphlet Series, 1993.

Dery, Mark, ed. *Flame Wars: The Discourse of Cyberculture.* Durham: Duke UP, 1994.

De Ste. Croix, G.E.M. *Athenian Democratic Origins and Other Essays.* Ed. David Harvey and Robert Parker. Oxford: Oxford University P, 1994.

Deutsche, Rosalyn. "Evictions: Art and Spatial Politics." Bridge and Watson, *Reader* 401–9.

Diogenes Laertius. *Lives of Eminent Philosophers.* Vol. 2, Book 6. Trans. R.D. Hicks. New York: Putnam, 1925. 224–47.

Dodge, Martin, and Rob Kitchin. *Atlas of Cyberspace.* Harlow, UK: Pearson, 2001.

Dos Passos, John. *Manhattan Transfer.* Boston: Houghton, 1925.

Dreiser, Theodore. *Dawn.* New York: Horace Liveright, 1931.

———. "Reflections." *Ev'ry Month* 3 (October 1896). Reprinted in *Sister Carrie* 409–13.

————. *Sister Carrie.* 1900. Ed. Donald Pizer. 2ⁿᵈ ed. New York: Norton Critical Editions, 1991.

Eby, Clare Virginia. *Dreiser and Veblen: Saboteurs of the Status Quo.* Columbia: U of Missouri P, 1998.

Ehrlich, Dimitri, and Gregor Ehrlich. "Graffiti in Its Own Words," *New York Magazine* July 3–10, 2006: 48–54, 124.

Elmer, Greg. "Spaces of Surveillance: Indexicality and Solicitation on the Internet." *Critical Studies in Mass Communication* 14 (1997): 182–91.

Enemy of the State. Dir. Tony Scott. Touchstone et al., 1998.

Ewen, Stuart, and Elizabeth Ewen. *Channels of Desire: Mass Images and the Shaping of American Consciousness.* New York: McGraw, 1982.

ExxonMobil. "Why ExxonMobil?" Accessed on 10 November 2008. <http://www.exxonmobil.com/Australia-English/HR/About/AU_HR_why.asp>.

Falling Down. Dir. Joel Schumacher. Alcor Films et al., 1993.

Fenske, Gail, and Deryck Holdsworth. "Corporate Identity and the New York Office Building: 1895–1915." Ward and Zunz 129–59.

Ferguson, Russell, ed. *At the End of the Century: One Hundred Years of Architecture.* Los Angeles: The Museum of Contemporary Art, 1998.

Finder, Alan. "Footloose Pedestrians Are Just about in Lock Step: They Hate Traffic Plan." *New York Times* 27 December 1997. Accessed on 1 August 2007. <http://select.nytimes.com/search/restricted/article?res=F00914FC3D550C748 EDDAB0994DF494D81>.

Fisher, Philip. *Hard Facts: Setting and Form in the American Novel.* New York: Oxford UP, 1985.

Fitting, Peter. "The Lessons of Cyberpunk." Penley and Ross 295–315.

Fitzgerald, F. Scott. *Tender Is the Night.* New York: Scribner's, 1982.

Flusty, Steven. *Building Paranoia: The Proliferation of Interdictory Space and the Erosion of Spatial Justice.* West Hollywood: Los Angeles Forum for Architecture and Urban Design, 1994.

————. *De-Coca-Colonization: Making the Globe from the Inside Out.* New York: Routledge, 2004.

"The Forbes Global 2000" (2005). *Forbes*.com. 31 March 2005. Accessed on 11 July 2007. <http://www.forbes.com/2005/03/30/05f2000land.html>.

"The Forbes 2000" (2006). *Forbes*.com. 30 March 30, 2006. Accessed on 11 July 2007. <http://www.forbes.com/lists/2006/18/06f2k_The-Forbes-2000_Rank. html>.

————. "Of Other Spaces: Utopias and Heterotopias." Leach 348–56.

Fotsch, Paul Mason. "The Building of a Superhighway Future at the New York World's Fair. *Cultural Critique* 48 (Spring 2001): 65–97.

Foucault, Michel. *Discipline and Punish: The Birth of the Prison.* Trans. Alan Sheridan. New York: Vintage, 1979.

Frampton, Kenneth. *Le Corbusier: Architect of the Twentieth Century.* New York: Harry N. Abrams, 2002.

Freud, Sigmund. "Character and Anal Eroticism." *Character and Culture.* New York: Macmillan, 1963. 27–33.

————. *Civilization and Its Discontents.* Ed. and trans. James Strachey. New York: Norton, 1961.

Freund, Peter E.S., and George Martin. *The Ecology of the Automobile.* Montreal and New York: Black Rose, 1993.

Friedman, Stephen. *City Moves: A User's Guide to the Way Cities Work.* New York: McGraw, 1989.

Friedmann, John. "The World City Hypothesis." *Development and Change* 4 (1986): 12–50.

Frisch, Max. *Homo Faber.* Trans. Michael Bullock. New York: Harvest, 1994.

Gabriel, Trip. "Virtual Downtown." *New York Times* 22 January 1995. Accessed on 8 November 2008. <http://query.nytimes.com/gst/fullpage.html?res=990CE2DD103AF931A15752C0A963958260&scp=1&sq=Virtual%20Downtown&st=cse>.

Garfield, Deborah. "Taking a Part: Actor and Audience in *Sister Carrie.*" *American Literary Realism* 16:2 (1983): 223–39.

Geddes, Norman Bel. *Magic Motorways.* New York: Random, 1941.

Gelernter, David. *Mirror Worlds: or, the Day Software Puts the Universe in a Shoebox . . . How It Will Happen and What It Will Mean.* New York: Oxford UP, 1991.

Gelfant, Blanche Housman. *The American City Novel.* Norman: U of Oklahoma P, 1954.

———. "What More Can Carrie Want? Naturalistic Ways of Consuming Women." *The Cambridge Companion to American Realism and Naturalism.* Ed. Donald Pizer. Cambridge: Cambridge UP, 1995. 178–210.

Geyh, Paula. "Jenny Holzer." Bertens and Natoli 173–79.

———. "Barbara Kruger." Bertens and Natoli 195–200.

Gibson, Todd. "*Manhattan Transfer* and the International Style: The Architectural Basis of Dos Passos's Modernism." *West Virginia University Philological Papers* 41 (1995): 65–70.

Gibson, William. *Burning Chrome.* New York: Ace, 1987.

———. *Neuromancer.* New York: Ace Books, 1984.

———. *Pattern Recognition.* New York: Putnam, 2003.

Gibson, William, and Timothy Leary. "'High Tech High Life': William Gibson and Timothy Leary in Conversation." *Mondo 2000.* Vol. 7 (Fall 1989). 58–64.

Gladwell, Malcolm. "The Terrazzo Jungle." *The New Yorker* March 15, 2004. 102–27.

Goldberger, Paul. "Architecture View: When Your Own Initials Aren't Enough." *New York Times* 7 August 1994. Accessed on 1August 2007. <http://query.nytimes.com/gst/fullpage.html?res=9E00E6D71531F934A3575BC0A962958260>.

———. "Robert Moses, Master Builder, is Dead at 92." *New York Times* (Obituary) 30 July 1981. Accessed on 1 August 2007. <http://select.nytimes.com/search/restricted/article?res=F20715FC3C5F0C738FDDAE0894D9484D81>.

———. "Uncommon Sense: Remembering Jane Jacobs, the 20th-Century's Most Influential City Critic." *The American Scholar* (Autumn 2006). Accessed on 10 July 2007. <www.theamericanscholar.org/archives/au06/uncommonsense-goldberger.html>.

Goldman, Robert, and Stephen Papson. *Sign Wars: The Cluttered Landscape of Advertising.* New York: Guilford P, 1996.

Goldman, Robert, Stephen Papson, and Noah Kersey. *Landscapes of Capital.* 1998–2003. Accessed on 30 June 2007. <http://it.stlawu.edu/~global/>.

Goldsmith, Jack, and Tim Wu. *Who Controls the Internet? Illusions of a Borderless World.* New York: Oxford UP, 2006.

Goodson, A. C. "*Manhattan Transfer* and the Metropolitan Subject." *Arizona Quarterly* 56.1 (Spring 2000): 89–103.

Google. "Company Overview." Accessed on 20 July 2008. <http://www.google.com/corporate/>.

———. "Our Philosophy." Accessed on 20 July 2008. <http://www.google.com/corporate/tenthings.html>.

Goss, Jon. "'We Know Who You Are and We Know Where You Live': The Instrumental Rationality of Geodemographic Systems." *The Consumption Reader.* Ed. David B. Clarke, Marcus A. Doel, and Kate M.L. Housiaux. London and New York: Routledge, 2003. 211–15.

Graham, Stephen, ed. *The Cybercities Reader.* Routledge Urban Reader Ser. London and New York: Routledge, 2004.

Graham, Stephen, and Simon Marvin. *Telecommunications and the City: Electronic Spaces, Urban Places.* New York: Routledge, 1996.

Grant, Jill. "The Dark Side of the Grid: Power and Urban Design." *Planning Perspectives* 16 (2001): 219–41.

Griffiths, Jay. "Life in the Fast Lane on the M41: Jay Griffiths Parties without Reservation at the Invitation of Reclaim The Streets." *The Guardian* (London). 17 July 1996. Accessed on 10 July 2007. <http://rts.gn.apc.org/sp'96/newsp.htm>.

Gunkel, David J., and Ann Hetzel Gunkel. "Virtual Geographies: The New Worlds of Cyberspace." *Critical Studies in Mass Communication* 14 (1997): 123–37.

Hackers. Dir. Iain Softley. United Artists et al., 1995.

Hafner, Katie. "After Subpoenas, Internet Searches Give Some Pause." *New York Times* 25 January 2006. Accessed on 1 August 2007. <http://www.nytimes.com/2006/01/25/national/25privacy.html?ex=1187150400&en=354ec5a05281 2db2&ei=5070>.

Hafner, Katie, and John Markoff. *Cyberpunk: Outlaws and Hackers on the Computer Frontier.* New York: Simon & Schuster, 1991.

Hafner, Katie, and Saritha Rai. "Governments Tremble at Google's Bird's Eye View." *New York Times* 20 December 2005. Accessed on 1 August 2007. <http://www.nytimes.com/2005/12/20/technology/20image.html?ex=1187150 400&en=ae015217e0a37dc3&ei=5070>.

Hanke, John. Address. 2005 O'Reilly Media *Where 2.0 Conference.* 30 June 2005. Accessed on 11 July 2007. <http://www.itconversations.com/shows/detail803.html>.

Hannerz, Ulf. "Cosmopolitans and Locals in World Culture." *Theory, Culture and Society* 7 (1990): 237–51.

Haraway, Donna J. "A Cyborg Manifesto: Science, Technology and Socialist-Feminism in the Late Twentieth Century." *Simians, Cyborgs, and Women: The Reinvention of Nature.* New York: Routledge, 1989. 149–81.

Harmon, Amy. "A Real-Life Debate on Free Expression in a Cyberspace City." *New York Times* 15 January 2004. Accessed on 1 August 2007. <http://www.nytimes.com/2005/12/20/technology/20image.html?ex=1187150400&en=ae0 15217e0a37dc3&ei=5070>.

Harpold, Terry. "Dark Continents: Critique of Internet Metageographies." *Postmodern Culture* 9.2 (1999).

Harvey, David. *The Condition of Postmodernity: An Enquiry into the Origins of Cultural Change.* Cambridge: Basil Blackwell, 1989.

———. *Spaces of Capital: Towards a Critical Geography.* New York: Routledge, 2001.

———. *Spaces of Global Capitalism: A Theory of Uneven Geographical Development.* New York: Verso, 2006.

Hayden, Dolores. *Building Suburbia: Green Fields and Urban Growth, 1820–2000.* New York: Vintage, 2004.

———. "Building the American Way: Public Subsidy, Private Space." Low and Smith 35–48.

———. "What Would a Non-Sexist City Be Like? Speculations on Housing, Urban Design, and Human Work." Stimpson 167–84.

Hayles, N. Katherine. *How We Became Posthuman: Virtual Bodies in Cybernetics, Literature, and Informatics.* Chicago: U of Chicago P, 1999.

Hegel, Georg Wilhelm Friedrich. *Phenomenology of Spirit.* Trans. A. V. Miller. Oxford: Oxford UP, 1979.

Herbert, Zbigniew. *Report from the Besieged City & Other Poems.* Trans. John Carpenter and Bogdana Carpenter. New York: Ecco P, 1985.

Higgins, Andrew, and Azeem Azhar, "China Begins to Erect Second Great Wall in Cyberspace." *The Guardian* (London). 5 February 1996.

Howard, June. *Form and History in American Literary Naturalism*. Chapel Hill: U of North Carolina P, 1985.

Huizinga, Johan. *Homo Ludens: A Study of the Play-Element in Culture*. 1938. Boston: Beacon P, 1955.

Huntington, Samuel P. *The Clash of Civilizations*. New ed. New York: Free P, 2002.

IBM. "The Future of Computing." Accessed on 1 July 2007. <http://www.ibm.com/IBM/ar95/sv_static/index.html>.

"International Covenant on Civil and Political Rights." Office of the High Commissioner for Human Rights. Adopted 16 December 1966. Accessed on 12 July 2007. <http://www.unhchr.ch/html/menu3/b/a_ccpr.htm>.

International Organization for Migration. "About Migration." Accessed on 11 July 2007. <http://www.iomdublin.org/about_us_facts_fig.htm>.

Internet Society of China. "Public Pledge on Self-Discipline for the Chinese Internet Industry." Accessed on 1 July 2007. <http://www.isc.org.cn/20020417/ca102762.htm>.

Internet World Stats. "Top Ten Languages Used on the Web." Accessed on 1 July 2007. <http://www.internetworldstats.com/stats7.htm>.

Irigaray, Luce. *Speculum of the Other Woman*. Trans. Gillian C. Gill. Ithaca: Cornell UP, 1985.

———. *This Sex Which Is Not One*. Trans. Catherine Porter. Ithaca: Cornell UP, 1985.

Iyer, Pico. *The Global Soul: Jet Lag, Shopping Malls, and the Search for Home*. New York: Vintage, 2001.

Jacobs, Jane. *The Death and Life of Great American Cities*. New York: Vintage, 1961.

Jameson, Fredric. "Cognitive Mapping." *Marxism and the Interpretation of Literature*. Ed. Cary Nelson and Lawrence Grossberg. Urbana: U of Illinois P, 1988. 347–57.

———. *Postmodernism, Or, The Cultural Logic of Late Capitalism*. Durham: Duke UP, 1991.

Jay-Z. *The Black Album*. Def Jam, 2003.

Johnny Mnemonic. Dir. Robert Longo. TriStar et al., 1995.

Jones, Steven G., ed. *CyberSociety: Computer-Mediated Communication and Community*. Thousand Oaks: Sage, 1995.

———, ed. *CyberSociety 2.0: Revisiting Computer-Mediated Communication and Community*. Thousand Oaks: Sage, 1998.

Jorn, Asger. Excerpt from *Image and Form*. Potlatch #15 (22 December 1954). Accessed on 11 July 2007. <http://www.notbored.org/SI-texts.html>.

Jump Britain. Dir. Mike Christie. Carbon Media, 2005.

Jump London. Dir. Mike Christie. Carbon Media, 2003.

Kant, Immanuel. *Groundwork of the Metaphysics of Morals*. Ed. and trans. Mary Gregor. Cambridge: Cambridge UP, 1998.

———. "Idea for a Universal History from a Cosmopolitan Point of View." *On History*. Ed. Lewis White Beck. Trans. Lewis White Beck, Robert E. Anchor, and Emil L. Fackenheim. New York: Bobbs-Merrill, 1963. 11–26.

———. "Perpetual Peace." *On History* 85–132.

Kaplan, Amy. *The Social Construction of American Realism*. Chicago: U of Chicago P, 1988.

Kay, Jane Holtz. *Asphalt Nation: How the Automobile Took Over America and How We Can Take It Back*. New York: Crown, 1997.

Kern, Stephen. *The Culture of Time and Space: 1880–1918*. Cambridge: Harvard UP, 1983.

Kerouac, Jack. *On the Road.* New York: Penguin, 1991.

Keunen, Bart. "The Plurality of Chronotopes in the Modernist City Novel: The Case of *Manhattan Transfer.*" *English Studies* 5 (2001): 420–36.

Kitto, H.D.F. *The Greeks.* Chicago: Aldine, 1965.

Klein, Naomi. *No Logo.* New York: Picador, 2000.

Kleingeld, Pauline. "Six Varieties of Cosmopolitanism in Late Eighteenth-Century Germany." *Journal of the History of Ideas* 60:3 (1999): 505–24.

Kleingeld, Pauline, and Eric Brown. "Cosmopolitanism." The Stanford Encyclopedia of Philosophy (Fall 2002 ed.). Ed. Edward N. Zalta. Accessed on 11 July 2007. <http://plato.stanford.edu/archives/fall2002/entries/cosmopolitanism/>.

Knabb, Ken, ed. and trans. *Situationist International Anthology.* Berkeley: Bureau of Public Secrets. 1981.

Kohn, Margaret. *Brave New Neighborhoods: The Privatization of Public Space.* New York: Routledge, 2004.

Kolson, Kenneth. "The Politics of SimCity." PS: Political Science and Politics 29:1 (1996): 43–46.

Kotányi, Attila, and Raoul Vaneigem. "Elementary Program of the Bureau of Unitary Urbanism." Knabb 65–67.

Krauss, Rosalind E. *The Originality of the Avant-Garde and Other Modernist Myths.* Cambridge: MIT P, 1985.

Kruger, Barbara. "An Interview with Barbara Kruger." By W.J.T. Mitchell. *Critical Inquiry* 17:2 (1991): 434–8.

———. *Love for Sale: The Words and Pictures of Barbara Kruger / Text by Kate Linker.* New York: Harry N. Abrams, 1990.

Kunz, William M. *Culture Conglomerates: Consolidation in the Motion Picture and Television Industries.* Lanham: Rowman, 2007.

Labaton, Stephen. "Congress to Take Up Net's Future." *New York Times* 10 January 2007. Accessed on 8 November 2008. <http://query.nytimes.com/gst/fullpage.html?res=9F0CE1DD1230F933A25752C0A9619C8B63&scp=1&sq=Congress%20to%20take%20up%20Net's%20Future&st=cse>.

———. "Protecting Internet Democracy." Editorial. *New York Times* 3 January 2007. Accessed on 10 November 2008. <http://www.nytimes.com/2007/01/03/opinion/03wed1.html?scp=1&sq=Protecting%20Internet%20Democracy&st=cse>.

Lacan, Jacques. *Écrits: The First Complete Translation in English.* Trans. Bruce Fink. New York: Norton, 2005.

———. "The Instance of the Letter in the Unconscious, or Reason Since Freud." *Écrits* 412–41.

———. "The Mirror Stage as Formative of the *I* Function as Revealed in Psychoanalytic Experience." *Écrits* 75–81.

LaFerla, Ruth. "Nests Imperial or Fashionably Feathered." *New York Times* 2 February 2006. Accessed on 1 August 2007. <http://www.nytimes.com/2006/02/02/garden/02fash.html?ex=1187150400&en=cbd93a0dc6ff0463&ei=5070>.

Latour, Bruno. *We Have Never Been Modern.* Trans. Catherine Porter. Cambridge: Harvard UP, 1993.

Law, Jaclyn. "PK and Fly." *This Magazine* May/June 2005. Accessed on 11 July 2007. <http://www.thismagazine.ca/issues/2005/05/>.

Leach, Neil, ed. *Rethinking Architecture: A Reader in Cultural Theory.* London and New York: Routledge, 1997.

Le Corbusier. *The Radiant City: Elements of a Doctrine of Urbanism to Be Used as the Basis of Our Machine-Age Civilization.* 1935. New York: Orion, 1967.

Le Corbusier, ed. *The Athens Charter.* 1943. Trans. Anthony Eardley. Introduction by Jean Giraudoux. Foreword by Josep Lluis Sert. New York: Grossman P, 1973.

Lefebvre, Henri. *Everyday Life in the Modern World.* Trans. Sacha Rabinovitch. New Brunswick: Transaction, 1984.

———. "Henri Lefebvre on the Situationist International." Interview with Kristen Ross. Trans. Kristen Ross. 1983. Accessed on 11 July 2007. <http://www.not-bored.org/lefebvre-interview.html>.

———. *The Production of Space.* Trans. Donald Nicholson-Smith. Cambridge: Blackwell, 1991.

———. "The Right to the City." *Writings on Cities.* Trans. Eleonore Kofman and Elizabeth Lebas. Cambridge: Blackwell, 1996.

Le Gall, Guillaume. *Atget, Life in Paris.* Trans. Brian Holmes. Paris: Éditions Hazan, 1998.

LeGates, Richard T., and Frederic Stout, eds. *The City Reader.* London and New York: Routledge, 1996.

Lehan, Richard. *The City in Literature: An Intellectual and Cultural History.* Berkeley: U of California P, 1998.

———. "The City, the Self, and Narrative Discourse." Pizer, ed. 65–85.

———. *Theodore Dreiser: His World and His Novels.* Carbondale: Southern Illinois UP, 1969.

Levy, Diane Wolfe. "City Signs: Toward a Definition of Urban Literature." *Modern Fiction Studies* 24:1 (1978): 65–73.

Lichtblau, Eric, and James Risen. "Spy Agency Mined Vast Data Trove, Officials Report." *New York Times* 24 December 2005. Accessed on 1 August 2007. <http://select.nytimes.com/search/restricted/article?res=FA0714F63E540C778 EDDAB0994DD404482>.

Lost in Translation. Dir. Sofia Coppola. Focus Features et al., 2003.

Low, Setha. *Behind the Gates: Life, Security, and the Pursuit of Happiness in Fortress America.* New York: Routledge, 2004.

———. "How Private Interests Take Over Public Space: Zoning, Taxes, and Incorporation of Gated Communities." Low and Smith 81–104.

Low, Setha, and Neil Smith, eds. *The Politics of Public Space.* New York: Routledge, 2006.

Lynch, Kevin. *The Image of the City.* Cambridge: MIT P, 1960.

Lyotard, Jean-François. "Answering the Question: What Is Postmodernism?" Trans. Régis Durand. *The Postmodern Condition* 71–82.

———. *The Differend: Phrases in Dispute.* Trans. Georges Van Den Abbeele. Theory and History of Literature 46. Minneapolis: U of Minnesota P, 1988.

———. *The Postmodern Condition: A Report on Knowledge.* Trans. Geoff Bennington and Brian Massumi. Theory and History of Literature 10. Minneapolis: U of Minnesota P, 1984.

Macek, Steve. "Gated Communities." *St. James Encyclopedia of Pop Culture.* Accessed on 10 July 2007. <http://findarticles.com/p/articles/mi_g1epc/is_tov/ai_2419100492>.

MacKinnon, Rebecca, and John Palfrey. "Opinion: Censorship Inc." *Newsweek International Edition* 27 February 2006. Accessed on 1 July 2007. <http://www.msnbc.msn.com/id/11437139/site/newsweek>.

Makimoto, Tsugio and David Manners. *Digital Nomad.* New York: Wiley, 1997.

Marchand, Roland. *Advertising the American Dream: Making Way for Modernity, 1920–1940.* Berkeley: U of California P, 1985.

Marcuse, Peter. "The Grid as City Plan: New York City and Laissez-Faire Planning in the Nineteenth Century." *Planning Perspectives* 2 (1987): 287–310.

———. "Not Chaos, but Walls: Postmodernism and the Partitioned City." Watson and Gibson 243–53.

———. "The Partitioned City in History." Of States and Cities: The Partitioning of Urban Space. Ed. Peter Marcuse and Ronald van Kempen. New York: Oxford UP, 2002. 11–34.

Marx, Karl. *Capital*. Vol. 1. Trans. Ben Fowkes. London: Penguin, 1990.

———. *Economic and Philosophic Manuscripts of 1844 and the Communist Manifesto*. Trans. Martin Milligan. New York: Prometheus, 1988.

———. "Theses on Feuerbach." *Karl Marx: A Reader*. Ed. Jon Elster. New York: Cambridge UP, 1986. 20–23.

Massey, Doreen. "Politics and Space/Time." *New Left Review* 196 (1992): 65–84.

The Matrix. Dirs. Andy and Larry Wachowski. Groucho II et al., 1999.

The Matrix Reloaded. Dirs. Andy and Larry Wachowski. Warner Bros. et al., 2003.

The Matrix Revolutions. Dirs. Andy and Larry Wachowski. Warner Bros. et al., 2003.

Max Headroom. Television series. Dirs. Janet Greek and Victor Lobl. ABC, 1987–88.

McFadden, Tim. "Notes on the Structure of Cyberspace and the Ballistic Actors Model." Benedikt 335–62.

McHale, Brian. *Postmodernist Fiction*. London and New York: Routledge, 1987.

McKenzie, Evan. *Privatopia: Homeowner Associations and the Rise of Residential Private Government*. New Haven: Yale UP, 1994.

McLuhan, Marshall, and Quentin Fiore. *The Medium is the Massage: An Inventory of Effects*. New York: Bantam, 1967.

McNamara, Kevin R. *Urban Verbs: Arts and Discourses of American Cities*. Stanford: Stanford UP, 1996.

"The Merchants of Cool: Media Giants." *Frontline*. PBS. WGBH, Boston. Accessed on 1 July 2007. <http://www.pbs.org/wgbh/pages/frontline/shows/cool/giants/>.

Michaels, Walter Benn. *The Gold Standard and the Logic of Naturalism*. Berkeley: U of California P, 1987.

Miles, Steven, and Malcolm Miles. *Consuming Cities*. New York: Palgrave Macmillan, 2004.

Miller, J. Abbott. *Inside Cars*. New York: Princeton Architectural P, 2001.

Milton S. Eisenhower Foundation. *'To Establish Justice, to Insure Domestic Tranquility': A Thirty-Year Update of the National Commission on the Causes and Prevention of Violence*. Washington, DC: Milton S. Eisenhower Foundation, 1999. Accessed on 1 July 2007. <http://www.eisenhowerfoundation.org/aboutus/publications/justice.html>.

Mishel, Lawrence, Jared Bernstein, and Sylvia Allegretto. *The State of Working America 2004–5*. Ithaca: Cornell UP, 2005. Accessed on 1 July 2007. <http://www.stateofworkingamerica.org>.

Mitchell, William J. *City of Bits: Space, Place, and the Infobahn*. Cambridge: MIT P, 1995.

Morgan, Richard. "Urban Tactics: Thread Counts, Yo." *New York Times* 13 November 2005. Accessed on 10 November 2008. <http://query.nytimes.com/gst/fullpage.html?res=9C01E6DF133EF930A25752C1A9639C8B63&sec=&spon=&&scp=1&sq=Urban%20Tactics:%20Thread%20Counts&st=cse>.

Morrison, Toni. *Beloved*. New York: Knopf, 1987.

Mueller, Milton L. *Ruling the Root*. Cambridge: MIT P, 2002.

Mumford, Lewis. *The City in History: Its Origins, Its Transformations, and Its Prospects*. New York: Harcourt, 1961.

———. *The Highway and the City*. New York: Harcourt, 1963.

———. "Mother Jacobs' Home Remedies for Urban Cancer." *The New Yorker* December 1, 1962. Repr. as "Home Remedies for Urban Cancer." *The Urban Prospect* 182–207.

———. *The Urban Prospect*. New York: Harcourt, 1968.

———. "What Is a City?" LeGates and Stout 183–88.

———. "Yesterday's City of Tomorrow." *The Urban Prospect* 116–127.

Munt, Sally R., ed. *Technospaces: Inside the New Media*. London: Continuum, 2001.

Muschamp, Herbert. "If the Cityscape Is Only a Dream." *New York Times* 2 May 1999. Accessed on 10 November 2008. <<http://query.nytimes.com/gst/fullpage.html?res=9804E3D6143DF931A35756C0A96F958260&scp=1&sq=I f%20the%20Cityscape%20Is%20Only%20a%20Dream&st=cse>.

———. "Service Not Included." Rothstein, Muschamp, and Marty 29–48.

Musil, Robert. *The Man Without Qualities*. Trans. Sophie Wilkins. New York: Vintage, 1996.

Nasaw, David. "Cities of Light, Landscapes of Pleasure." Ward and Zunz 273–86.

Negroponte, Nicholas. *Being Digital*. New York: Random, 1995.

Newman, Oscar. *Creating Defensible Space*. Washington, DC: Dept. of Housing and Urban Development, 1996.

———. *Defensible Space: Crime Prevention through Urban Design*. New York: Collier, 1973.

Newman, Peter W. G., and Jeffrey R. Kenworthy. *Cities and Automobile Dependency: An International Sourcebook*. Aldershot, UK: Gower, 1989.

———. *Sustainability and Cities: Overcoming Automobile Dependence*. Washington, DC: Island P, 1999.

———. "Urban Design to Reduce Automobile Dependence." *Opolis* 2:1 (2006): 35–52.

Nietzsche, Friedrich. *On the Genealogy of Morals and Ecce Homo*. Trans. Walter Kaufmann and R. J. Hollingdale. New York: Vintage, 1989.

———. *Thus Spoke Zarathustra: A Book for All and None*. Modern Library Ed. Trans. Walter Kaufmann. New York: Random, 1995.

Nunn, Samuel. "Cities, Space, and the New World of Urban Law Enforcement Technologies." *Journal of Urban Affairs*, Vol. 23.3–4: 259–78.

Nye, David E. *Electrifying America: Social Meanings of New Technology, 1880–1900*. Cambridge: MIT P, 1990.

Ogilvy, David. *Confessions of an Advertising Man*. New York: Atheneum, 1963.

OpenNet Initiative. Accessed on 1 July 2007. <http://www.opennetinitiative.org/modules.php?op=modload&name=Archive&file=index&req=viewarticl e&artid=5>.

Owens, Mitchell. "Saving Neighborhoods One Gate at a Time." *New York Times* 25 August 1994. Accessed on 1 August 2007. <http://query.nytimes.com/gst/fullpage.html?res=9F06E3DA1339F936A1575BC0A962958260>.

Penley, Constance and Andrew Ross, eds. *Technoculture*. Minneapolis: U of Minnesota P, 1991.

Piranesi, Giovanni Battista. *The Prisons (Le Carceri)*. New York: Dover, 1973.

Pizer, Donald. *Dos Passos's U.S.A.: A Critical Study*. Charlottesville: U of Virginia P, 1988.

———. *Realism and Naturalism in Nineteenth-Century American Literature*. Carbondale: Southern Illinois UP, 1984.

Pizer, Donald, ed. *New Essays on Sister Carrie*. Cambridge: Cambridge UP, 1991.

Plato. *Protagoras*. Trans. W.K.C. Guthrie. *Plato: The Collected Dialogues*. Ed. Edith Hamilton and Huntington Cairns. Bollingen Series LXXI. Princeton: Princeton UP, 1961. 308–52.

Plotnitsky, Arkady. *The Knowable and the Unknowable: Modern Science, Nonclassical Thought, and the "Two Cultures."* Ann Arbor: U of Michigan P, 2002.

Porter, Eduardo. "The Divisions that Tighten the Purse Strings." *New York Times* 29 April 2007. Accessed on 1 November 2008. <http://www.nytimes.

com/2007/04/29/business/yourmoney/29view.html?sq=DivisionsthatT-ightenPurseStrings&st=cse&adxnnl=1&scp=1&adxnnlx=1225584209-mNfl8cr3kuGirDiZg7ttbw>.

Pynchon, Thomas. *The Crying of Lot 49*. 1965. New York: Bantam, 1966.

———. *Mason & Dixon: A Novel*. New York: Picador, 2004.

Raban, Jonathan. *Soft City*. London: Harvill, 1974.

Rabaté, Jean-Michel. *Jacques Lacan: Psychoanalysis and the Subject of Literature*. New York: Palgrave, 2001.

Reporters Without Borders. "China." Accessed on 1 July 2007. <http://www.rsf. org/article.php3?id_article=10749>.

———. "'Living Dangerously on the Net': Censorship and Surveillance of Internet Forums." 12 May 2003. Accessed on 1 July 2007. <http://www.rsf.org/article. php3?id_article=6793>.

Rheingold, Howard. *The Virtual Community: Homesteading on the Electronic Frontier*. Rev. ed. Cambridge: MIT P, 2000.

Rosen, Jeffrey. "The Eroded Self." *New York Times Magazine* 30 April 2000. Accessed on 1 August 2007. <http://query.nytimes.com/gst/fullpage.html?sec=t echnology&res=990CE0DD1530F933A05757C0A9669C8B63>.

Ross, Andrew. "Hacking Away at the Counterculture." Penley and Ross 107–134.

Rothstein, Edward, Herbert Muschamp, and Martin E. Marty. *Visions of Utopia*. New York: Oxford UP, 2003.

Rousseau, Jean-Jacques. *Of the Social Contract or Principles of Political Right*. 1762. Trans. Charles M. Sherover. New York: Harper, 1984.

"Rush Hour." BBC One trailer. Dir. Tom Carty. BBC, 2002. Accessed on 10 November 2008. <http://www.youtube.com/watch?v=SAMAr8y-Vtw>.

Rushdie, Salman. *Imaginary Homelands*. New York: Penguin, 1992.

Sachs, Wolfgang. *For the Love of the Automobile: Looking Back into the History of Our Desires*. Trans. Don Reneau. Berkeley: U of California P, 1992.

Sadler, Simon. *The Situationist City*. Cambridge: MIT P, 1998.

Sammy and Rosie Get Laid. Dir. Stephen Frears. Channel Four Films et al., 1987.

Sassen, Saskia. *The Global City: New York, London, Tokyo*. 2nd ed. Princeton: Princeton UP, 2001.

Saussure, Ferdinand de. *Course in General Linguistics*. New York: McGraw, 1966.

Schaub, Thomas H. *Pynchon: The Voice of Ambiguity*. Urbana: U of Illinois P, 1981.

Schivelbusch, Wolfgang. *Disenchanted Night: The Industrialization of Light in the Nineteenth Century*. Trans. Angela Davis. Berkeley: U of California P, 1988.

Schone, Mark. "Building Rome in a Day." *The Village Voice*. May 31, 1994: 50–51.

Schwarzer, Mitchell. *Zoomscape: Architecture in Motion and Media*. New York: Princeton Architectural P, 2004.

Schwartz, Joel. *The New York Approach: Robert Moses, Urban Liberals, and Redevelopment of the Inner City*. Columbus: Ohio State UP, 1993.

Scuri, Piera. *Late-Twentieth-Century Skyscrapers*. New York: Van Nostrand, 1990.

Sen, Amartya. *Identity and Violence: The Illusion of Destiny*. New York: Norton, 2006.

———. "What Difference Can Ethics Make?" Address. Intl. Meeting on "Ethics and Development." Inter American Development Bank in Collaboration with the Norwegian Government. Accessed on 10 November 2008. <http://www. iadb.org/Etica/Documentos/dc_sen_queimp-i.pdf>.

Sennett, Richard. *The Fall of Public Man*. London and Boston: Faber, 1977.

Sex and the City. Television series. HBO, 1998–2004.

Sharpe, William, and Leonard Wallock, eds. *Visions of the Modern City: Essays in History, Art, and Literature*. New York: Columbia Univ., Heyman Center for the Humanities, 1983.

Shaw, Marybeth. "Promoting an Urban Vision: Le Corbusier and the Plan Voisin." Master's Thesis, MIT 1991. Accessed on 10 July 2007. <http://dspace.mit.edu/bitstream/1721.1/36421/1/25571430.pdf>.

Short Cuts. Dir. Robert Altman. Avenue Pictures et al., 1993.

Shulman, Robert. *Social Criticism & Nineteenth-Century American Fictions.* Columbia: U of Missouri P, 1987.

Smith, Adam. *An Inquiry into the Nature and Causes of the Wealth of Nations.* 1776. Ed. Edwin Canaan. New York: Modern Lib., 1994.

———. *The Theory of Moral Sentiments.* 1759. New York: Garland, 1971.

Smith, Carl. *Urban Disorder and the Shape of Belief: The Great Chicago Fire, the Haymarket Bomb, and the Model Town of Pullman.* Chicago: U of Chicago P, 1995.

Smith, Elizabeth A.T. "Re-examining Architecture and Its History at the End of the Century." Ferguson 22–99.

Sobchak, Vivian. "The Scene of the Screen: Towards a Phenomenology of Cinematic and Electronic Presence." *Post-Script* 10 (1990): 50–59.

Soja, Edward W. *Postmetropolis.* Critical Studies of Cities and Regions. Oxford: Blackwell, 2000.

———. *Postmodern Geographies: The Reassertion of Space in Critical Social Theory.* London and New York: Verso, 1989.

———. "Postmodern Urbanization: The Six Restructurings of Los Angeles." Watson and Gibson 125–37.

———. *Thirdspace: Journeys to Los Angeles and Other Real-and-Imagined Places.* Oxford: Blackwell, 1996.

Sorkin, Michael, ed. *Variations on a Theme Park: The New American City and the End of Public Space.* New York: Noonday P and HarperCollins, 1992.

Spence, Edward. "Cosmopolitanism and the Internet." Paper delivered at the Second International Conference of the Australian Institute of Computer Ethics. November 2000. Accessed on 1 August 2007. <http://crpit.com/confpapers/CRPITV1Spence.pdf >.

Squiers, Carol. "Diversionary (Syn)tactics—Barbara Kruger Has Her Way with Words." *Art News* 86:2 (1987): 77–85.

St. John, Warren. "A Store Lures Guys Who Are Graduating from Chinos." *New York Times* July 14, 2002: Sections 9:1 and 9:6 Sunday Styles.

Stallybrass, Peter, and Allon White. *The Politics and Poetics of Transgression.* Ithaca: Cornell UP, 1986.

Stearn, Gerald Emanuel, ed. *McLuhan Hot & Cool.* New York: Penguin, 1968.

Steinhauer, Jennifer. "For $82 a Day, Booking a Cell in a 5-Star Jail." *New York Times* 29 April 2007. Accessed on 1 August 2007. <http://select.nytimes.com/search/restricted/article?res=F10E15FC385A0C7A8EDDAD0894DF404482>.

Stephenson, Neal. *Snow Crash.* New York: Bantam, 1992.

Sterling, Bruce. Preface. *Burning Chrome.* By William Gibson. New York: Ace, 1986.

Stevens, Mark. "California Dreaming." *New York Magazine* 9 August 2004. Accessed on 10 November 2008. <http://nymag.com/nymetro/arts/art/reviews/9565/>.

Stewart, Rory. *The Places in Between.* New York: Harcourt, 2004.

Stimpson, Catherine R., ed. *Women and the American City.* Chicago: U of Chicago P, 1981.

Stone, Allucquere Rosanne. "Will the Real Body Please Stand Up?: Boundary Stories about Virtual Cultures." Benedikt 81–118.

Stone, Brad. "How Much for a Jetpack?" *Newsweek* 17 October 2005. Accessed on 10 November 2008. <http://services.newsweek.com//search.aspx?offset=0&pageSize=10&sortField=pubdatetime&sortDirection=descending&mode=su

mmary&q=How+Much+for+a+Jetpack&site-search-submit.x=27&site-search-submit.y=3>.

———. "New Flights of Fancy: Google and Microsoft Aim to Give You a 3-D World." *Newsweek* November 20, 2006: 82–89.

Story, Louise. "Anywhere the Eye Can See, It's Now Likely to See an Ad." *New York Times* 15 January 2007. Accessed on 1 August 2007. <http://select.nytimes.com/search/restricted/article?res=F30E1EFD3B540C768DDDA80894DF404482>.

Sullivan, Danny. "A Picture Says 1000 Words about Google's Censorship in China" at "Revealing China Censorship via Google Images," 30 January 2006. Accessed on 10 November 2008. <http://www.seroundtable.com/archives/003212.html>. Original post 1 July 2007 <http://blog.searchenginewatch.com/blog/060130–080248>.

"Surveillance Camera Project." New York Civil Liberties Union. Accessed on 1 July 2007. <http://www.mediaeater.com/cameras/summary.html>.

Sussman, Elizabeth, ed. *On the Passage of a Few People through a Rather Brief Moment in Time: The Situationist International, 1957–1972.* Cambridge: MIT P and Institute of Contemporary Arts, Boston, 1989.

Taylor, Chris. "Google Moves into Virtual Worlds." *Business 2.0 Magazine* on CNNMoney.com. 14 December 2006. Accessed on 11 July 2007. <money.cnn.com/2006/05/11/technology/business2_futureboy_0511>.

Taylor, Peter J. *World City Network: A Global Urban Analysis.* London: Routledge, 2004.

Taylor, William R., ed. *Inventing Times Square: Commerce and Culture at the Crossroads of the World.* New York: Russell Sage Foundation, 1991.

The Tenth Victim (La Decima Vittima). Dir. Elio Petri. Compagnia Cinematografica Champion et al., 1965.

Terdiman, Daniel. "Meet the Metaverse, Your New Digital Home." *CNET News* 13 April 2007. Accessed on 1 July 2007. <http://news.com.com/2100–1025_3–6175973.html>.

Things to Come. Dir. William Cameron Menzies. London Film Productions, 1936.

Tomas, David. "Old Rituals for New Space: Rites de Passage and William Gibson's Cultural Model of Cyberspace." Benedikt 31–48.

Tritch, Teresa. "The Rise of the Super-Rich." *New York Times* 19 July 2006. Accessed on 1 August 2007. <http://select.nytimes.com/2006/07/19/opinion/19talkingpoints.html>.

Tron. Dir. Steven Lisberger. Lisberger/Kushner and Walt Disney Productions, 1982.

Turkle, Sherry. *Life on the Screen: Identity in the Age of the Internet.* New York: Simon & Schuster, 1995.

"Unitary Urbanism at the End of the 1950s." Sussman. (Orig. publ. in *Internationale Situationniste* #3, December 1959; also avail. in a slightly diff. transl. at <http://www.notbored.org/UU.html>.)

United Nations. "Human Development Report 1998." Accessed on 10 July 2007. <http://hdr.undp.org/reports/global/1998/en/>.

United States. Dept. of Commerce, Census Bureau News. "Quarterly Retail e-Commerce Sales, First Quarter, 2006." Table 3. "Estimated Quarterly U.S. Retail Sales (Adjusted): Total and E-commerce." Accessed on 20 July 2008. <http://www.census.gov/mrts/www/data/html/06Q1.html>.

———. *National Commission on the Causes and Prevention of Violence.* Washington, DC: GPO, 1969.

Urry, John. "The Global Media and Cosmopolitanism." Lancaster UK: Department of Sociology, Lancaster University, 2003. Accessed on 11 July 2007. <http://www.comp.lancs.ac.uk/sociology/papers/Urry-Global-Media.pdf>.

———. "Inhabiting the Car." Lancaster, UK: Department of Sociology, University of Lancaster, 2003. Accessed on 10 July 2007. <http://www.comp.lancs.ac.uk/sociology/papers/Urry-Inhabiting-the-Car.pdf>.

Veblen, Thorstein. *The Theory of the Leisure Class.* 1899. Mineola: Dover, 1994.

Venturi, Robert, Denise Scott Brown, and Steven Izenour. *Learning from Las Vegas: The Forgotten Symbolism of Architectural Form.* Cambridge: MIT P, 1977.

Virilio, Paul. "Dromoscopy, or the Ecstasy of Enormities." *Wide Angle* 20:3 (1998). 11–22.

———. *Speed and Politics: An Essay on Dromology.* Trans. Mark Olizzotti. New York: Semiotext(e), 1987.

Wachs, Martin, and Margaret Crawford. *The Car and the City: The Automobile, the Built Environment, and Daily Urban Life.* Ann Arbor: U of Michigan P, 1991.

Waldman, Diane. *Jenny Holzer.* New York: The Solmon R. Guggenheim Foundation, 1989.

Waldron, Jeremy. "Minority Cultures and the Cosmopolitan Alternative." *University of Michigan Journal of Law Reform* 25 (1992): 751–93.

———. "Multiculturalism and Mélange." *Public Education in a Multicultural Society.* Ed. Robert Fullinwider. Cambridge: Cambridge UP, 1996.

Wallace, Mark. "The Game Is Virtual. The Profit Is Real." *New York Times* May 29, 2005: Sect. 7 Business.

Ward, David, and Olivier Zunz, eds. *The Landscape of Modernity: Essays on New York City.* New York: Russell Sage Foundation, 1992.

Ward, Stephen V. *Planning the Twentieth-Century City: The Advanced Capitalist World.* Chichester: Wiley, 2002.

Watson, Sophie, and Katharine Gibson, eds. *Postmodern Cities and Spaces.* Oxford: Blackwell, 1995.

Le Week-end. Dir. Jean-Luc Godard. Cinecidi et al., 1967.

Wells, H.G. *Shape of Things to Come.* New York: Penguin Classics, 2006.

Westendorf, Michael, and Uta Krogmann. "Horses and Manure." *Fact Sheet #36.* New Brunswick: Equine Science Center at Rutgers University, 2004. Accessed on 30 June 2007. <http://www.esc.rutgers.edu/publications/stablemgt/FS036.htm>.

Wetmore, Alex. "The Poetics of *Pattern Recognition*: William Gibson's Shifting Technological Subject." *Bulletin of Science, Technology & Society* 27:1 (2007): 71–80.

Wexelblat, Alan, ed. *Virtual Reality: Applications and Explorations.* Cambridge: Academic P Professional, 1993.

White, E.B. "Here Is New York." *Essays of E.B. White.* New York: Harper, 1934. 118–33.

Whyte, William H. *The Social Life of Small Urban Spaces.* Washington, DC: The Conservation Foundation, 1980.

Wiener, Jon. "Free Speech on the Internet." *The Nation* June 13, 1994: 825–28.

The Wild One. Dir. Laslo Benedek. Stanley Kramer Productions, 1953.

Wilkin, Peter. *The Political Economy of Global Communication: An Introduction.* London: Pluto P, 2001.

Williams, Raymond. *The Country and the City.* New York: Oxford UP, 1973.

———. *Keywords: A Vocabulary of Culture and Society.* 1976. Rev. ed. New York: Oxford UP, 1983.

———. *Marxism and Literature.* New York: Oxford UP, 1977.

Williams, Rosalind H. *Dream Worlds: Mass Consumption in Late Nineteenth-Century France.* Berkeley: U of California P, 1982.

Wirth, Louis. "Urbanism as a Way of Life." LeGates and Stout 189–97.

Wollen, Peter, and Joe Kerr, eds. *Autotopia: Cars and Culture*. London: Reaktion, 2002.

Wood, Daniel B. "On the Rise in American Cities: The Car-Free Zone." *The Christian Science Monitor* 2 May 2007. Accessed on 8 November 2008. <http://www.csmonitor.com/2007/0502/p01s03-ussc.html>.

Woolf, Virginia. *Jacob's Room & The Waves*. New York: Harcourt, 1931.

Yamakasi: Les Samouraïs des temps modernes. Dirs. Ariel Zeitoun and Julian Serin. Europa Corp. et al., 2001.

Yates, Frances A. *The Art of Memory*. Chicago: U of Chicago P, 1966.

Young, Iris Marion. "The Ideal of Community and the Politics of Difference." Bridge and Watson, *Reader* 430–39.

Zukin, Sharon. *The Cultures of Cities*. Cambridge: Blackwell, 1995.

Zunz, Olivier. "Inside the Skyscraper." *Making America Corporate: 1870–1920*. Chicago: U of Chicago P, 1990. 103–24.

Index